Proceedings of the Eighth International Symposium on

Human Aspects of Information Security & Assurance (HAISA 2014)

Plymouth, UK
8-9 July 2014

Editors

Nathan Clarke
Steven Furnell

Centre for Security, Communications & Network Research
Plymouth University

ISBN: 978-1-84102-375-5

Preface

It is now widely recognised that technology alone cannot provide the answer to security problems. A significant aspect of protection comes down to the attitudes, awareness, behaviour and capabilities of the people involved, and they often need support in order to get it right. Factors such as lack of awareness and understanding, combined with unreasonable demands from security technologies, can dramatically impede their ability to act securely and comply with policies. Ensuring appropriate attention to the needs of users is therefore a vital element of a successful security strategy, and they need to understand how the issues may apply to them and how to use the available technology to protect their systems.

With the above in mind, the Human Aspects of Information Security and Assurance (HAISA) symposium series specifically addresses information security issues that relate to people. It concerns the methods that inform and guide users' understanding of security, and the technologies that can benefit and support them in achieving protection.

This book presents the proceedings from the 2014 event, held in Plymouth, United Kingdom, during July 2014. A total of 20 reviewed papers are included, spanning a range of topics including user attitudes and awareness, management and modelling of security, and the suitability of technologies that people are expected to use. All of the papers were subject to double-blind peer review, with each being reviewed by at least two members of the international programme committee.

We would like to thank the authors for submitting their work and sharing their findings, and the international programme committee for their efforts in reviewing the submissions and ensuring the quality of the resulting event and proceedings. We would also like to thank the local organising committee for making all the necessary arrangements to enable this symposium to take place. Special thanks go to Paul Dowland as the local host, for organising the venue and other facilities. Thanks are also due to the British Computer Society and Emerald (publishers of the sponsoring journal, *Information Management & Computer Security*) as the co-sponsors of the event.

Nathan Clarke and Steven Furnell
Symposium Co-Chairs, HAISA 2014

Plymouth, July 2014

International Programme Committee

William Buchanan	Napier University	United Kingdom
Jeff Crume	IBM	United States
Dorothy Denning	Naval Postgraduate School	United States
Ronald Dodge	United States Military Academy	United States
Paul Dowland	Plymouth University	United Kingdom
Jan Eloff	SAP	South Africa
Simone Fischer-Huebner	Karlstad University	Sweden
Stefanos Gritzalis	University of the Aegean	Greece
John Howie	Cloud Security Alliance	United States
William Hutchinson	Edith Cowan University	Australia
Murray Jennex	San Diego State University	United States
Andy Jones	Edith Cowan University	Australia
Vasilios Katos	Democritus University of Thrace	Greece
Sokratis Katsikas	University of Piraeus	Greece
Costas Lambrinoudakis	University of Piraeus	Greece
Michael Lavine	Johns Hopkins University	United States
Javier Lopez	University of Malaga	Spain
George Magklaras	University of Oslo	Norway
Maria Papadaki	Plymouth University	United Kingdom
Malcolm Pattinson	University of Adelaide	Australia
Corey Schou	Idaho State University	United States
Rossouw von Solms	Nelson Mandela Metropolitan University	South Africa
Kerry-Lynn Thomson	Nelson Mandela Metropolitan University	South Africa
Theodore Tryfonas	University of Bristol	United Kingdom
Kim Vu	California State University	United States
Jeremy Ward	Hewlett Packard	United Kingdom
Merrill Warkentin	Mississippi State University	United States
Wei Yan	Trend Micro	United States
Louise Yngstrom	Stockholm University	Sweden
Mary Ellen Zurko	IBM	United States
Ibrahim Zincir	Yasar University	Turkey

Contents

Developing Contextual Understanding of Information Security Risks

M. Sadok[1], V. Katos[2] and P. Bednar[3]

[1]Higher Institute of Technological Studies in Communications in Tunis, Tunisia
[2]Democritus University of Thrace, Greece
[3]School of Computing, Portsmouth University, United Kingdom
e-mail: moufida.sadok@gmail.com; vkatos@ee.duth.gr; peter.bednar@port.ac.uk

Abstract

Given the uncertainty and complexity of security risk analyses, there is a great need of tools for contextual inquiry supporting assessment of risk with multi-value scales according to different stakeholders' point of view. Such tools can be used at individual level to help develop the understanding of a problem space. At the collective level, they can be used as a mean of communication to support the discussion, comparison and exploration of different understandings. The exploration of multiple perspectives of contextual understanding avoids entrapment in various types of reductionism and eliminates tendencies towards a deterministic reasoning and the pursuit of one optimum solution. A critical challenge is first developing a large spectrum of alternatives and then managing how the differences and similarities between alternatives will be handled to efficiently support decisions in information systems security (ISS). To address the aforementioned challenges, this paper seeks to explore the potential relevance of cognitive maps use in an ISS context to support the exploration of individual understanding leading to richer elaboration of problem spaces.

Keywords

Risk analysis, Systemic risk, Cognitive map, Contextual analysis, Information security, Uncertainty

1. Introduction

In information systems security (ISS), the objectives of the risk analysis process are to help to identify new threats and vulnerabilities, to estimate their business impact and to provide a dynamic set of tools to control the security level of the information system. In their practices, organisations employ and balance between prevention and response security management approaches (Baskerville et al., 2014). Many of the existing risk analysis models and frameworks focus mainly on the technical modules related to the development of security mitigation and prevention and do not pay much attention to the influence of contextual variables affecting the reliability of the provided solutions (Samela, 2008; Siponen and Willison, 2009). Moreover, Siponen and Iivari (2006) identified a gap in research on ISS policies when it comes to handle exceptional situations of business. The importance of context for systemic analysis has been widely recognized (e.g. Checkland, 1981; Checkland and Poulter, 2006; Ulrich, 1983). A systemic view of security would result in a better understanding of

1

organizational stakeholders of the role and application of security functions in situated practices and an achievement of contextually relevant risk analysis (Bednar and Katos, 2010). The study of Spears and Barki (2010) provides a particular application of this view in the context of regulatory compliance and confirms the conclusion that the engagement of users in ISS risk management process contributes to more effective security measures and better alignment of security controls with business objectives.

Given the uncertainty and complexity of security risk analyses, there is a great need of tools for contextual inquiry supporting assessment of risk with multi-value scales according to different stakeholders' point of view. Such tools can be used at individual level to help to develop the understanding of a problem space. At the collective level, they can be used as a mean of communication to support the discussion, comparison and exploration of different understandings. The exploration of multiple perspectives of contextual understanding avoids entrapment in various types of reductionism and eliminates tendencies towards a deterministic reasoning and the pursuit of one optimum solution. A critical challenge is first developing a large spectrum of alternatives and then managing how the differences and similarities between alternatives will be handled to efficiently support decisions in ISS.

To address the aforementioned challenges, this paper seeks to explore the potential relevance of cognitive maps use in ISS context to support the exploration of individual understanding leading to richer elaboration of problem spaces. A case study is used to illustrate the concept.

The remainder of this paper is organized as follows. In the section 2, a short review of existing ISS models found in the literature is provided. Section 3 discusses the need for particular tools for contextual inquiry under uncertainty and complexity. In Section 4 a case study is given to illustrate the use of cognitive maps. Finally, the conclusive remarks are presented in section 5.

2. Related literature

A number of researchers have addressed the uncertainty and complexity related to ISS applying several theories as well as operations research techniques. The involvement of security experts has been a significant input in many of the models proposed. In Feng and Li (2011), an improved version of the evidence theory is used to deal with the uncertainty in ISS risk assessment. The proposed model requires experts' beliefs inputs to establish the ISS index system and quantify index weights. However, the authors recognise the need to better elicit practitioners' assessments of the strength of the evidence. In practice, the evaluation of risk under uncertainty through index weights appears to be highly structured reductionist and simplistic passing over the subjectivity inherent to any human problem solving process. It is also important to define relevant stakeholders in specific situation of risk analysis. In Ryan *et al.* (2012), the security expert judgment elicitation method is applied to quantify information security risks "where the experts' weights are derived from the experts' responses to a set of seed variables whose values are known by the analyst and which are used to "calibrate" the accuracy of the experts' opinions". This method of codification is based on a list of a pre-determined questions and answers; however, in real world situations a problem space is not 'given' but created by the interest of relevant stakeholders who make use of their own norms and values, derived through experience, in the context of risk analysis. Moreover, it is limiting to disqualify out of context any understanding or analysis developed by any of the involved stakeholders or creates any kind of discrimination between them. All the contextual (and situated) perspectives should be considered as relevant. The concept of weight has also been used in Gupta *et al.* (2006) who propose a genetic algorithm approach to match security technologies to vulnerabilities. Without applying real case studies the techniques described in their approach, the authors argue that the estimation of weights depends on the types and preferences of the organization which will influence the decisions regarding the number of vulnerabilities covered and the cost of implemented security solutions.

Based on the expert's experience and a database of observed cases, Feng *et al.* (2014) develop a security risk analysis model using Bayesian network techniques and ant colony optimisation algorithms. The developed model identifies causal relationships of risk factors and vulnerability propagation analysis. In spite of the interest of the proposed model, it is difficult to apply it in practice to cope with unpredictable risks and more complex security risk analysis problems as the database of observed cases can only support the prediction of already know risks. It is also not apparent how to obtain the data to do so. The judgment of security risks cannot be only based on the security expert experience and knowledge, as the risk is contextually situated (Katos and Bednar, 2008).

Another stream of research in ISS risk assessment draws up on the estimation of likelihood occurrences and impact of vulnerabilities and threats. Sommestad *et al.* (2010) provide an overview of several studies and methods based on probabilistic assessment of security incidents and their potential consequences. However, the discrete and non-linear nature of security failures limits the usefulness and relevance of an assessment based on probabilities (Brooke and Paige, 2003). Sun *et al.* (2006) propose to use the notion of plausibility of a negative outcome to measure ISS risk as it covers residual uncertainty. The authors suggest, for example, Delphi techniques to obtain consensus about values of evidence strength and recognise that the structure of their model is dependent on users' understanding of the interrelationships between risk factors. However, as a consequence of subjectively known contextual dependencies, consensus about values of evidence is not necessarily achievable.

We suggest therefore that two issues need to be further investigated in the field of ISS risk management. First, traditional probability theory is handicapped in the sense that it cannot capture and represent events in an uncertain domain. That is, probabilistic analysis requires that the probability distributions are known for all events. This limitation was initially addressed by Dempster (1967) and further refined by Shafer (1976). According to the Dempster Shafer mathematical theory of evidence (DST), classical probability is extended in such a way that events can be described at a higher level of abstraction, without requiring one to resort to assumptions within the evidential set. Furthermore, Dempster and Shafer developed an algebraic system to combine events and produce measures for events that can be contradictory.

Classic probability could be viewed as a special case of DST. In DST hypotheses are represented as subsets of a given set. A hypothesis is a statement which holds with some probability. An interesting feature in DST is that the probability assigned to a hypothesis need not be calculated or proven in the classic probability sense. Therefore, a probability can be a person's view on the validity of the respective hypothesis (Katos and Bednar, 2008). Second, the description of a problem space which is uncertain and complex requires the generation of multi-perspectives and mutually inconsistent possible alternatives. Unique perspectives of individual stakeholders may be particularly important in highlighting aspects of a problem situation which may have become 'invisible' due to over-familiarity (Bednar and Welch, 2006). At a collective level, it is important to recognise and consider each individual's unique perspectives without temptation to unify or integrate the differences in a shared understanding of a problem space, to seek a premature consensus or to set up an artificial imposed scale of agreement.

3. Use of cognitive maps for ISS risk analysis

One manoeuvre for coping with uncertainty and unstructured situations involves sense-making and interpretation processes (Weick, 1995). To support such processes of reflection that assign meaning to data cognitive maps are constructed (Daft and Weick, 1984). A cognitive map (CM) consists of nodes and relations an individual uses to develop his/her understanding in specific problem space. When the relations are limited to causality effect cognitive map is the so-called cause map. The nodes are variables that may be continuous or dichotomous and can take on different values (Weick, 2001). Cognitive maps, as a model of thinking, may act as a tool to facilitate decision-making, problem-solving, and negotiation within the context of organizational intervention (Den, 1992).

In the specific context of security risks, each breach provides the opportunity to develop understanding of risk in a way that incrementally allows the improvement of security practices. The development of understanding may not necessarily prevent the next breach but can support the learning about how to manage and respond to unpredictable risks. It is argued in this paper that the exploration and understanding of issues are not only conducted by technical experts in security but also by experts in context such as managers or end users engaged in a specific problem space. Furthermore, given that there are many cases in information security where exceptions need to be made due to the increased complexity of the problem; experts have to face contradicting opinions and problem descriptions. All complex problems suffer from this. For example, conceptual maps and rich pictures are used in Soft Systems Methodology (Checkland, 1981; Checkland and Poulter, 2006) to address complex problems and to support dialogue and conversation about problematic situations. As such, documenting the individual's view of a problem by the means of cognitive maps may help in the development of more appropriate and flexible security policies and controls.

As there is increased complexity and uncertainty, it is possible that each individual can make more than one description of potential problem issue due to more than one understanding of potential issue (Bednar, 2000; 2007) and so each individual could come up with more than one cognitive map. This would result in more sophisticated cognitive maps at an individual level. Still each individual would potentially end up having more than one cognitive map. The result would be that a group would potentially have more than three cognitive maps to discuss and compare. The following discussion and systematic analysis between individuals could focus on similarities and differences of understanding of individual cognitive maps. Some cognitive maps may be recognized by all individuals in a group as easy to understand but not necessarily to agree upon. Some cognitive maps may be recognized as not easy to understand in the same way but all participants and so should not be aligned with each other. Instead they should be developed and categorized further using heuristics.

Such systematic analysis might support learning about threats and risk. And develop a number of additional and contextually relevant heuristics for continuity of inquiry - a kind of knowledge that the team through these conversations develop a better language for dialogue. It is learning about learning and heuristics which support this learning process. This help the team of professionals to get a better and more developed overview and insight into complexities of problem space and also their common and diverse understandings of the problem space they are interested in.

In terms of security policies and controls, it may mean that there should not be a single policy that will cover the needs of all the involved stakeholders in the risk analysis process. As such, trying to force compliance with one policy (i.e. no exceptions) could lead to problematic security as people will be driven to circumvent the underlying security controls or to give up on their own professional best practices.

4. Case study

In this section we describe three CMs as produced by three stakeholders respectively following a security breach.

ACME Ltd. like many other companies suffered a data breach. Following a preliminary assessment from the security expert, the company was exposed to an Advanced Persistent Threat, as it seemed that the attack was targeted and custom made to exploit the particular security gaps of the company. More specifically the external security expert – who was in fact commissioned to conduct an audit for the company a couple of years ago and had some good knowledge on the security posture of the company – was not surprised, as he had identified several vulnerabilities, most of which were not fully addressed. His view of the possible causes of the breach is captured with the CM as shown in Figure 1.

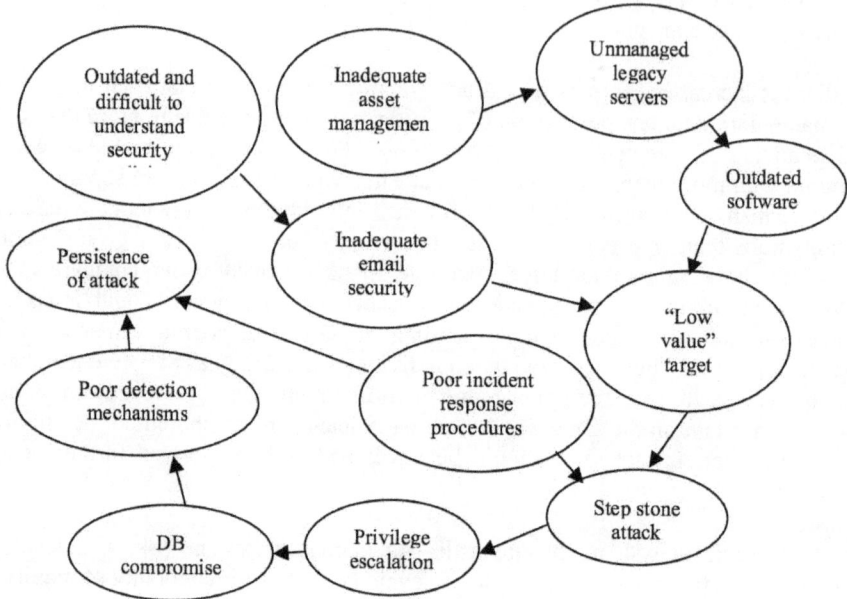

Figure 1: Security expert' CM

However, the systems administrator had a different view of the cause of the attack vector. He did not agree with the security consultant, mainly because the latter had an outdated view of the infrastructure; two years ago the Bring Your Own Device (BYOD) paradigm was not as prevalent and the infrastructure has dramatically changed ever since.

The network perimeter is completely different as many users bring their portable devices in their job environment bypassing most security controls: the firewall is not capable of inspecting and filtering all network traffic, documents and saved on smartphones and laptops in unencrypted forms, users are addicted to downloading a number of apps on the smartphones. As such the administrator is very upset with the plethora of functionality and applications he has no control of and his view of the problem stems from the adoption of BYOD where the company was unprepared to embrace. His CM is presented in Figure 2.

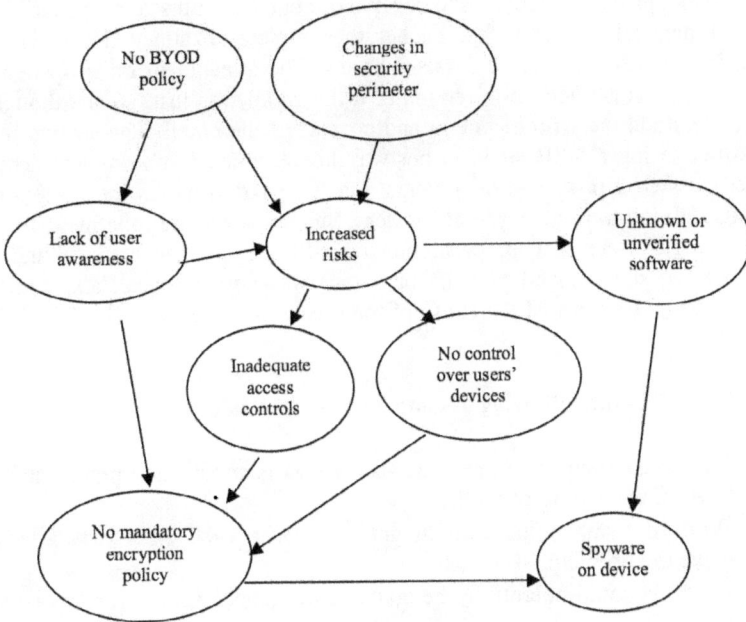

Figure 2: Systems administrator' CM

One of the end users feels somewhat responsible for the breach, as she recalled of two incidents that she did not considered being of significant importance.

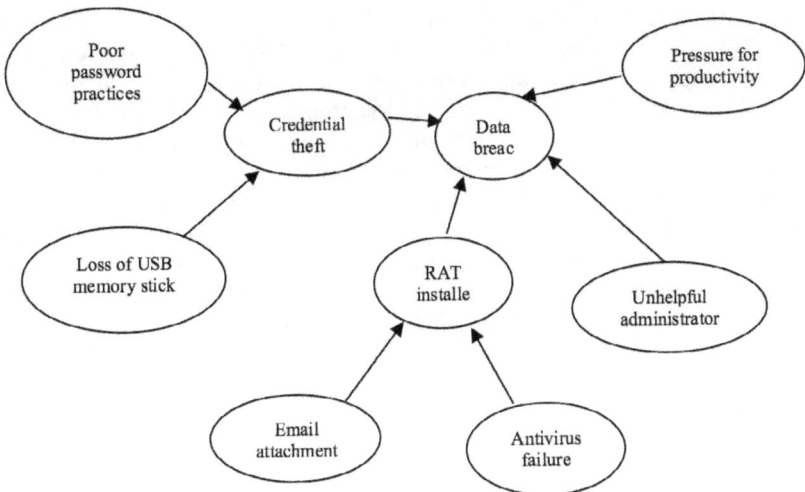

Figure 3: End user' CM

The first incident was an email she received about 8 months ago appearing to be from the Finance Department asking her to complete an attached file with some personal information to receive a salary bonus. The attachment once opened cause her computer to crash and upon rebooting it the email was lost, so she thought that she misunderstood the whole content and context of the email. The second incident involved her losing a USB stick on her way home, about 6 months ago. The USB contained password protected documents, but the password was the same with the one she uses to log into the corporate system. She never reported the incident before, because she did use password protection on USB device, but after talking to the security expert, she realized that the password was perhaps weak and could have been recovered. Her view of the cause of the breach is captured in the CM in Figure 3.

For the above CMs the following assumptions can be made:

- Each stakeholder assumes that his/her CM is correct and represents his/her true understanding of reality,
- While the stakeholders might not agree with each other they all want to solve the problem,
- All CMs could potentially be contextually relevant, more or less correct or wrong.

The benefit of having multiple CMs supports the exploration of a wider problem space from multiple perspectives. This is particularly useful in the case where the attack vector is unknown.

The involved stakeholders try to understand and compare through structured discussions the similarities and differences between their views of the problem space as described by their respective CMs. Each stakeholder can identify relationships between all of the CMs and categorize similarities and differences. The categorization can be made using an appropriate reasoning tool such as paraconsistent logic that allows ambiguity and uncertainty in judgement to be expressed. This can also be done by the application of methods such as the Diversity Network (e.g. Katos *et al.* 2006). As the three CM's describe three potentially different and incompatible understandings of what ought to be a relevant attack vector to address, more than one security policy could be delivered. Furthermore more than one perspective allows the organization to better identify vulnerabilities and threats, and eventually implement more appropriate security controls and policies.

5. Conclusion

This paper explored security risk analysis as an example of an inquiry into a complex, ambiguous and uncertain problem space. As such the process needs to support stakeholders to develop a widening of problem understanding before stakeholders commit to a problem definition. This is done through developing multiple contextual understandings of information security risks by using CMs which then are used by stakeholder in a dialogue for the discovery and description of relationships between the CMs as understood by each stakeholder. The objective with this effort is not to merge, integrate or combine different CMs as it might lead to framing stakeholders' perspectives and views. Instead we argue that there must be recognition in the problem identification process that stakeholders may have different subjective and potentially valid problem experiences. We suggest the consideration of multiple security policies to reflect the differing CMs of experts, managers and users. We recognise that there is a limit to how many CMs will be used in practice. Then a relevant question for future research would be how to determine and incorporate the chosen CMs.

This work would benefit from further developing of how frameworks such as Strategic Systemic Thinking (e.g. Bednar, 2000) and methods such as diversity networks could be applied in the identification process of similarities and differences between multiple CMs. It would also aid in the decision making processes among the involved stakeholders.

6. References

Baskerville, R., Spagnoletti, P. and Kim, J. (2014), "Incident-centered information security: Managing a strategic balance between prevention and response", *Information & Management*, Vol. 51, pp138-151.

Bednar, P. and Katos, V. (2010), "Digital forensic investigations: a new frontier for Informing Systems", in D'Atri, A. and Sacca, D. (Ed.) *Information Systems: People, Organizations, Institutions and Technologies*, Springer Physica-Verlag, Berlin Heidelberg, ISBN: 978-3-7908-2147-5.

Bednar, P. and Welch, C. (2006), "Structuring uncertainty: sponsoring innovation and creativity", in Adam, F. et al. (Ed.) *Creativity and Innovation in Decision Making and Decision Support*, London, Decision Support Press, ISBN: 1-905800-00-2.

Bednar, P.M. (2000), "A Contextual Integration of Individual and Organizational Learning Perspectives as part of IS Analysis", *Informing Science Journal*, Vol. 3, No. 3, pp145-156.

Bednar, P.M. (2007), "Individual emergence in contextual analysis", *Problems of Individual Emergence: Special issue of Systemica*, Vol. 14, pp23-28.

Brooke, P.J. and Paige, R.F. (2003), "Fault trees for security system design and analysis", *Computers & Security*, Vol. 22, No. 3, pp256-264.

Checkland, P. (1981), Systems Thinking, Systems Practice, John Wiley & Sons, Chichester, ISBN 0471279110.

Checkland, P. and Poulter J. (2006), Learning for Action, John Wiley & Sons, Chichester, ISBN 100470025549.

Daft, R.L. and Weick, K.E. (1984), "Toward a Model of Organizations as Interpretation Systems", *Academy of Management Review*, Vol. 9, No. 2, pp284-295.

Demspster, P. (1967), "Upper and lower probabilities induced by a multivalued mapping", *Annals of Statistics*, Vol. 28, pp325-339.

Den, C. (1992), "On the nature of cognitive maps", Journal of Management Studies, Vol. 293, pp261-265.

Feng, N. and Li, M. (2011), "An information systems security risk assessment model under uncertain environment", *Applied Soft Computing*, Vol. 11, pp4332–4340.

Feng, N., Wang, H. and Li, M. (2014), "A security risk analysis model for information systems: Causal relationships of risk factors and vulnerability propagation analysis", *Information Sciences*, Vol. 256, pp57–73.

Gupta, M., Rees, J., Chaturvedi, A. and Chi, J. (2006), "Matching information security vulnerabilities to organizational security profiles: a genetic algorithm approach", *Decision Support Systems*, Vol. 41, pp592-603.

Katos, V. and Bednar, P. (2008), "A cyber-crime investigation framework", *Computer Standards & Interfaces*, Vol. 30, pp223–228.

Katos, V., Bednar, P. and Welch, C. (2006), "Dealing with epistemic uncertainty in the SST framework", in Adam, F. et al. (Ed.) *Creativity and Innovation in Decision Making and Decision Support*, London, Decision Support Press, ISBN: 1-905800-00-2.

Ryan, J.J.C.H., Mazzuchi, T.A., Ryan, D.J., Lopez de la Cruz, J. and Cooke, R. (2012), "Quantifying information security risks using expert judgment elicitation", *Computers & Operations Research*, Vol. 39, pp774–784.

Salmela, H. (2008), "Analysing business losses caused by information systems risk: a business process analysis approach", *Journal of Information Technology*, Vol. 23, pp185-202.

Shafer, G. (1976), *A Mathematical Theory of Evidence*, Princeton University Press, ISBN: 9780691100425

Siponen, M. and Iivari, J. (2006), "Six design theories for IS security policies and guidelines", *Journal of the Association for Information systems*, Vol. 7, No. 7, pp 445-472.

Siponen, M. and Willison, R. (2009), "Information security management standards: Problems and solutions", *Information & Management*, Vol. 46, pp267-270.

Sommestad, T., Ekstedt, M. and Johnson, P. (2010) "A probabilistic relational model for security risk analysis", *Computers & Security*, Vol. 29, pp659-679.

Sun, L., Srivastava, R.P. and Mock, T.J. (2006) "An Information Systems Security Risk Assessment Model Under Dempster-Schafer Theory of Belief Functions", *Journal of Management Information Systems*, Vol. 22, No. 4, pp109-142.

Ulrich, W. (1983), *Critical Heuristics of Social Planning*, Wiley, Chichester, ISBN: 0-471-95345-8.

Weick, K. (1995), *Sense-making in Organizations*, Sage Publications, London, ISBN:0-8039-7176-1.

Weick, K. (2001), *Making sense of the organization*, Blackwell Publishers, Oxford, ISBN: 0-631-22317-7.

Information Security Policy Development and Implementation: A Content Analysis Approach

T. Tuyikeze[1] and S. Flowerday[2]

[1]Walter Sisulu University, East London, South Africa
[2]University of Fort Hare, East London, South Africa
e-mail : ttuyikeze@wsu.ac.za; sflowerday@ufh.ac.za

Abstract

The literature clearly agrees that the major threat to an organization's information security is caused by careless insider employees who intentionally or unintentionally misuse the organization's information assets (Bulgurcu *et al.*, 2010). This paper posits that one important mechanism to encounter insider threats is through the development of an effective information security policy. The research question posed by this paper is what processes organizations should follow in developing an effective information security policy. In order to answer this question, the paper follows the steps of the content analysis research technique. The primary objective of this paper is to define a model for the formulation, implementation and enforcement of an information security policy in an organization. A content analysis on current information security policy development and implementation methods is conducted from secondary sources in order to obtain a deep understanding of the processes that are critical to the information security policy development life cycle. The proposed model provides the various steps required in the development, implementation and evaluation of an effective information security policy.

Keywords

Information security policy, information security policy development and implementation, content analysis research technique

1. Introduction

Organizations are enormously dependent on Information Technology (IT) as it supports day-to-day transactions and many critical business functions. IT stores confidential information such as organizations' financial records, medical records, job performance reviews, trade secrets, new product developments and marketing strategies, which all must be protected to ensure organization survival. However, this dependency has unfortunately resulted in an increase of potential threats to the organization's information (Edwards, 2011). The literature review indicates that both intentional and unintentional insider threats are considered as one of the top ranked threats to information security over the past decade (Richardson, 2009). The Cybersecurity Watch Survey (2011) found that the damage caused by insider (employees or contractors with authorized access) attacks was bigger than outsiders (those without authorized access to network systems and data). The most common insider e-crimes were: unauthorized access to corporate information (63%);

unintentional exposure of private or sensitive data (57%); virus, worms, or other malicious code (37%); theft of intellectual property (32%).

This paper argues that one important mechanism to encounter the insider threats is through the formulation, implementation and enforcement of effective information security policies. According to Bacik (2008), information security policy architecture is a set of documents, comprising policies, guidelines, standards, procedures, and memorandums that collectively contributes to the protection of organizational assets. The remainder of this paper is organized as follows: In the next section, a discussion of the challenges pertaining to information security development is provided. Section 3 and its sub-sections explore the steps of the content analysis research technique and how they have been applied in this research paper in order to answer the research question. Finally, section 4 concludes the paper.

2. Challenges in developing effective information security policy

Maynard and Ruighaver (2006) argue that the major potential problem in the current security policy development practice is attributed to the lack of guidance as to how to develop security policy contents. We found no evidence that shows step-by-step processes of developing and implementing an information security policy. The literature concentrates on the description of the structure and the content of the security policy, but in general, fails to describe the processes used to generate the output of the information security policy. Due to the lack of the security policy development guidance, security policy developers often use commercially available sources or templates available from the internet in order to develop their policies (Karin and Eloff, 2004). The resulting policy document will, however, not give proper direction for information security protection. In this case, the policy statements developed may not be directly attributed to the risks they are designed to nullify; therefore, they do not combat the security threats that the specific organization is facing.

Furthermore, Tuyikeze and Flowerday (2013) compared a sample of existing security policy development methods. Their finding revealed basic steps for the development of a security policy document. It also showed some similarities where there is an agreement on the same steps, while also showing differences on the importance of the steps to be followed. Having noticed that there is a gap in the current security policy development methods; and that the literature does not offer comprehensive methodology or mechanisms that show in detail the processes of developing an information security policy, a more pragmatic strategy becomes a necessity. A content analysis of security policy development is conducted from secondary sources in order to uncover the processes necessary for the formulation, implementation and application of an effective information security policy.

3. A content analysis of information security policy development

This paper uses a content analysis research technique to find the solution of the questions raised in this paper. Krippendorff (2004) defines content analysis as: "a research technique for making replicable and valid inferences from text to their context of use, with the purpose of providing knowledge, new insights, a representation of facts and a practical guide to action". Having mentioned that content analysis is a research technique, it must follow a well-structured process to ensure reliability and validity (Du Preez, 2010). Krippendorff (2004) highlights six steps that should be followed while conducting a content analysis. These are: *Unitizing, Sampling, Coding, Reducing, Inferring and Narrating.* Each of the six steps of the content analysis is discussed on how it has been applied in this research paper.

3.1. Unitizing

The process of content analysis begins with the creation of a scheme of categories composed of the various analysis units (Elo and Kyngas, 2007). A unit of analysis can be a word, sentence, or portion of words (Elo and Kyngas, 2007). 'Unitizing' refers to a systematic approach for distinguishing segments of texts that are of interest to a content analysis (Krippendorff, 2004). For the nature of this study, a search string like: "information security policy", "security policy development", "security policy implementation" and "security policy formulation" was used to gather information regarding the security policy development methods from the literature.

3.2. Sampling

Krippendorff (2004) highlights that sampling enables the content analyst to save on the research efforts by cutting observations to a manageable subset of units that are statistically or conceptually representative of the whole population. A combination of various publications sources was utilized in order to answer the question posed in this research paper. A total number of 21 documents were chosen for the sample of this paper. These documents constitute the top cited papers on Google. The category of these samples varies from journal article papers, conference proceedings papers, industry policy publications and industry policy reports. During the selection of the sample, the reputation of the author, depending for example on the number of people who cited the article, was taken into account. Secondly, the reputation of the journal or the conference was considered. More importantly, the publications that provided relevant contents directly related to the research topic under study were highly selected. This entails an extensive analysis of the literature review. After the process of selecting the sample has been established, the coding process commences.

3.3. Coding

Coding entails the process of converting texts from the sample into analysable units (Krippendorff, 2004). In order to avoid human errors, the coding step was conducted by the use of the MAXQDA software package. The twenty one sample documents were imported into the MAXQDA. Each document was individually coded by highlighting the sentence or the paragraph that mentions the process of developing security policy. On completion of the coding process, a total number of 36 codes emerged and 552 accumulative codes. There was a variation of the codes from general to specific. General code was for example security policy construction, while the specific ones were draft the policy, write policy and write policy procedure. The general codes are grouped under one category in the next stage referred as the reducing step.

3.4. Reducing

The main objective of reducing is to decrease the number of codes into categories that can be easily interpreted (Du Preez, 2010). Most of the codes that have high frequency of occurrence were related to the process of constructing the policy, management support and information security policy compliance and enforcement. The 36 codes that emerged during the coding process were reduced to 10 categories. For example, the codes labelled "identification of vulnerabilities", "identification of threats" and "identification of assets to be protected" were grouped under one category named 'risk assessment' as they are all part of evaluating the security risk processes.

Category label	Number of tags	Cumulative tags
1. Information security policy construction	85	85
2. Management support	78	163
3.Information security policy compliance and enforcement	72	235
4. Information security policy implementation	68	303
5. Risk assessment	63	366
6. Information security policy monitoring, review and assessment	54	420
7. Employee support	51	471
8. International security standards	32	503
9. Information security policy stakeholders	28	531
10. Law and regulation requirements	21	552

Table 1: List of categories identified

In the next section, the last 2 steps of the content analysis are discussed.

3.5. Inferring and Narrating

In order to answer the research question posed in this paper, the 10 categories were analyzed and interpreted so that a model for information security policy development can be inferred from these categories.

3.5.1. Risk assessment

The literature provides different activities that need to be carried out during the risk assessment process. First, the assets that the organization needs to protect must be identified (Kadam, 2007). Secondly, a list of all the threats that can cause harm to the organization's assets is identified. Thirdly, the likelihood of threats exercising system vulnerability is determined. Information can have multiple vulnerabilities, for instance terminated employees' system identifiers (ID) that were not removed from the system (NIST, 2012). Fourth, the threats and vulnerabilities which cause a security failure and the associated impacts are assessed in terms of the organization's loss of integrity, availability and confidentiality. The risk assessment helps to make decision on which risks the organization is willing to accept and the ones it must mitigate. Lastly, the controls that must be implemented in order to mitigate the risks are identified (NIST, 2012). For example, an information security policy should be chosen as the main control to mitigate the risk of insider employees who negligently put the organization's information assets at risk. Once the risk assessment process is accomplished, the information security policy construction process begins.

3.5.2. Information security policy construction

One of the categories that emerged during the coding process with the highest number of codes is the writing of the security policy. Since the chosen sample deals with the information security policy development, it is not surprising that there was an enormous number of codes. The following constitute the activities of constructing a security policy: Executive management provides *high level security policy* that contains directives. These directives give a sense of the company's overall security policy philosophy (Diver, 2007). The high level information security policies emanating from the executive management are transformed into *organizational standards and guidelines* (Von Solms *et al.,* 2011). Organizational standards are detailed statements of what should be done to comply with the policy (Grobler and Von Solms, 2004), but not how to do it (Mauritian Computer Emergency Team, 2011). Lastly, the detailed information security policies are supported by lower level security policies also called procedures (Von Solms *et al.,* 2011). Procedures provide the step-by-step detailed instructions on how to carry out the requirements of an information security policy (Diver, 2007). Once the information security policy construction is complete, the next stage deals with its implementation across all levels of the organization.

3.5.3. Information security policy implementation

After the creation of the security policy is complete, the most difficult part of the policy development process is rolling it out to the organization (Kadam, 2007). The introduction of a new information security policy brings changes in the way employees behave in handling the organization's information. The whole idea is to gain support from the organization's community to accept the new changes. This can be achieved by educating and training employees on the new information security policy requirements. The objective of the information security awareness is to make sure that all stakeholders are aware and understand their responsibilities towards the security policy requirements (Talbot and Woodward, 2009). In order to reach such an audience, different business communication (notices, intranet, posters, newsletters, etc.) should be used to promote security policy awareness. Information security researchers agree that the Security Education, Training and Awareness (SETA) program are three important pillars that are crucial to control the information security misuse (D'Arcy *et al.,* 2009). D'Arcy *et al.* (2009) states that "SETA program extends beyond just "awareness of security policy and often includes on-going efforts to (1) convey knowledge about information risks in the organizational environment, (2) emphasize recent actions against employees for security policy violations, and (3) raise employee's awareness of their responsibilities regarding organizational information resources". Once the information security policy has been implemented in the organization and all employees have been trained and educated on the new information security policy requirements, it is crucial to put mechanisms in place that ensure the compliance and enforcement of the new information security policy.

3.5.4. Information security policy compliance and enforcement

A number of theories have been developed underlying employees' behavioural intention towards the compliance of information security policies. Within the chosen sample, Bulgurcu *et al.* (2010) argue that the General Deterrence Theory (GDT) and Theory of Planned Behaviour (TPB) are examples of theories that ensure information security policy compliance. GDT predicts that the increase in the severity of punishment on those who violate the rules of the organization reduce some criminal acts (Blumstein *et al.,* 1978). A study conducted by Siponen *et al.* (2010) found that the use of sanctions is a good approach to encounter the employees who violate information security policy and consequently reduce the computer abuse. Based on the TPB, Bulgurcu *et al.* (2010) posit that an employee's intention to comply with the organization's security policy is influenced by *normative norms, perceived behavioural control* and *attitude* toward compliance. The theory explains the intention of an individual to perform a given behaviour (Fishbein and Ajzen, 1975). Normative beliefs reflect normative expectations of peers or colleagues (Fishbein and Ajzen, 1975). These constitute the social pressures from the employees' managers, information security policy development team and colleagues.

3.5.5. Information security policy monitoring, review and assessment

The need to periodically or non-periodically review and update the security policy is indispensable to the organization (Talbot and Woodward, 2009). Hong (2006) suggests that the information security policy should be evaluated and reviewed on regular basis to make sure that the latest threats, new regulations and government policies are kept up to date. To facilitate the security policy review and maintenance, Talbot and Woodward (2009) advise the use of an automated system of review scheduling which timely alerts when a major change to the existing security practices have occurred. Importantly, the security violations, deviations, and audit information should also be reviewed (Diver, 2007) as the result of this process help to identify the area where the policy was not enforced or where frequent policy deviations occurred.

3.5.6. Management support

Bayuk (2009) argues that the first step in composing a security policy is to get the top management's opinions on how they understand security in the organization.

"The implementation of security policy must start from the executive management" (Bayuk, 2009). Johnson and Merkow (2010) posit that: "without executive support, policies are just words. To have meaning, they must be given the right priority and be enforced". Indeed, top management is important in enforcing information security policy so that employees can take the policy requirements seriously. Furthermore, management plays key role in approving the policy and making sure that there is enough budget to cover all resources required.

3.5.7. Employee support

Employee support consists of end-users who carry out different activities in an organization. Maynard *et al.* (2011) suggest that the end-user community needs to be part of the development effort to ensure that the multidisciplinary nature of the organization is incorporated in the information security policy development process. Diver (2007) recommends that the end-users must be involved earlier in the policy development so that they can identify errors and difficulties and correct them before the security policy deployment. "If the policy documents are hard to understand, users may not read them fully or may fail to understand them correctly" (Diver, 2007). In order to have an effective information security policy, everyone in the organization must practice them. If employees practice the information security policy requirements day-to-day, it helps to create a security culture that protects the organization's information.

3.5.8. International security standards

Diver (2007) and Hong *et al* (2006) agree that international standards such as ISO 27002 are good starting point to implement the information security policy which therefore improves an organization's information security. In addition, Bayuk (2009) supports the idea of using international standards as a baseline framework because they increase trust with the organization's stakeholders. Bayuk (2009) states "…this is a reasonable approach as it helps to ensure that that the policy will be accepted as adequate not only by company management, but also by external auditors and others who may have a stake in the organization's information security program". Undoubtedly, an international security standard that has been approved by security experts can definitely provide the basis requirements to start developing an information security policy.

3.5.9. Regulations requirements

The main reason to develop information security policy is to mitigate the various security risks that organizations face. One of the risks that organizations face is the increasing legal requirements (Doherty *et al.*, 2009). Edwards (2011) argues that organizations must first identify and understand all regulatory requirements that dictate the creation of such policies before writing the information security policy. Avolio and Scott (2007) suggest that information security policy developers should familiarize themselves with penalties of non-compliance with laws, as this will aid the organizations to prioritize their policies and implement the proper level of discipline to employees who violate the policies. Therefore, it is necessary that organizations obtain legal advice to ensure that their policies are legally binding (Maynard *et al.*, 2011) and the employees violating such policies will be legally liable of their behaviour.

3.5.10. Information security policy stakeholders

The development of an effective security policy requires a combination of different skills emanating from different stakeholders experiences (Diver, 2007). Maynard *et al.* (2011) recommend the involvement of ICT Specialists and security specialists in the policy development process because they have technical knowledge of the systems that the information security policy intends to protect as well as the security of these systems. Diver (2007) posits that the human resource department should review and/or approve the security policy based on how the policy relates to organization's existing policies. This is necessary to make sure that there is a consistency between the organization's security policies with the standard organizational practices (Maynard *et al.*, 2011). The inclusion of multiple stakeholders is crucial to the organization because it gives the whole organization a sense of security policy ownership and facilitates the security policy acceptance and adoption. The next section discusses the model construction.

4. Model construction

Based on the analysis and interpretation of the ten categories discussed, different dimensions of the model are proposed. The first dimension is the security policy development as it encompasses the processes needed to develop an information security policy such as risk assessment, policy construction, policy implementation, policy compliance and policy monitoring, assessment and review. The second dimension is the security policy drivers as it is composed of threats that put the organization under pressure to have mechanisms to protect their information. The third dimension is the security policy guidance because it is constituted by security standards that guide organizations in constructing an information security policy. The fourth dimension is concerned with the support of the policy. Management, employees and stakeholders need to support the security policy in order for it to survive and attain its objectives. Lastly, the organization needs to use existing theories to understand the employees' behavioral intention with regard to information security policy compliance. These dimensions are shown in the proposed model in Figure 1.

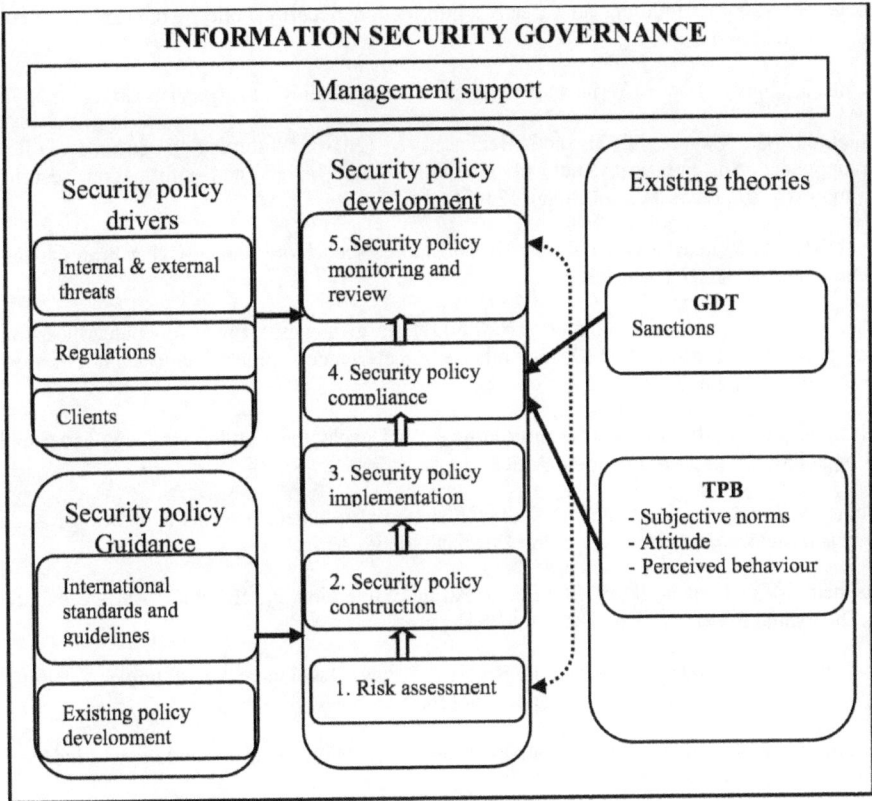

Figure 1: Information security policy development model

The different components that are shown in Figure 1 are considered to be the main pillars of the information security policy development processes.

5. Conclusion

The research question posed by this paper is what processes organizations need to follow in developing and implementing an effective information policy. The list of the ten categories that emerged during the reducing stage of the content analysis was analysed and interpreted so that a model for information security policy development could be inferred from the emerged ten categories. The proposed model provides the different dimensions that a specific organization needs to take into account during the information security policy development and implementation process. It ensures both comprehensive and sustainable information security policies.

6. References

Avolio, M. and Scott, P. (2007). "Producing your network security policy". *WatchGuard Technologies, Inc.*

Bacik, S. (2008). Buildling an Effective Information Security Policy Architecture . *Boca Raton: CRC Press.*

Bayuk, J. (2009). "How to Write an Information Security Policy". *Computerworld.*

Bulgurcu, B., Cavusoglu, H. and Benbasat, I. (2010). "Information Security Policy Compliance: An empirical study of rationality-based beliefs and information security awareness". *MIS Quarterly,* 34(3), pp. 523-548.

Cybersecurity Watch Survey. (2011). "Organizations Need More Skilled Cyber Professionals to Stay Secure". *CSO Magazine.*

D'Arcy, J., Hovav, A. and Galletta, D. (2009). "User awareness of security countermeasures and its impact on information systems misuse: A deterrence approach". *Information Systems Research,* 20(1), pp. 79-98.

Diver, S. (2007). "Information Security Policy – A Development Guide for Large and Small Companies". *SANS Institute.* South Africa.

DuPreez, R. (2010). "A model for green IT strategy: a content analysis approach". *Nelson Mandela Metropolitan University:* Port Elizabeth, South Africa.

Fishbein, M. and Ajzen, I. (1975). "Belief, Attitude, Intention and Behavior: An Introduction to Theory and Research": MA, Addison-Wesley.

Kadam, A. W. (2007). "Information Security Policy Development and Implementation". *Information Systems Security,* 16(5), pp. 246-256.

Krippendorff, K. (2004). "Content analysis: an introduction to its methodology" (2nd ed.). Sage Publications, Inc.

Mauritian Computer Emergency Team. (2011). "Guidelines on Information Security Policy". *Mauritius: National Computer Board.* CMSGu2011-04.

Maynard, S., Ruighaver, A. and Ahmad, A. (2011). "Stakeholders in security policy development". *Proceedings of the 9th Australian Information Security Management Conference.* Perth Western, Australia.

Richardson, R. (2009). "CSI Computer Crime & Security Survey". *Computer Security Institute.*

Talbot, S. and Woodward, A. (2009). "Improving an organisations existing information technology policy to increase security". *Proceedings of the 7th Australian Information Security Management Conference.* Perth, Western Australia.

Tuyikeze, T. and Flowerday, S. (2013). "Information Security Policy Maturity Model (ISPMM) ". *Joint International Conference on Engineering Education and Research and International Conference on Information Technology.* Cape Town, South Africa.

Von Solms, R., Thomson, K.-L. and Maninjwa, M. (2011). "Information security governance control through comprehensive policy architectures". *ISSA.* Johannesburg, South Africa.

Engaging Stakeholders in Security Design:
An Assumption-Driven Approach

S. Faily

Software Systems Research Centre, Bournemouth University
e-mail : sfaily@bournemouth.ac.uk

Abstract

System stakeholders fail to engage with security until comparatively late in the design and development process. User Experience artefacts like personas and scenarios create this engagement, but creating and contextualising them is difficult without real-world, empirical data; such data cannot be easily elicited from disengaged stakeholders. This paper presents an approach for engaging stakeholders in the elicitation and specification of security requirements at a late-stage of a system's design; this approach relies on assumption-based personas and scenarios, which are aligned with security and requirements analysis activities. We demonstrate this approach by describing how it was used to elicit security requirements for a medical research portal.

Keywords

Personas, Scenarios, Requirements, Risks, Context

1. Introduction

When building systems, it is generally agreed that its stakeholders should be engaged in security as early in the design process as possible. However, all too often, security is considered an after-thought, and security requirements are not properly considered until comparatively late in a project's lifecycle.

Engaging the stakeholders is difficult. The right stakeholders may be heavily in demand, and motivated by innovation rather than security. For example, a software developer may be required to dedicate significant time and resources to understanding the complexity of a problem domain, leaving themselves little time for applying standard security design techniques. Such stakeholders may also find security a distant topic, with media reports on security threats and privacy invasions as somehow irrelevant to a system they are trying to build.

One way of engaging the security unengaged is rely not only on evocation, but also people's natural bias towards personified, rather than anonymous, risk (Schneier, 2012). Software developers may gloss over stories about the loss or public disclosure of patient medical data, but highlighting *their* contribution towards such losses may draw their attention. User Experience (UX) artefacts can evoke by contextualising or personifying these losses, but building them requires real-world empirical data; this can only be collected when stakeholders are engaged, thereby leading to a `chicken-and-egg' situation.

Recent work (Dray, 2014) has highlighted the power of assumptions when engaging developers. Using UX research to challenge assumptions helps developers recognise why such issues need to be addressed, and focus their curiosity towards addressing them. To explore the power of challenging such assumptions, this paper presents an approach for eliciting and specifying security requirements using assumption-based personas, scenarios, and risks to engage system developers to think more about security for a medical research portal, particularly how the portal might be misused. In Section 2, we briefly describe the related work upon which this approach is based, before presenting the approach in Section 3. We describe a case study where this approach was applied in Section 4, before concluding with some implications for security design in Section 5.

2. Related Work

2.1. Personifying Security Expectations

The *personas* technique is a popular UX approach for personifying users to understand their goals and needs (Cooper et al, 2007). Personas are models that provide a specification of archetypical user behaviour. By designing software to satisfy the expectations of these personas, software developers need not rely on their own assumptions about users, which may be unwarranted. In recent years, personas have also been used to support secure system design interventions. For example, (Faily and Fléchais, 2010) found that personas not only provided empathy about the security challenges of hard-to-reach user groups, but were useful for eliciting unforeseen user characteristics if stakeholders felt a persona didn't match reality.

Personas are data-driven, and collecting the empirical data necessary to build them is difficult if stakeholders are not engaged enough to provide or facilitate access to such data. Given these difficulties, (Pruitt and Adlin, 2006) proposes the use of *assumption personas*; these are sketches that articulate assumptions about a user population. Once created, assumption personas allow stakeholders to see the value of personas, and how assumptions may colour their characteristics.

2.2. Contextualising Personas in Secure System Design

Personas build empathy, but their goals and expectations need to be put in context. For this reason, personas are often paired with scenarios; these centre around activities performed by users, rather than around the users themselves. For example, (Rosson and Carroll, 2002) used scenarios to describe how hypothetical stakeholders tackle current practice; these scenarios may be based on empirical data or assumptions. More recently, (Parkin et al, 2010) successfully engaged senior managers using low-fidelity prototypes of security management tools, and a collection of scenarios illustrating their use.

Together, personas and scenarios illustrate security problems, but understanding these problems is not enough to specify solutions that address them: we need to carry out a more formal security and requirements analysis. Personas and scenarios supplement these analyses by illustrating how risks are realised, and how specification decisions are operationalized. In doing so, the human implications of security design decisions in different contexts of use can be better perceived.

To illustrate how these different approaches can work together, the Integrating Requirements and Information Security (IRIS) Framework (Faily and Fléchais, 2010, 2011) was devised; the framework demonstrates how the elements constituting personas, scenarios, requirements, and risks might be aligned, and the application of security, usability, and requirements techniques can complement each other.

3. Approach

Using personas and scenarios, we have developed an approach for eliciting and specifying security requirements that engages stakeholders in security concerns. This approach not only captures information about how usability and security concerns impact requirements, it also accommodates a lack of end-user access, limited access to project stakeholders, and the need to make assumptions about users as transparent as possible during design.

The approach is tool-supported by the open-source Computer Aided Integration of Requirements and Information Security (CAIRIS) requirements management tool (Faily, 2013). CAIRIS was developed to support the IRIS Framework; it allows the capture of security, usability, and requirements data as the techniques are applied, guides the creation of personas, and automatically evaluates risks for different contexts of use (Faily and Lyle, 2013; Faily and Fléchais 2010b).

3.1. Assumption Persona Development

The first stage of the approach involves specifying the expectations held about a system's prospective user-community. Implicit assumptions in the available documentation are identified, and used to form the basis of assumption personas. Not only do these assumption personas clarify expectations about end-users, subsequent discussion around these confirm a useful scope of analysis for the subsequent stage.

For each role relevant to the scope of analysis, the available documentation is reviewed to elicit factoids for each role. These are used to establish persona characteristics and, based on these, assumption persona narratives. Once the assumption personas are developed, these are presented to the project team for review. Any issues raised by the team are used to revise the assumption personas or correct any misinterpretations held about the system. The process for building these personas is described in more detail in (Faily and Fléchais, 2010a).

3.2. Design Sessions

This stage entails holding small focus groups with project team members. Each session focuses on the use of scenarios, requirements, or risk analysis.

A scenario session involves modelling scenarios carried out by the assumption personas in their respective contexts. Like the personas, these scenarios are grounded in assumptions identified from project documentation, or from analysis undertaken during other design sessions. Some of these scenarios focus on *misusability*, by illustrating how unintentional misuse of the system might lead to security problems.

A requirements session involves using the KAOS goal-oriented requirements engineering approach (van Lamsweerde, 2009) to elicit and specify requirements needing to be satisfied in order for the scenarios to be realised. Requirements are modelled as goal trees and, in addition to being refined to sub-goals, goals may conflict with obstacles: conditions representing undesired behaviour and preventing an associated goal from being achieved (van Lamsweerde and Letier, 2000). Such obstacles may arise from intentional, as well as accidental, obstacles, thereby making it possible for them to model threats (van Lamsweerde, 2004).

Risk analysis sessions involve using AEGIS (Appropriate and Effective Guidance for Information Security): a participative design process (Fléchais et al, 2007). This entails the team members jointly modelling the system's assets in different contexts; these assets are modelled using UML class diagrams, where classes represent different assets. The assets are evaluated according to values held by the participants about them. Vulnerabilities, threats, and risks affecting these assets are elicited, before possible security controls mitigating these risks are selected. Although one of many risk analysis processes, AEGIS's diagrammatic notation is useful for engaging stakeholders about security, providing useful discussion about asset values, and eventually yielding relevant security requirements (Fléchais, 2005).

In all sessions, assumption personas are used as an authority for user expectations; these are modified if aspects of the analysis challenge their characteristics.

During the sessions, elicited requirements and security analysis elements are specified within CAIRIS, and the resulting models are discussed with the session participants. After the final session, each requirement is examined and assigned a responsible role. Following this, a specification document is generated and sent to project team members for their review.

4. Case Study

This approach was evaluated by using it to elicit security requirements for a portal that facilitated the sharing of medical study data. The study data consisted of long-running, longitudinal studies of people sharing some specific characteristic. By providing an accessible interface to such studies, the portal ensured that research data and meta-data could be re-used by researchers, thereby reducing the need for running unnecessary and expensive long-term studies.

Two particular user roles dominated the design of the portal. The first of these were academic researchers; these would use the portal to find datasets of interest. The project sponsors were keen to maximise take-up by the researcher community, and initiatives encouraging this would be looked upon kindly. The second class of users were data managers; these were responsible for curating data sets, which would be available via the portal. The perception held by the project team was that data managers were portal's key user community.

The portal design was dominated by two contexts of use. The *Research* context was concerned with researchers interacting with the portal as part of their day-to-day research. The *Study* context was concerned with data managers' interaction with the portal to curate their datasets, and managing requests for accessing them.

Although empirical data from representative stakeholders would have made an invaluable contribution to the usability and security analysis, there was no scope for collecting data from research end-users. Similarly, time constraints meant that data managers from the study exemplars would also not be available. Fortunately, the development team agreed to act as user proxies because of the time they had spent working with data managers from the exemplar studies, and their domain knowledge based on previous, related research. However, given that the development team had little direct experience of the researcher community, it was important that any assumptions that were made about both data managers and researchers needed to be as transparent as possible.

Unfortunately, limited access to stakeholders also extended to the development team. Despite the project team being small with only 4 developers, it faced several tight deadlines; this made opportunities to work with the project team severely limited. Consequently, it was essential to be parsimonious with regards to team member access, while at the same time ensuring that the intervention had an impact on the development of the portal.

4.1. Assumption Persona Development

When the study began, only two documents were available for eliciting assumptions: a requirements specification for the portal, and a technical annexe to the portal's contract signed by all project partners.

After a review of the documentation, three roles were evident: researchers, data managers, and gateway administrators. Based on these roles, the documentation was analysed to elicit assumptions. Assumptions were elicited about behaviour, which could be reasonably assumed if the documentation accurately represented the concerns of the particular stakeholder role. For example, a requirement indicating that first-line support to the portal would be provided between the hours of 9 am to

5.30pm might reasonably suggest that the authors believe researchers work only during commercial office hours.

Three skeleton assumption personas were created for each of these roles: Alex (an academic researcher), Brian (a data manager), and Colin (an administrator for the Data Gateway). For each persona's characteristic, a narrative was written commensurate with it. For example, based on persona characteristics summarised by *In no hurry* and *Looking to apply data-set once discovered*, the following narrative describing Alex's motivation was written:

Alex is looking to use a dataset as soon as he discovers it is suitable. He isn't in a particular hurry, so is prepared to wait for his registration to the Data Gateway and the respective data set to be approved.

The results of this initial analysis to date were presented to the project team. This presentation described the scope assumed for the analysis, provided an overview of the work carried out, and Alex, Brian, and Colin were presented. Each persona selected particular persona characteristics. The third characteristic was chosen as the most divisive, in order to stimulate lively discussion about the persona. At the end of this session, it was agreed that Colin's activities were not relevant to the scope of analysis, and this persona was dropped from the remainder of the intervention.

Despite the nature of the documentation used, it was possible to elicit a surprising amount of data about both the possible activities and attitudes of personas. Moreover, many persona characteristics were elicited during the design sessions. As such, the personas evolved throughout the design sessions, concurring with best practice in the use of personas, which suggests that personas should be fostered throughout a project's lifecycle (Pruitt and Adlin, 2006).

Although identifying the basis for characteristics was straightforward, justifying them was more difficult. Prior to their initial validation, many of the characteristics were based exclusively on individual pieces of empirical data. As such, value judgements about the source data and context were directly reflected in these characteristics.

Although the initial workshop surfaced a number of these issues, it was usually not until the personas were directly written into scenarios in design sessions that certain invalid characteristics were identified. Applying the personas within a specific context did, however, help identify missing data about behaviour not identified during their creation and initial presentation to the team.

4.2. Design Sessions

Four design sessions were held over the course of a month. The first was a scenario session followed, a day later, by a requirements session. A risk analysis session took place the following week, followed by a final risk analysis session the week after.

Due to project deadlines, rather than having access to multiple developers per session, only a single developer was available. The same developer was consistently used for each session, and was available for email clarification when queries arose outside at other times. In addition to the allocated portal developer, a non-project domain expert participated in the second session. Although this participant was only partially knowledgeable in the on-going project, she was aware of the problem domain in general.

The approach taken during each session was more flexible than originally envisaged. In practice, multiple techniques were used when the situation deemed it useful. For example, KAOS was used in each of the first sessions when it was felt most appropriate. Similarly, elements of AEGIS were also used in the first two sessions to elicit assets, their relationships, and concerns arising from goals and scenarios. Switching from the use of one technique to another did not seem to hinder the thought processes of participants in the sessions.

During the sessions, the personas were progressively refined and embellished with further characteristics from the documentation as new insights were gleaned.

The amount of data elicited from the risk analysis sessions was comparatively small. This was mainly due to the resolution of many security and usability problems during the requirements and scenarios sessions. Another reason for the small number of explicit risks was a tendency by the project team to dismiss security issues deemed out of scope. On more than one occasion, assets identified as in scope, such as portal documentation about the use of some functionality, was de-scoped. This issue of passing responsibility for out-of-scope issues was also apparent from the threats and vulnerabilities highlighted in both contexts of use.

The issue of scope deferral was also contextual. Most of the risk analysis elements were elicited from the Research context; these were associated with assets deemed out of the project scope. The few risk analysis elements not concerning the Study environment were also marginalised. For example, of four risks elicited, only one - a Man-in-the-Middle attack - concerned the Study environment. Upon discussing resolutions to this, it was agreed that the portal relied on a secure channel between some of its components. Consequently, responsibility for mitigating more general Man-in-the-Middle attacks was delegated to the administration team responsible for one of these components.

Although the project team were reluctant to take a defence-in-depth approach to tackling security problems, security concerns were eventually identified. This was possible by focusing attention on goal obstruction within the Study environment; unlike the Research environment, this environment concerned concepts that *were* within the project scope. This allowed threats and vulnerabilities to be mitigated at the design level when considered in context with other portal requirements. This was especially useful because, besides the generic internet-facing threats and vulnerabilities, it was not entirely clear what the threat model facing the portal might be.

5. Conclusion

In this paper, we presented an approach where assumptions were used to ground an approach for engaging project team members when eliciting and specifying security requirements. The case study example demonstrated that, in lieu of research on a target system's users, assumptions afford the creation of personas that engage developers in security while they building a system. Moreover, these personas can be used in design sessions, which elicit or draw attention to security requirements without disrupting a project's on-going development activities. Based on the lessons learned applying this approach, three security design implications can be taken away.

First, engagement can follow by focusing on the indirect, rather than direct, consequences of security. One of the difficulties in completing this study arose from the lack of engagement with the project team. Although the project team appeared to be genuinely interested in the approach and the analysis being carried out, their time was too limited to properly integrate this analysis into the day-to-day running of the project. The case study showed that focusing on the impact of non-security design decisions is a more effective technique for engaging developers in security issues rather than relying on fear of more generic threats, particular when these threats may or may not be relevant (or perceived relevant) to the scope of analysis.

Second, as much as security should be considered at the outset of a project, we may need to develop design approaches for treating it at a comparatively late stage. This study reinforced the need for innovative thinking to ensure that important security issues were built into the system. This is an important finding as the individual techniques used were designed on the basis that they would be used early in the design process. In contrast, not only were they applied at a comparatively late stage; they were used in parallel with other design activities.

Finally, our findings lead us to conclude that when a security design process is devised, its techniques should scale to working with less than optimal input data. Moreover, the process should attempt to carry out as much analysis as reasonably possible carried out without disrupting other project activities.

6. References

Cooper, A., Reimann, R., and Cronin, D. (2007). About Face 3: The Essentials of Interaction Design. John Wiley & Sons.

Dray, S. M. (2014). Questioning Assumptions: UX Research That Really Mat- ters. interactions, 21(2):82–85.

Faily, S. (2013). CAIRIS web site. http://github.com/failys/CAIRIS.

Faily, S. and Fléchais, I. (2010). A Meta-Model for Usable Secure Requirements Engineering. In Proceedings of the 6th International Workshop on Software Engineering for Secure Systems, pages 126–135. IEEE Computer Society.

Faily, S. and Fléchais, I. (2010). Barry is not the weakest link: eliciting secure system requirements with personas. In Proceedings of the 24th BCS Interaction Specialist Group Conference, BCS '10, pages 124–132. British Computer Society.

Faily, S. and Fléchais, I. (2010a). The secret lives of assumptions: Developing and refining assumption personas for secure system design. In Proceedings of the 3rd Conference on Human-Centered Software Engineering, volume LNCS 6409, pages 111–118. Springer.

Faily, S. and Fléchais, I. (2010b). Towards tool-support for Usable Secure Requirements Engineering with CAIRIS. International Journal of Secure Software Engineering, 1(3):56–70.

Faily, S. and Fléchais, I. (2011). Eliciting Policy Requirements for Critical National Infrastructure using the IRIS Framework. International Journal of Secure Software Engineering, 2(4):114–119.

Faily, S. and Lyle, J. (2013). Guidelines for integrating personas into software engineering tools. In Proceedings of the 5th ACM SIGCHI symposium on Engineering interactive computing systems, EICS '13, pages 69–74. ACM.

Fléchais, I. (2005). Designing Secure and Usable Systems. PhD thesis, University College London.

Fléchais, I., Mascolo, C., and Sasse, M. A. (2007). Integrating security and usability into the requirements and design process. International Journal of Electronic Security and Digital Forensics, 1(1):12–26.

Parkin, S., van Moorsel, A., Inglesant, P., and Sasse, M. A. (2010). A stealth approach to usable security: helping it security managers to identify work- able security solutions. In Proceedings of the 2010 workshop on New security paradigms, NSPW '10, pages 33–50. ACM.

Pruitt, J. and Adlin, T. (2006). The persona lifecycle: keeping people in mind throughout product design. Elsevier.

Rosson, M. B. and Carroll, J. M. (2002). Usability engineering: scenario-based development of human-computer interaction. Academic Press.

Schneier, B. (2012). Liars & Outliers: Enabling the Trust That Society Needs to Thrive. John Wiley & Sons.

van Lamsweerde, A. (2004). Elaborating security requirements by construction of intentional anti-models. In Proceedings of the 26th International Conference on Software Engineering, pages 148–157. IEEE Computer Society.

van Lamsweerde, A. (2009). Requirements Engineering: from system goals to UML models to software specifications. John Wiley & Sons.

van Lamsweerde, A. and Letier, E. (2000). Handling obstacles in goal-oriented requirements engineering. IEEE Transactions on Software Engineering, 26(10):978–1005.

Using Actions and Intentions to Evaluate Categorical Responses to Phishing and Genuine Emails

K. Parsons[1], A. McCormac[1], M. Pattinson[2], M. Butavicius[1] and C. Jerram[2]

[1] Defence Science and Technology Organisation, Edinburgh, Australia
[2] Business School, University of Adelaide, Australia
e-mail: {kathryn.parsons; agata.mccormac;
marcus.butavicius}@dsto.defence.gov.au; {malcolm.pattinson;
cate.jerram}@adelaide.edu.au

Abstract

While many studies have investigated people's susceptibility to phishing emails, little attention has been paid to how behavioural responses translate into overall intent when users are not informed they are undertaking a phishing study. This paper examines how well the quantitative multiple-choice categorisation used in such studies reflects the underlying reasoning of the users. The results of a role play scenario in which 117 participants were asked to manage 50 emails are presented. The users' multiple-choice actions were recoded based on their response to the question, *"What aspect of this email influenced your decision?"* using the Action-Intention Email Response Framework. According to this framework, intention incorporates the use of security-based reasoning, usefulness and phishing assessment. Results indicated that recoding did not significantly influence overall accuracy scores, which provides empirical support for the multiple-choice categorisation as a method of indirectly testing phishing susceptibility. However, closer examination revealed that combining the user's recommended actions with their qualitative responses provided significantly more detail on user's intent which, in many cases, changed the coding of the user's response to the email. Implications for the analysis of user performance in similar studies are discussed.

Keywords

Information security (InfoSec), Information risk, Phishing, Social engineering, Human behaviour

1. Introduction

The online threat posed by phishing has received widespread attention for almost a decade, but it remains a significant problem today (Furnell, 2013). Phishing describes a malicious attempt to deceptively acquire personal or financial information, and phishing attacks can have direct consequences to an individual or organisation, such as financial loss, as well as indirect consequences, such as damaged reputation (Parsons, McCormac, Pattinson, Butavicius, & Jerram, 2013). Recent research has demonstrated that when people are primed about phishing risks, they adopt a more diligent approach to screening emails (Pattinson, Jerram, Parsons, McCormac, & Butavicius, 2012). This has implications for the interpretation of previous studies of users' susceptibility to phishing, as it is likely that studies in which the concept of phishing was mentioned to participants may have underestimated users' susceptibility.

Hence, to more accurately assess the level of susceptibility expected in the real world (where people are infrequently reminded about the risks of phishing), it is necessary to utilise a method where participants are not directly told to make a decision regarding the legitimacy of an email. However, such studies make assumptions about a users' underlying thought process, and it may be difficult to reflect the complexity of user behaviour without revealing that participants are undertaking a phishing study.

1.1. Previous research

A number of studies have assessed users' susceptibility by directly asking participants to make a phishing decision. For example, Furnell (2007) provided respondents with the options 'illegitimate', 'legitimate' or 'don't know', and other studies asked participants to rate an email's authenticity on a five point scale, from 'Certainly phishing' to 'Certainly not phishing' (Jakobsson, Tsow, Shah, Blevis, & Lim, 2007; Tsow & Jakobsson, 2007) or asked participants to indicate if an email was a phishing attempt (Robila & Ragucci, 2006). A more recent study provided participants with the options to mark emails as important, leave them in the inbox or delete, but this study informed participants that they were assessing the legitimacy of emails (Hong, Kelley, Tembe, Murphy-Hill, & Mayhorn, 2013).

Several researchers have used a role play scenario, in which participants are not directly informed that they are taking part in a phishing study. Instead, participants are told they are participating in a study about email use or computer use. For example, Wang, Chen, Herath, Vishwanath and Rao (2012) asked participants about their likelihood to respond to an email on a five-point scale from 'Not At All Likely' to 'Very Likely'. Pattinson et al. (2012) provided participants with the options 'Leave the email in the inbox and flag for follow up', 'Leave the email in the inbox', 'Delete the email' or 'Delete the email and block the sender'.

Downs, Holbrook and Cranor (2006) presented users with eight emails, and asked them to react as they normally would in their own life. The options chosen naturally (e.g., reply by email, contact the sender by phone or in person, delete the email, save the email, click on the link, copy and paste the URL, or type the URL into a browser window) were then provided to participants in future experiments (Downs, Holbrook, & Cranor, 2007; Sheng, Holbrook, Kumaraguru, Cranor, & Downs, 2010). Although these options are comprehensive and likely to allow for the complexity of user behaviour, the specificity may indirectly prime participants about the fact the study is interested in phishing susceptibility.

1.2. Aim of this paper

The aim of this paper is to validate the quantitative multiple-choice categorisation utilised by Parsons, McCormac, Pattinson, Butavicius & Jerram (2013). To achieve this, we developed a framework, the Action-Intention Email Response Framework, through which user action and intention could be recoded. Results based on the raw (quantitative, multiple-choice) method are then compared with the recoded mixed method (quantitative and qualitative) results (Tashakkori & Teddlie, 2003) to validate and evaluate the methodology of Parsons et al. (2013).

The structure of this paper is as follows. The next section describes the research method and details of the emails utilised. This is followed by the results, in which the categories of the framework are introduced and described, and the recoded results are presented and compared to the raw scores. Finally, the conclusions summarise the significance of these findings in the context of previous literature.

2. Method

Fifty emails, consisting of 25 genuine emails and 25 phishing emails, were utilised. All emails were either actual emails received by the authors, or were found online. The emails represented a range of topics such as banking, shopping and social networking, and an effort was made to select comparable genuine and phishing emails for each topic. The emails were altered to include the details of a fictitious character, 'Sally Jones', as if she was the recipient of the emails. A role play based method was utilised, in which participants were told that they were viewing emails from the inbox of 'Sally Jones' and that the experiment was designed to study how people manage emails.

The participants consisted of 117 students from the University of Adelaide. The majority were female (90) and in the first year of their university study (93). The sample included 64 business students and 54 psychology students. They received $25 cash for their participation. Participants were presented with randomised images of 50 email messages sequentially. For each email, participants were asked to respond to the question, *"How would you manage this email?"* with one of the four replies: A) leave the email in the inbox and flag for follow up; B) leave the email in the inbox; C) delete the email; or D) delete the email and block the sender. Participants were also required to respond to the question *"What aspect of this email influenced your decision?"* in an open text field. More information regarding this scenario-based method (Erickson, 1995) is reported in Parsons et al. (2013).

3. Results

In Parsons et al. (2013) a phishing email was deemed to be correctly managed if participants responded with 'delete the email' or 'delete the email and block the sender'. A genuine email was deemed to be correctly managed if participants responded with 'leave the email in the inbox and flag for follow up' or 'leave the email in the inbox'.

However, a preliminary analysis of qualitative responses to the question, *"What aspect of this email influenced your decision?"* revealed that some responses did not correspond with the assumption that a phishing email would be *deleted* or *deleted and blocked*, and a genuine email would be *left in the inbox* or *flagged for follow up*. Some participants flagged emails for follow up to alert Sally to a potential security risk that should be investigated.

In order to examine the decision-making process more closely, a second-order analysis was conducted (Shkedi, 2004). This involved deriving the participants' underlying reasoning from their qualitative response which, in turn, was used to modify the first order responses (i.e., the categorical responses). Of the 5850 responses (50 responses for each of the 117 participants), 5817 (or 99%) included enough information to enable recoding. The other 33 responses were either insufficient or unclear, and those responses were removed from further analysis.

3.1. Reasoning provided by participants

An analysis of the responses provided by participants, together with the multiple-choice option chosen, identified four important aspects, namely:

- the action recommended by participants (e.g., to delete or keep the email),
- whether participants mentioned or implied the use of security-based reasoning,
- whether participants appeared to believe the email was phishing, and
- whether participants appeared to believe the email was useful.

These aspects were used to develop the Action-Intention Email Response Framework, which represents the possible reasons for participants' decisions. The framework consists of eight categories, as shown in Table 1. It is important to highlight that categorisation for the security factor was based on whether the participant mentioned or implied the use of security-based reasoning, even if the aspects of security specified were incorrect or incorrectly implemented. For example, one participant chose to *delete and block* a genuine email from a bank, and responded with, *"There is no [bank name] logo or anything which represents the company itself. This email is very suspicious"*. This is classified as security-based reasoning, even though the assumption that a genuine email should have a professional looking logo is flawed, and the reasoning utilised did not help the individual to correctly manage the email in question.

Category Identification	Action	Security-based reasoning?	Perceived to be phishing?	Perceived to be useful?
1a	Deleted	Yes	Yes	No
1b	Deleted	Yes	No	No
2a	Kept	Yes	No	Yes
2b	Kept	Yes	Yes	No
2c	Kept	Yes	Conditional	Conditional
3a	Deleted	No	No	No
3b	Deleted	No	No	Yes
4a	Kept	No	No	Yes

Table 1: Categories of the Action-Intention Email Response Framework

Every response to the question, *"What aspect of this email influenced your decision?"* was then examined by one of three judges and was assigned a category. To ensure valid and consistent categorisation, Taylor's (1976) hermeneutics approach was utilised. Random subsets of the responses were re-examined by a second judge and contentious cases were then examined by all three judges to reach a consensus.

QUADRANT 1: SECURITY / DELETED		QUADRANT 2: SECURITY / KEPT	
DELETE AND BLOCK	**DELETE**	**LEAVE IN INBOX**	**FLAG FOR FOLLOW UP**
[1a] *"link is fake. does not take you to [company name] website"*	[1a] *"Be careful - no logos or sender details, error in spacing after full stop, asking for credit card details."*	[2a] *"Informational email from [company name], no threat."*	[2a] *"Accurate looking email information, trusted sender, doesn't look like phishing."*
[1a] *"There is no [company name] logo or anything which represents the company itself. This email is very suspicious"*	[1b] *"Does not appear to be a harmful email however is pretty useless and not worth keeping."*	[2b] *"seemed dodgy, maybe ring bank to confirm"*	[2b] *"Sally needs to call the card company immediately and double check."*
[1b] *"It's not a phishing e-mail but it's advertising and it's unimportant when managing a workplace inbox."*	[1b] *"This is not a sinister email but contains irrelevant information."*	[2c] *"The e-mail address looks legitimate, and if Sally really does have this account, then she may respond to it"*	[2c] *"If Sally has created an account at [company name], it should be trustable."*

QUADRANT 3: NO SECURITY / DELETED		QUADRANT 4: NO SECURITY / KEPT	
DELETE AND BLOCK	**DELETE**	**LEAVE IN INBOX**	**FLAG FOR FOLLOW UP**
[3a] *"Personal. She will not have time to read it, so just delete it."*	[3b] *"It just requires confirming details, can be deleted once done."*	[4a] *"This email contain account number and some information related to the phone, so should leave it in the inbox."*	[4a] *"It says the credit card has expired so you would need to follow up and replace the details."*
[3a] *"Don't really want to join and wouldn't want to keep receiving these e-mails being asked to join."*	[3a] *"I get emails like this from card companies and department stores all the time. It is just random junk which doesn't concern me & it seems to be a time waster."*	[4a] *"regarding important information so it should be kept for later reference"*	[4a] *"Confirm the email identity otherwise the account will be blocked. It is an important email."*
[3a] *"Personal. It is advertisement. She will not want to waste time, so just delete and block it."*	[3b] *"after activating your account, this email is no longer required & therefore should be deleted."*	[4a] *"personally i would leave this email in my inbox, as you are able to earn money simply by participating in an online survey."*	[4a] *"This is an official email from [company name] which requires an action from Sally Jones."*

KEY: SHAPE – Oval: Participant thought it was phishing; Rectangle: Participant thought it was real |
BACKGROUND – Grey: Participant thought it was useful | **OUTLINE:** Solid line: Real email; Dotted line: Phishing email

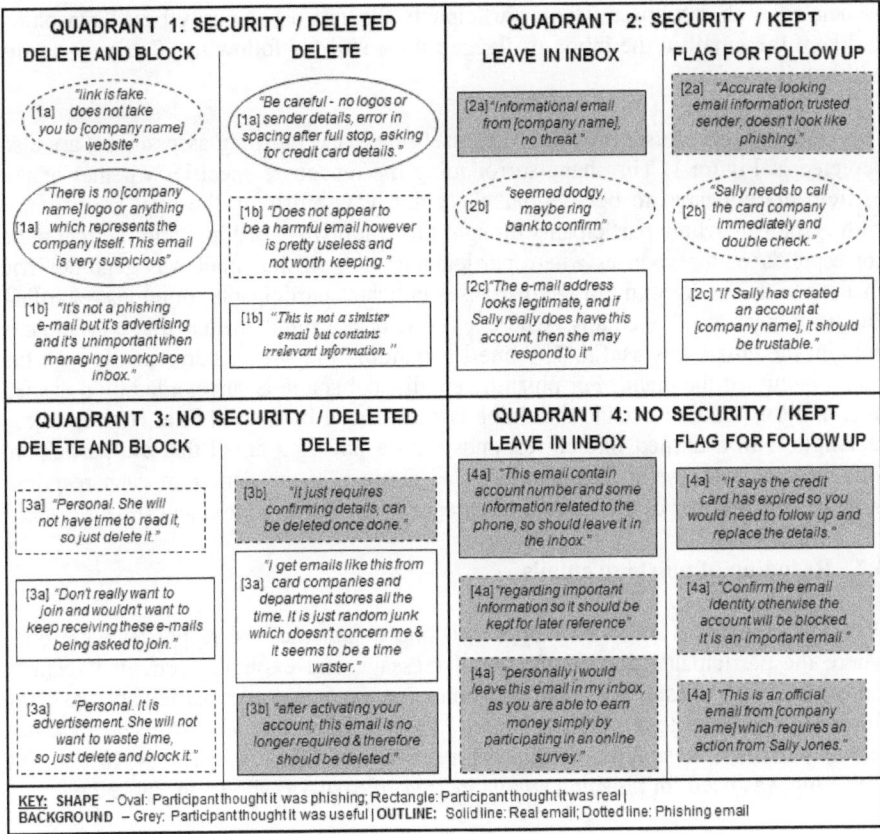

Figure 1: Illustration of the Action-Intention Email Response Framework, showing examples of the different responses within the four quadrants

Figure 1 provides an illustration of the Action-Intention Email Response Framework, based on two factors: the action recommended by participants (i.e., whether to keep or delete the email) and the degree to which participants used security-based reasoning. These two factors (recommended action and use of security-based reasoning) were used to plot the different categories within the two-factor space, resulting in four quadrants.

The upper left quadrant (Quadrant 1) of the factor-space is associated with responses where participants used security-based reasoning and chose to *delete* or *delete and block* the email. Categories 1a and 1b fit within this quadrant. The upper right quadrant (Quadrant 2) is associated with cases where participants used security-based reasoning and chose to keep the email in the inbox or flag the email for follow up. Categories 2a, 2b and 2c fit within this quadrant. The lower left quadrant (Quadrant 3) is associated with responses where participants did not use security-based reasoning and chose to *delete* or *delete and block* the email. Categories 3a and 3b fit within this quadrant. Finally, the lower right quadrant (Quadrant 4) is associated with responses where participants did not use security-based reasoning and kept the email in the inbox or flagged the email for follow up. Category 4a fits within this quadrant.

The other aspects of user intention (i.e., usefulness and phishing assessment) are also depicted in Figure 1. The shape surrounding the responses specifies whether or not participants appeared to believe that the email was phishing; the oval corresponds with responses where participants thought the email was phishing, and the rectangle corresponds with responses where participants thought the email was genuine. The shading in the background of the responses indicates participants' opinions regarding the usefulness of the emails, where a grey background means that participants thought the email was useful. The line surrounding the shapes corresponds with the actual nature of the email. For phishing emails, the shape is surrounded by a dashed line, and for genuine emails, the shape is surrounded by a solid line. Hence, a grey rectangle with a dashed line corresponds with a phishing email that the participant thought was both useful and genuine. The number in the corner of each response indicates the number of the associated category (see Table 1 for categories).

3.2. Recoding of phishing emails

When participants were faced with a phishing email, the best responses were ones where the participants deleted the email message and explicitly provided security concerns as the reason for their decision. For example, one participant gave the following response to a phishing email: *"link is fake. does not take you to [bank name] website"*. Responses of this nature were classified as category 1a and this reasoning was used for phishing emails in 26% of cases, as shown in Table 2.

There were a minority of cases where participants kept an email, but did so because they wanted to alert Sally to a possible security threat that she should follow up with the purported company or organisation. When faced with phishing emails, responses of this nature are also extremely positive, as they suggest that the participant has a useful awareness of security. For example, one participant responded with: *"Address looks dodgy, don't' click link – call [organisation name] for confirmation"*. Responses of this nature were classified as category 2b, and this reasoning was used for phishing emails in 6% of cases.

The worst possible responses to phishing emails were ones where participants kept an email because they believed it was valid. For example, a participant responded to a phishing email with: *"I am confident in this email and will follow it up, as I know it is not a scam"*. This is particularly concerning, as it indicates that the participant is conscious of security, but has an inaccurate knowledge of what constitutes a security concern. Responses of this nature were classified as category 2a, and this category of response was provided for phishing emails in 10% of cases.

Also of concern were category 4a responses, where participants appeared to simply take emails at face value. For example, one participant gave the following response to justify a decision to keep an email: *"This is a requirement, as [company] users* have to prove their id. If individuals have to use [company], they have to follow this email's instruction". This therefore suggests that the participant did not consider security when deciding how to manage that email. This was the most common response for phishing emails, and was chosen in 32% of cases.

3.3. Recoding of genuine emails

When participants were faced with genuine emails, the best response was when participants kept the email because they believed it was valid. For example, one participant gave the following (successful) response to a genuine email: *"Clearly legit, tells Sally to enter the URL herself and warns her not to click on links"*. Responses of this nature were classified as category 2a, and were given for genuine emails in 19% of cases. Category 2c responses were similar and were given in 6% of cases. These emails were kept on the basis of security reasoning, but the participants required further information before deciding whether to trust the email. An example to this is, *"The e-mail address looks legitimate, and if Sally really does have this account, then she may respond to it"*.

There were cases where participants decided to delete a genuine email, but made it clear it was not because the email was phishing, but rather, because they did not believe it was useful for Sally. For example, one participant responded to a genuine email with: *"No motivation to participate in the lengthy survey. Although it is a valid sender email address"*. This therefore indicates a good security aware decision. These responses were given for only 2% of genuine emails and were classified as category 1b.

In contrast, the worst possible response was when participants deleted a genuine email because they believed that it was illegitimate. The following provides an example of this type of response: *"The layout of the email looks illegitimate - there is no logo and the email is very short"*. Responses of this nature were classified as category 1a, and genuine emails were managed using this reasoning in 10% of cases.

3.4. Analysis of Raw and Recoded Decisions

The qualitative analysis and framework provided above captures the complexity of the decision-making process that is often overlooked in most phishing research, and the reason second-order analysis (Shkedi, 2004) was used in this study. To understand the significance of this data, the raw results based on the multiple-choice categorisation (first-order analysis) were compared to the recoded results (second-order analysis), that take into account both user action and intention (and quantitative and qualitative data). The percentage of responses in each of the raw and recoded categories can be seen in Table 2.

	Category	Phishing	Genuine
Raw	Delete and Block	15%✓	7%
	Delete	33%✓	33%
	Leave in inbox	25%	36%✓
	Flag for follow up	27%	25%✓
	Accuracy	*48%*	*60%*
Recoded	1a	26%✓	10%
	1b	2%	2%✓
	2a	10%	19%✓
	2b	6%✓	3%
	2c	4%	6%✓
	3a	16%✓	25%
	3b	4%	3%✓
	4a	32%	32%✓
	Accuracy	*48%*	*62%*

✓ Denotes a category that was deemed to be correct

Table 2: Percentage of responses in raw and recoded data

To determine whether the recoding significantly influenced the accuracy scores for the 50 emails, paired samples t-tests were conducted. For phishing emails, there was no significant difference in mean accuracy between the raw ($M = 48.03$, $SD = 12.00$) and recoded scores ($M = 48.37$, $SD = 10.41$, $t(24) = -.27$, $p = .789$, Cohen's $d = -0.03$). There was also no significant difference in mean accuracy between the raw ($M = 60.17$, $SD = 11.48$) and recoded scores ($M = 61.86$, $SD = 10.82$, $t(24) = -1.95$, $p = .063$, Cohen's $d = -0.15$) for genuine emails. This means that the quantitative multiple-choice categorisation provides an accurate reflection of the underlying reasoning or intent of users based on overall accuracy scores.

However, this must be interpreted with caution. Results were examined on an individual level to determine how much the recoding changed the accuracy scores of participants. For 23 participants (20%) the recoding changed accuracy scores by less than 1%. Accuracy scores were changed by between 1-5% for a further 59% (50%) of participants. This means that, in the majority of cases, the raw results provided by the multiple-choice categorisation was appropriate. But for almost a third (30%) of participants, the recoding revealed that their underlying intentions were not captured by the raw results. Instead, accuracy scores changed by between 6-10% for 21 participants, between 11-15% for 11 participants, and by over 20% for 3 participants.

Furthermore, the recoding facilitates closer and more useful examination of results. For example, although the overall accuracy score for phishing emails is 48%, only 32% were accuracy decisions made with security reasoning. Less than half (27%) of the correct results for genuine emails were made for security-based reasons. This information regarding incorrect security-based reasoning is also very informative. Recoded results indicate that 16% of decisions made for phishing emails and 13% of decisions made for genuine emails incorrectly used security reasoning. This has important implications for education and training, which will be highlighted in Section 4.

4. Conclusions

This study provides support for the categories 'leave the email in the inbox and flag for follow up', 'leave the email in the inbox', 'delete the email' and 'delete the email and block the sender' as a method of indirectly measuring phishing susceptibility. A role-play scenario was presented to 117 participants, and their overall accuracy scores, based on the multiple-choice options above, did not differ significantly when the results were recoded based on the Action-Intention Email Response Framework. This provides some validation of the multiple-choice categories utilised in Parsons et al. (2013).

However, since just one successful phishing attack can cause extensive damage to an individual or their organisation, examining only overall accuracy scores is not sufficient. A closer inspection of results indicated that the recoding changed accuracy scores by 11% or more for 14 of the 117 participants (12%). This means that the raw scores failed to accurately reflect the intentions of a minority of users.

The Action-Intention Email Response Framework also provides information regarding the type of mistake made by participants, which can be used for training and education purposes. An examination of the incorrect results for genuine emails revealed that 13% inaccurately used security-based reasoning, whereas 36% made no reference to security. Approximately 16% of incorrect decisions regarding phishing emails inaccurately used security-based reasoning, whereas 25% made no reference to security. It is likely that what constitutes effective training would differ based on the type of mistake made. For users who did not consider security, a simple awareness seminar might be sufficient, whereas users who considered security but inaccurately implemented the knowledge might need a more in-depth explanation of the security rules.

It is important to note that the participants in our sample consisted of business and psychology students, most of whom were in the first year of their studies. It is possible that the findings may differ in a sample of participants from a wider range of disciplines or employees rather than students. Further research into what individual differences, such as personality, experience or decision-making style, may influence the consideration of security information is warranted.

Hence, although user actions themselves are a rich source of data for analysing the results of psychological studies and inferring user intent from user action, user actions looked at in isolation may not always indicate users' underlying thought processes. A simple multiple choice response does not allow for the complexity of human reactions to phishing emails. This study highlights that researchers should not make assumptions about decision-making processes, and should instead delve deeper into the reasoning behind users' actions in phishing experiments. The methodology of this paper, in which action and intention are combined, could be applied in future studies to validate and evaluate user performance.

5. References

Downs, J.S., M. Holbrook & Cranor, L.F. (2007, October). Behavioral response to phishing risk (pp. 37-44). Proceedings of the anti-phishing working groups 2nd annual eCrime researchers summit, ACM.

Downs, J.S., M.B. Holbrook & Cranor, L.F. (2006, July). Decision strategies and susceptibility to phishing. Proceedings of the second symposium on Usable privacy and security (pp. 79-90), ACM.

Erickson, T. (1995). Notes on design practice: Stories and prototypes as catalysts for communication, Scenario-based design: envisioning work and technology in system development. New York: John Wiley & Sons, Inc.

Furnell, S. (2013). Still on the hook: the persistent problem of phishing. Computer Fraud & Security, 2013(10), 7-12.

Furnell, S. (2007). Phishing: can we spot the signs? Computer Fraud & Security, 2007(3), 10-15.

Hong, K.W., Kelley, C.M., Tembe, R., Murphy-Hill, E., & Mayhorn, C.B. (2013, September). Keeping Up With The Joneses Assessing Phishing Susceptibility in an Email Task. In Proceedings of the Human Factors and Ergonomics Society Annual Meeting (Vol. 57, No. 1, pp. 1012-1016). SAGE Publications.

Jakobsson, M., Tsow, A., Shah, A., Blevis, E., & Lim, Y.K. (2007). What instills trust? a qualitative study of phishing. In Financial Cryptography and Data Security (pp. 356-361). Springer Berlin Heidelberg.

Parsons, K., McCormac, A., Pattinson, M., Butavicius, M. & Jerram, C. (2013). Phishing for the truth: A scenario-based experiment of users' behavioural response to emails. In L.J. Janczewski, H. Wolf, and S. Shenoi (Eds.): Security and Privacy Protection in Information Processing Systems - IFIP Advances in Information and Communication Technology (Vol. 405, pp. 366-378). Springer Berlin Heidelberg.

Pattinson, M., Jerram, C., Parsons, K.M., McCormac, A., Butavicius, M.A. (2012). Why do some people manage phishing emails better than others? Information Management & Computer Security, 20(1), 18-28.

Robila, S.A., & Ragucci, J.W. (2006, June). Don't be a phish: steps in user education. In ACM SIGCSE Bulletin (Vol. 38, No. 3, pp. 237-241). ACM.

Sheng, S., Holbrook, M., Kumaraguru, P., Cranor, L. F., & Downs, J. (2010, April). Who falls for phish?: a demographic analysis of phishing susceptibility and effectiveness of interventions. In Proceedings of the SIGCHI Conference on Human Factors in Computing Systems (pp. 373-382). ACM.

Shkedi, A. (2004). Second-order theoretical analysis: A method for constructing theoretical explanation. International Journal of Qualitative Studies in Education, 17(5), 627-646.

Tashakkori, A., & Teddlie, C. (Eds.). (2003). Handbook of mixed methods in social & behavioral research. Sage.

Taylor, C. (1976). Hermeneutics and politics. Critical sociology, selected readings, 153-193.

Tsow, A., & Jakobsson, M. (2007). Deceit and Deception: A Large User Study of Phishing. Technical report TR649, Indiana University.

Wang, J., Chen, R., Herath, T., Vishwanath, A., & Rao, H. R. (2012). Phishing Susceptibility: An Investigation into the Processing of a Targeted Spear Phishing Email. IEEE Transactions on Professional Communication, 55(4), 345-362.

A Framework to Assist Email Users in the Identification of Phishing Attacks

A. Lötter and L. Futcher

Nelson Mandela Metropolitan University, Port Elizabeth, South Africa
email : {andries.lotter ; lynn.futcher}@nmmu.ac.za

Abstract

This paper proposes a framework to address the problem that email users are not well informed or assisted by their email clients in identifying possible phishing attacks, thereby putting their personal information at risk. Furthermore, it argues that email clients should make use of feedback mechanisms to present security related aspects to the users, so as to make them aware of the characteristics pertaining to such attacks. This paper therefore addresses the human weakness (i.e. the user's lack of knowledge of phishing attacks which causes them to fall victim to such attacks) as well as the software related issue of email clients not visually assisting and guiding the users through the user interface.

Keywords

Email client security, phishing attacks, usable security, user awareness

1. Introduction

A fact that cannot be disputed is that the Internet is an ever growing craze. Every day new users are adopting the Internet for the first time. The global Internet population (as of 2012) represented just over 2.4 billion people compared to the 360 million Internet users in late 2000 (Miniwatts Marketing Group, 2012). Along with this growth of users, the content on the Internet also expands every minute.

Unfortunately, along with any popular phenomenon comes an increase in exploitation thereof. Phishing can be seen as such, and a paper on "Social Phishing" defines phishing as: *"a form of social engineering in which an attacker attempts to fraudulently acquire sensitive information from a victim by impersonating a trustworthy third party"* (Jagatic, Johnson, Jakobsson, & Menczer, 2005). Recent statistics have found that, in the second half of 2011 alone, 83 083 unique phishing domains were registered worldwide. Other findings indicated that 3% of all phishing emails were opened, that eight victims are yielded for every 100 000 targeted users and that the average phishing victim produces around $2 000. Furthermore, 500 million phishing emails appear in user inboxes every day (Orloff, 2012). From this it is discernible that 40 000 people (worldwide) will fall victim to a given phishing attack every day, resulting in daily damages of approximately $80 million.

Phishing attacks are undoubtedly a popular way in which cyber-criminals conduct their crimes. It is argued that part of the blame for why phishing attacks are so successful could be shifted towards email clients. Email clients should therefore implement an effective and secure protection mechanism to protect email users in this regard.

This paper addresses the problem that email users are not well informed or assisted by their email clients in identifying possible phishing attacks, thereby putting their personal information at risk. In addressing this problem, this paper presents a framework to assist email clients and their users in the identification of phishing attacks. A literature study was carried out to determine the characteristics common to phishing attacks and to understand the security mechanisms currently employed in email clients. Furthermore, argumentation and modelling techniques contributed towards the development of the framework. This paper follows on from a paper published at the 2013 ZAWWW Conference (Lötter & Futcher, 2013). The said paper was a work in progress towards the development of the framework presented in this paper.

The results of the literature reviewed are presented in Sections 2 and 3 respectively. Whereas Section 4 presents the framework as a mental model that can assist users in the identification of common forms of phishing attacks, Section 5 discusses how this framework can be implemented in the email client.

2. Email client security

Anyone with an email account is a potential phishing target. Therefore, because of the great reach of phishing emails, it can be deduced that most email users may fall victim to such attacks. However, in order to realistically mitigate phishing attacks, the burden of identifying such attacks should not only lie in the software side; users also require a certain level of awareness. The email client software should therefore be designed and developed in such a way, that it "educates" the users. According to Furnell (2005, p.276), the software should at all times *"provide a visible indication of the security status"* as this is one of the primary causes that leads to the users feeling insecure about the security of their software.

Email clients do implement a reasonable amount of security. At the very least, they implement protection mechanisms such as password protection when accessing one's inbox and make use of spam filters to prevent users from coming into contact with unsolicited email messages. The problem here lies in the fact that these spam filters are not 100% accurate (Spamhaus, 2010). Sometimes legitimate messages get flagged as spam and fraudulent messages pass through the filters. It is at this stage that the user needs to be sufficiently aware of the criteria for identifying fraudulent email, so that they do not fall victim to a potential attack.

Currently, email clients simply place any email message it deems sufficiently suspicious into a "Junk" folder. Thus, it is left to the user's imagination to discern why a certain message was flagged as "Junk". There is no feedback mechanism to identify the portions of the email that caused the email client to believe that the said message is fraudulent. Even when users peruse their "Junk" folder, they may find emails in the said folder that they know does not belong. Often they are left puzzled at the email client's inability to have foreseen that certain messages were in fact genuine. The user interface of an email client should therefore be designed in such a way that it provides feedback to the user. All received email messages should be represented (in a minimalistic manner) according to its level of suspicion. Security dialogs should not be verbose and tedious as to deter the user from learning; however, compact and to-the-point explanations should be available as per the user's request. Therefore, the next time a potential phishing attack bypasses the spam filters, the user should be aware of the criteria to look out for when identifying potential fraudulent email. Thus, the risk that a user will fall victim to a specific phishing attack is further mitigated.

There exist vulnerabilities in email clients which phishers exploit in order for their phishing attacks to succeed. It is thus these vulnerabilities that need to be managed in order to mitigate phishing attacks. What causes a phishing attack to succeed is a combination of the software (email client) that was unable to flag the email as a phishing attack, and the user's gullibility in believing that the email is genuine. A paper on "Why users cannot use security" by (Furnell, 2005, pp. 274-279) states that *"Some clear awareness issues still need to be overcome, and there is unfortunately ample evidence to show that users do not actually understand security very well in the first place"*. From this it is clear that the usable security aspect of email clients must be addressed, as it should be a goal of the email client to prevent users from coming into contact with fraudulent email. It is argued that phishing attacks will only be successfully mitigated, once the average email user has the knowledge to differentiate a legitimate email from its fraudulent counterpart. The user interface in email clients should therefore implement security mechanisms that address the manner in which users perceive and understand security.

3. Understanding Phishing attacks

Phishing can be seen as a type of online identity theft. It is usually conducted by means of sending email messages to (thousands of) potential victims (Ayodele et al., 2012, p. 208). These emails are typically sent out in bulk to act as "bait", claiming to be from individuals or companies that the receiver of the message may trust, asking for confidential and sensitive information. The content of these emails are thus designed to deceive the receiver into divulging their personal details. These details can then be used by the phisher to gain access to the victim's financial accounts.

A variation of this attack, which encompasses much of the same deception techniques, but functions slightly differently, is known as "spear phishing". In a paper specifically focussing on spear phishing, Wang et al. (2012, p. 345) describes spear phishing as being more content specific in comparison to normal phishing attacks. They further explain that spear phishing attacks are perceived to originate from an existing organisation, thereby establishing the sender of the attack as relevant and true. A common use among phishers is to impersonate well-known financial institutions like banks (Chen & Guo, 2006). Spear phishing is effective, because it functions on the statistical fact that a large percentage of the targeted population will have an account with a company with a huge market share. Therefore, spear phishing attacks appear to come from an organisation that the targeted user could possibly have an account with. Phishers can therefore employ this technique by looking up the Chief Executive Officer (CEO) of a company on its website, and send emails to the accounts in the same corporate domain, seemingly from the CEO (Janssen, n.d.).

From the literature studied (Ledford, n.d.; Wang et al., 2012), several characteristics have been identified that can indicate the likelihood of an email message being a potential phishing attack. These characteristics include:

1. **Urgent wording in message:** Phishing attacks in general stress the urgency of the email as to make the victim uneasy and get results quickly.

2. **Request for personal and sensitive information**: Phishing attacks, by definition, aim to deceive victims into trusting the phishers, thereby gaining access to the victim's personal details with which to commit identify theft.

3. **Sender is unknown:** However, spear phishing is, by definition, a more concentrated attack. The phisher often impersonates a co-worker or executive member in the same corporate domain.

4. **Fake (deceiving) hyperlinks embedded**: The hyperlinks usually point to a phishing domain.

5. **Message body is an image:** Spear phishing, on the other hand, is more text-based, and would not necessarily use this evasive technique.

6. **Unrealistic promises:** Although spear phishing does not contain empty promises. They are to the point, to retain credibility.

7. **Poor language and punctuation:** Phishing attacks in general tend to be badly constructed.

8. **Visually represents impersonation:** As mentioned, spear phishing is more text-based, because it "comes from a co-worker" or trusted entity.

9. **Contains malware as attachments:** Generally phishing may try to install malware upon opening attachments.

10. **Emails are sent out at random to large number of random email addresses:** Spear phishing attacks, however, are concentrated, thus the victims are chosen carefully.

Phishing attacks undoubtedly pose a noteworthy problem. It is therefore important to understand the characteristics of these attacks in order to identify them. These characteristics are fundamental to the framework presented in the following section.

4. The Framework as a Mental Model

The framework presented in this section has been developed to simulate the thought process of the user of an email client when determining the legitimacy of a specific email. However, it can easily be adapted to be implemented into email clients (the software) as discussed in Section 5.

The framework depicted in Figure 1 illustrates a sequence of nine steps that the user of an email client should ask him or herself when determining whether an email should be trusted or not. The framework acts as a flowchart in that it guides the user through all nine steps. Only by answering "no" to each question (except for the last), can the positive outcome of "Email should be safe" be reached. The questions posed were determined based on the common characteristics of phishing attacks as described in Section 3.

The questions in this framework have been ordered to range from highly significant to less significant. Thus, a "Yes" answer to the former questions could lead to a higher probability of the email in question being fraudulent. The reason for this particular order is because this framework imitates the thought process of the human mind. Therefore, the most significant characteristics of a phishing attack are considered first. Upon finding that a certain characteristic is present, the framework opts out and classifies the email as a likely phishing attack without considering the other (less significant) characteristics.

This framework can classify a given email in four different ways. If an email contains a highly significant characteristic, it can either be classified as having a high or medium risk of being a phishing attack. Similarly, if the email contains a less significant characteristic, it can be classified as having a low risk of being a phishing attack or as cautious. The cautious classification serves as an intermediate between low risk and medium risk. When an email is classified as such, it advises the user that they should have an elevated sense of caution, since some less significant phishing characteristics are present.

A characteristic that is often present in phishing attacks is the abundance of spelling and grammar errors. However, an email should not be deemed a phishing attack based solely on the presence of such mistakes. One needs to consider that a specific phishing attack may be so meticulously thought out and refined, that it does not contain any spelling and grammar errors. Similarly, a normal, everyday email from one peer to another is often full of spelling and grammar errors, since emails often tend to be sent out in haste. For these reasons, the question asking whether spelling and grammar errors are present is considered with each of the other questions posed. If an email is already deemed suspicious and the email also contains many spelling and grammar errors, the likelihood (risk) of the said email being a phishing attack is increased. Otherwise, if suspicion is never raised about the legitimacy of an email, the spelling and grammar characteristic is never brought into consideration.

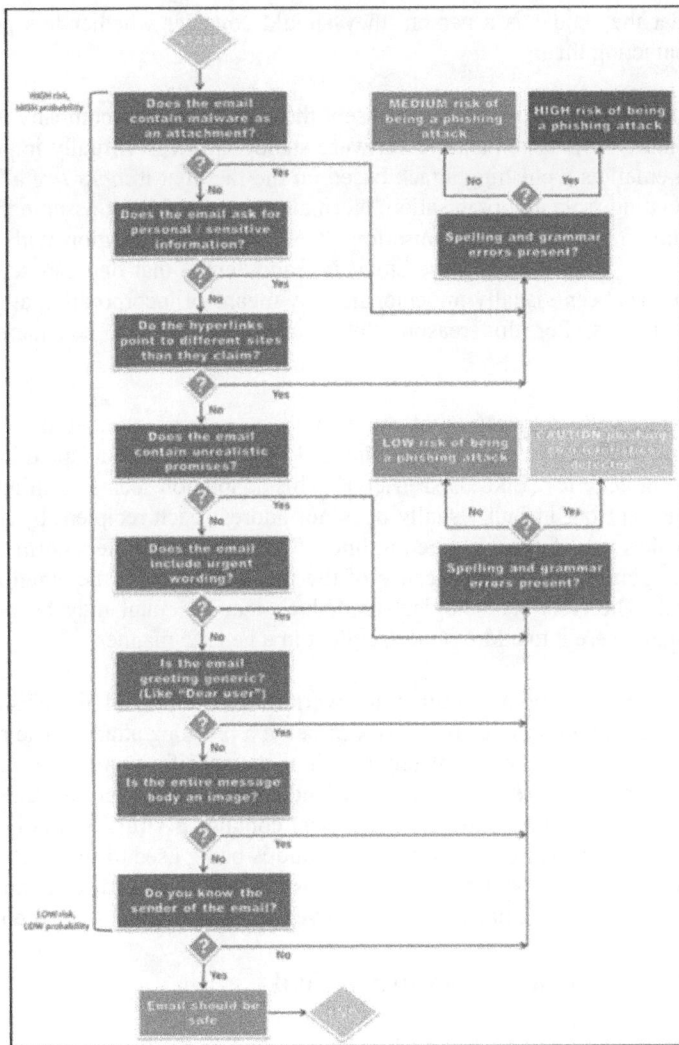

Figure 1: A framework to identify phishing attacks (mental model)

The terminating question, "Do you know the sender of the email?" can be somewhat questioned for phishing emails seldom impersonates a person. Recall that phishing is a "form of social engineering in which an attacker attempts to fraudulently acquire sensitive information from a victim by impersonating a trustworthy third party" (Jagatic et al., 2005). This "trustworthy third party" could thus refer to either a person or a company. Therefore, by answering this question, the user needs to consider all types of phishing attacks. They should thus consider whether they know the company that may have sent them the email. Does it make logical sense for this company to have contacted them (i.e. do they have a connection to this company)? In the case that the sender is a person, they should consider whether this person has merit in contacting them.

Phishing attacks normally visually represent the organisation or company it is trying to impersonate. From a human and software standpoint, it is virtually impossible to identify an email as a phishing attack based on the fact that it *looks like* a legitimate email originating from an organisation. Normally, one would just assume that it is in fact an email from the said organisation. It is thus in combination with the other characteristics – after realizing the email is fraudulent – that one can see how the organisation has been visually impersonated, by means of incorporating a lot of their logos and images. For this reason, this characteristic is not considered in the framework.

Phishing attacks are normally sent out in bulk to a large number of users. This characteristic, despite not rigidly appearing in Figure 1, has been adapted into "Is the email greeting generic? (Like 'Dear user')". This adaptation seems befitting since an email that is sent out in bulk usually does not address each recipient by name, and therefore makes use of generic greeting lines. Furthermore, phishers normally do not have the recipient's real name because of the manner in which the email addresses are obtained. Therefore, it is logical to deduce that an email may be a potential phishing attack were it to address the recipient in a generic manner.

Lastly, the termination points to this framework make use of "indefinite" statements, such as "Email *should* be safe" or "...*risk* of being a phishing attack". The reason for this is that one can never be completely certain that a specific email poses no security threat whatsoever. An email from a friend may contain an attachment that (unbeknownst to both the sender and receiver) contains a virus. Similarly, a user's email account could have been compromised and is being used to send out malicious emails to all its trusted contacts. For these reasons, one should always consider that an email may still be potentially dangerous, even if all signs point to the contrary.

5. The Framework as a Software Tool

Email clients make use of various techniques in filtering out spam messages, such as rule-based and Bayesian spam filtering. The main purpose of the proposed framework developed is not to improve the existing filtering techniques, but rather to improve the way in which any irregularities present in an email is reported back to the user. Thus, from a software standpoint, the framework can be implemented in the user interface of email clients so as to increase the awareness of users with regard to phishing attacks.

Figure 2 illustrates how the security level of email messages (as they would appear in the inbox) can be conveyed to the user in a minimalistic manner. As seen in this figure, the email items are all associated with a specific colour (as seen by the leftmost border and the rightmost shield icon).

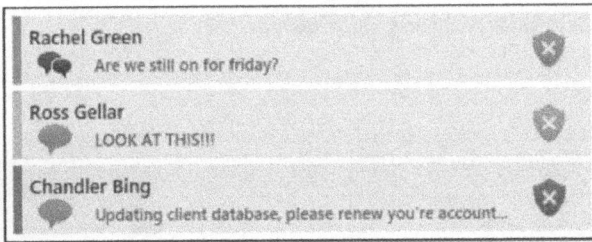

Figure 2: Indicating security level of received emails in a minimalistic manner

These colours (much like traffic lights) instinctively conveys to the users whether an email is considered safe or not, without them having to read a single word. Logically, green would represent a message which is considered safe, orange would indicate that there is some doubt regarding the safety of the message, and red would indicate that the message is most likely a phishing attack. Should the user like to know why an email is considered safe, doubtful or dangerous respectively, they can find the information by clicking on the shield icon. Figure 3 depicts how the information could be presented to the user by means of a context menu.

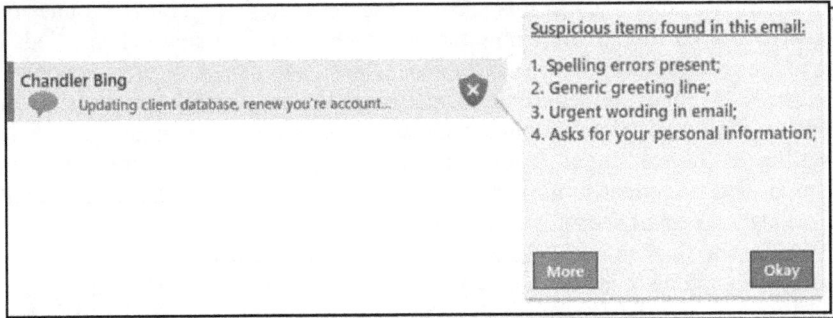

Figure 3: Additional phishing characteristics identified displayed in a context menu

As can be seen in Figure 3, the user is now presented with a list of suspicious characteristics identified by the framework. Thus, security is placed at the forefront of the user interface. The user does not have to read tedious security dialogs full of jargon and terminology which they do not understand. Users are often not motivated to use security, because of jargon and terminology which they do not understand. As mentioned above, Figure 3 shows the suspicious aspects of a specific email in short, easy to understand terms thus appealing to the user's sense of simplicity. However, detailed explanations should also be provided per the user's request. Figure 4 shows this detailed explanation which can be accessed by the user upon clicking on the "*more*" button seen in Figure 3.

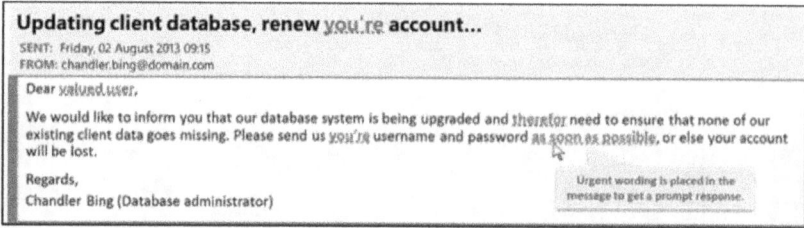

Figure 4: Detailed explanation of the aspects identified in the suspicious email

As evident in Figure 4, the entire email message is displayed with all the suspicious aspects identified by the framework shaded in red and underlined. The message border is also red, so as to keep displaying the security level to the user. When the user hovers over one of the suspicious aspects, a tooltip is displayed describing the characteristic that was found. Thus, the email is no longer simply placed in a *"junk"* folder without explanation. Through this method, and the ones described previously in this section, the users can be made aware of the characteristics pertaining to phishing attacks.

All of the figures discussed in this section (Figures 2 to 4) rely on the framework developed in order to determine how the user interface of the email client needs to adapt to the security level of a specific email. The email client software should work procedurally through the sequence of questions to see which characteristics are present in the email. If a certain characteristic is found, it should increase the probability of the said email being a phishing attack based on a pre-determined weighting. It is important to note that the weightings for each characteristic should not be equal. An email does not deserve the same penalty for including spelling and grammar errors, than should it contain malware as an attachment. Afterwards, the framework should be followed in moving on to the next question in the sequence and will follow this paradigm until all the characteristics in the framework have been considered. This results in a final score, which is the probability of the email being fraudulent, being presented as output. The user interface of the email client can then be adjusted accordingly based on this score, i.e. the email messages in the inbox can be colour coded as seen in Figure 2.

The colour code that a certain email should be associated with (green, orange or red) can be determined by the probability score. The email client implementing the framework can make it a business decision as to what the ranges are for safe (green), doubtful (orange) and dangerous (red) classifications. It should be noted that an email displayed in green can still have items in its context menu (should the user wish to see it). Figure 5 illustrates a gauge that can be used to determine the ranges for these classifications. As can be seen in this figure, if the resultant probability score is lower than 0.1, it can be deemed as safe. If the score ranges between 0.1 and 0.49, the email may be deemed doubtful. Lastly, if the score is higher than 0.5, the email is deemed dangerous and a potential phishing attack.

SAFE	Doubtful	Dangerous
0 to 0.9	0.1 to 0.49	0.5 to 0.98

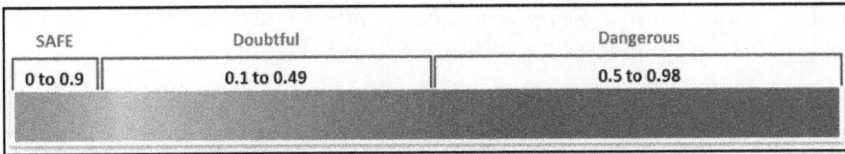

Figure 5: A colour gauge indicating the security level of emails

As stated, determining these ranges can be made a business decision by the email client implementing the framework. Moreover, the email client may even allow the user to define these ranges. As guidance, the email client may have certain default values for these ranges (like the ones specified in Figure 5), but then allow more paranoid or trusting users to redefine these ranges to a level that they are comfortable with.

6. Conclusion

This paper presents a framework that specifically addresses the threat of phishing attacks to email users and is based on the common characteristics found in phishing attacks. Although it was initially developed to be used as a mental model by email users, it can easily be adapted for implementation in email clients. The users of email clients should have a visual indication of security status at all times. Only through user awareness can scams like phishing be successfully mitigated. Through implementation of this framework the user's level of awareness can be raised by presenting to them the aspects identified as being suspicious. Users will therefore be made more aware of the characteristics pertaining to phishing attacks and in so doing this threat could be mitigated.

Future research is required to address other security threats relating to email users in order to ensure that email clients cater for all aspects of security that put email users and their information at risk.

7. References

Ayodele, T., Shoniregun, C., & Akmayeva, G. (2012). Anti-Phishing Prevention Measure for Email Systems. *Internet Security (WorldCIS)*, (pp. 208-211). Guelph.

Chen, J., & Guo, C. (2006). Online Detection and Prevention of Phishing Attacks. *Communications and Networking in China, 2006. ChinaCom '06. First International Conference*, (pp. 1-7). Beijing.

Furnell, S. (2005). Why users cannot use security. *Computers & Security* (24), 274-279.

Jagatic, T., Johnson, N., Jakobsson, M., & Menczer, F. (2005, December 15). Social Phishing. Bloomington.

Janssen, C. (n.d.). *Spear Phishing*. Retrieved April 29, 2013 from Techopedia: http://www.techopedia.com/definition/4121/spear-phishing

Spamhaus. (2010, January). *Whitepapers: Effective filtering.* Retrieved July 16, 2013 from Spamhaus: http://www.spamhaus.org/whitepapers/effective_filtering/

A Trust Domains Taxonomy for Securely Sharing Information: A Preliminary Investigation

N.A.G. Arachchilage and A. Martin

Department of Computer Science
University of Oxford
Wolfson Building, Parks Road
Oxford, UK, OX1 3QD
e-mail: {nalin.asanka; andrew.martin}@cs.ox.ac.uk

Abstract

Information sharing has become a vital part in our day-to-day life due to the pervasiveness of Internet technology. In any given collaboration, information needs to flow from one participant to another. While participants may be interested in sharing information with one another, it is often necessary for them to establish the impact of sharing certain kinds of information. This is because certain information could have detrimental effects when it ends up in wrong hands. For this reason, any would-be participant in a given collaboration may need to establish the guarantees that the collaboration provides, in terms of protecting sensitive information, before joining the collaboration as well as evaluating the impact of sharing a given piece of information with a given set of entities. In order to address this issue, earlier work introduced a trust domains taxonomy that aims at managing trust-related issues in information sharing. This paper attempts to empirically investigate the proposed taxonomy through a possible scenario (e.g. the ConfiChair system). The study results determined that *Role, Policy, Action, Control, Evidence* and *Asset* elements should be incorporated into the taxonomy for securely sharing information among others. Additionally, the study results showed that the ConfiChair, a novel cloud-based conference management system, offers strong privacy and confidentiality guarantees.

Keywords

Trustworthiness; Trust Domains; Information Security; Usable Security; Human Factor in Security

1. Introduction

Human trust is subjective (Bizer and Oldakowski, 2004, Wang and Emurian, 2005). Therefore, it is worth evalating the human aspect of trust in a system in order to better design trustworthiness systems for eveyone. In our day to day life, we use a wide range of trust decisions. These decisions depend on the specific situation, our experience, subjective preferences, and also the trust relevant information displayed by the system. For example, we might trust to buy a particular item only from sellers on Amazon who have more than 100 positive ratings. Therefore, it is important to display measureable trust characteristics from the system to attract customers for the business.

Information sharing plays an important role in any business process. Organizations and individuals exchange information daily for the purpose of service delivery, communication and collaboration. For example, two law enforcement agencies working on similar cases may require sharing information about the evidence of a crime. However, each agency may need to share such information with only a selected list of other agencies or individuals from these agencies. While participants may be interested in sharing information with one another, it is often necessary for them to establish the impact of sharing certain kinds of information. This is because certain information could have detrimental effects when it ends up in wrong hands. For this reason, any would-be participant in a collaboration may need to establish the guarantees that the collaboration provides, in terms of protecting sensitive information, before joining the collaboration as well as evaluating the impact of sharing a given piece of information with a given set of entities.

Arachchilage, et al. (Arachchilage *et al.* 2013), proposed a concept of a trust domains that aims at managing trust-related issues in information sharing. It is essential for enabling efficient collaborations. Authors introduced a taxonomy for trust domains with measurable trust characteristics, which provides security-enhanced, distributed containers for the next generation of composite electronic services for supporting collaboration and data exchange within and across multiple organisations. Then the proposed taxonomy applied to a possible real world scenario, in which the concept of trust domains could be useful. Kirkham, et al. (Kirkham *et al.* 2013), describes individuals are transient on the Internet, but the data is permanent. Individuals exist only at the outside of the architecture, and behind a browser, application, service, or device. Authors argued that the indispensability of a user-centric architecture where individuals need some kind of unified, permanent, and controllable representation of themselves (Kirkham *et al.* 2013). Therefore, it is important to understand how users trust perceptions towards the taxonomy since it developed for them to securely share the information among the others. On the other hand, they are ultimately responsible of sharing information among others. It can therefore be argued that it's worth understanding their trust perceptions before actually implementing the taxonomy in the real world. Therefore, our purpose in the current study is to validate the taxonomy by exploring users' trust perceptions of the ConfiChair system scenario.

Kelton, et al. (Kelton *et al.* 2008), assert that there is a strong need for empirical research on the end user's trust perception of using systems within the field of information science. So far, there has been little research work on the human aspect of trustworthiness systems designing and modeling (Baptista *et al.* 2008, Donaldson and Fear, 2011, Missier *et al.* 2008 and Weng *et al.* 2007). We know to our cost that none of the existing models or systems has been empirically tested with end-users before their implementation. Furthermore, It has been shown that previous end-user studies underscore the importance of human-centered systems modeling in determining the trustworthiness of systems (Baptista *et al.* 2008, Chapman *et al.* 2010, Gil and Artz, 2007, Hartig and Zhao, 2009, Lauriault *et al.* 2008, Missier *et al.* 2008 and Sexton *et al.* 2004). It is worth empirically testing those systems and models before the implementation takes place since they were designed for end-users. However, there has been little empirical research on exploring those assumptions. The research work reported in this paper attempts to empirically investigate the proposed taxonomy (Arachchilage *et al.* 2013), for trust domains through users based on the ConfiChair system scenario. The concept of trust domains is used for proving a foundation (evidence) for securely sharing information (how, when and with whom) among a group of entities. This enables the parties involved and the observers to understand the level of trust before going ahead with sharing data. Therefore, the current study empirically investigates what key elements that should be incorporated into the trust domains taxonomy for securely sharing information among others. Furthermore, it interprets why these elements should be incorporated into the trust domains taxonomy.

The developed taxonomy enables individuals and organizations to securely collaborate across functions, geographies and corporate boundaries by providing collaborating parties (or participants) the means to create online environments designed to prevent information from leaking and where their resources can be shared as they specify.

The reminder of this paper is structured in the following manner. Section II describes the proposed taxonomy for trust domains. In section III, the proposed taxonomy is applied to a possible scenario (in this case the ConfiChair system scenario). We then discuss the methodology employed in this research to empirically evaluate the taxonomy through the ConfiChair system scenario in section IV. Section V describes the results analysis. Then the trust domains taxonomy is formed through an empirical investigation in section VI. In section VII, a detailed discussion of the findings is presented. Section VIII provides conclusions and opens up opportunities for future work that may extend the research work reported in this paper.

2. Proposed trust domains taxonomy

In this section of the paper, we discuss how the models were combined to create the trust domains taxonomy (Arachchilage *et al.* 2013). We illustrate the concepts that can be used to integrate the models and discuss how the semantic gap in the usage of these concepts can be bridged.

2.1. Fundamental Concepts and Relations

The proposed model consists of a number of concepts, such that each concept captures a class of things that may either exists in a trust domain, be used to build a trust domain and used within a trust domain. Though all these concepts may be used in different instances of a trust domain, a few of them can be identified as being fundamental to the existence of a trust domain. We identify the *Data, Policy, Controls, Roles, Actions* and *Evidence* as being fundamental concepts necessary to build a trust domain.

As depicted in Figure 1, a *Role* owns *Data* that will exist within a trust domain and establishes a *Policy* that constrains *Actions*.

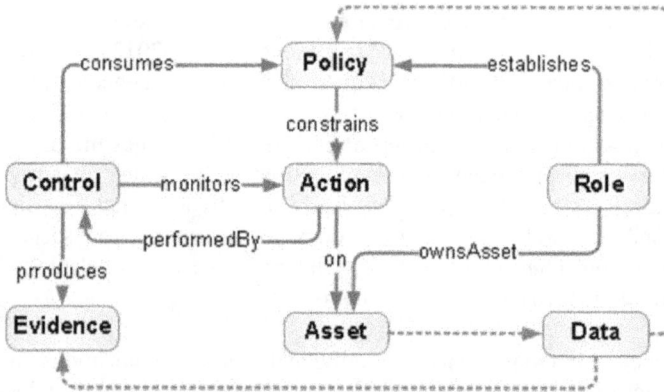

Figure 1: Fundamental concepts in the trust domain taxonomy

As mentioned in the fundamental model, a *Role* establishes one or more *Policies* within the domain. However, any given policy can only be established by one *Role*. This means that if two roles establish identical policies, then both policies are treated as a unique entity, which can be linked through the equivalence property.

Actions are performed by a given role or by an agent that represents a particular role. These actions are monitored by *Controls* to ensure that the policy is being upheld. These controls produce *Evidence* to indicate that actions have been performed in accordance to the policies. Both *Evidence* and *Policy* can be considered to be a form of data, which can be manipulated in the same way as other data and may be subject to the same information flow restrictions.

3. Application Scenario

We consider a scenario, which focuses on the particular cloud computing application of conference management. Existing conference management systems like EasyChair and Editor's Assistant (EDAS) pose the specific security and privacy risks. The Cloud service provider (e.g. the cloud system administrator who administrates the system for all conferences) has access to all the data, and could accidentally or deliberately discloses it to the public. On the other hand, an individual conference chair (who is concerned with a single conference) has access to the data only for the particular conference of which one is chairing. Furthermore, an author or reviewer that chooses to participate in the conference can be assumed to be willing to trust the chair (it can therefore be argued if he didn't, he would not participate); but there is no reason to assume that he trusts or even knows the conference management system provider. Therefore, those conference management systems raise privacy and confidentiality issues. Arapinis, et al. (Arapinis *et al.* 2012), proposed a conference management system called ConfiChair (as shown in Figure 2) to address those issues.

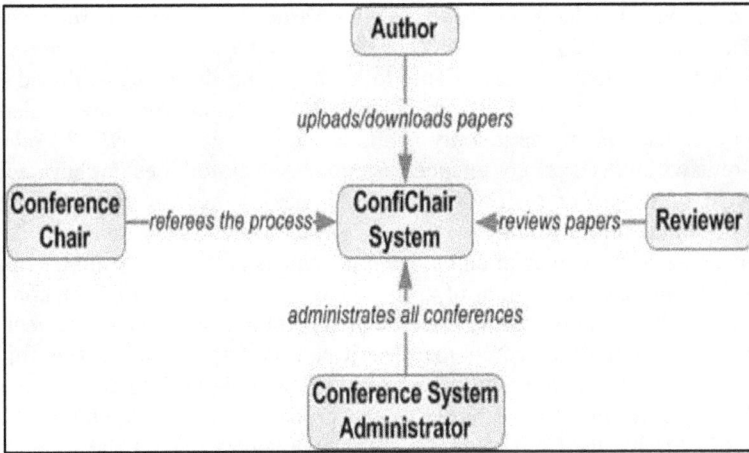

Figure 2: ConfiChair conference management system

ConfiChair is a cloud-based conference management protocol, which is proposed to address a set of privacy and confidentiality requirements for conference management. In ConfiChair, authors, reviewers, and the conference chair interact through their browsers with the cloud, to perform the usual tasks of uploading and downloading papers and reviews. Authors claimed that the ConfiChair system offers strong privacy and confidentiality gurantees. Therefore, we use the ConfiChair system as the application scenario to empirically investigate the proposed taxonomy in Figure 1 (Arachchilage *et al.* 2013).

3.1. Data Flow Relations & Trust Domains Application

In this section of the paper, we attempt to apply the proposed trust domains taxonomy to the above-mentioned scenario (in this case ConfiChair system scenario). This is achieved by identifying the boundaries that exist with respect to data flows within the setup.

According to the ConfiChair system scenario shown in Figure 2, authors, reviewers, and the conference chair interact through their browsers with the cloud, to perform the usual tasks of uploading and downloading papers and reviews. Additionally, the conference system administrator is responsible of administrating the ConfiChair system for all conferences. Therefore, the *Role* element in the taxonomy is represented in the ConfiChair system scenario. Various roles carry some actions developed by the ConfiChair system. Author upload/download papers, reviewer reviews papers, conference chair referees the process and the conference system administrator administrates all conferences are a few examples. Therefore, the *Action* element in the taxonomy is represented in the ConfiChari system scenario. A set of policies developed within the ConfiChair system. For example, (a) a reviewer doesn't see other reviewers of a paper before writing her own, (b) the Conference System Administrator does not have access to the content of papers or reviews, or the numerical scores give by the reviewers to papers and (c) the conference system administrator does have access to the names of authors and the names of reviewers;

however, he does not have ability to tell if a particular author was reviewed by a particular reviewer. The *Policy* element in the taxonomy is, therefore, represented in the ConfiChair system scenario. The following controls also developed in the ConfiChair system in order to monitor actions: (a) the login procedure implemented relies on each user having an identity *id* and a secret password *pswid;* (b) secrecy of papers, reviews and scores: conference system administrator does not have access to the content of papers or reviews, or the numerical scores given by reviewers to papers; (c) unlinkability of author-reviewer: conference system administrator does not have access to the names of authors and the names of reviewers and (d) however, all sensitive data (e.g. encryption of each review or score) is seen by the conference system administrator only in encrypted form. Therefore, the *Control* element in the taxonomy is also represented in the ConfiChair system scenario. The following evidence such as information produced by uploading/downloading papers, reviewing papers, refereeing the ConfiChair system process and also administrating all conferences through the ConfiChair system is maintained by the ConfiChair system. The *Evidence* element in the taxonomy is therefore represented in the ConfiChari system scenario. Finally, data such as authors, reviewers, conference chairs and conference system administrator information; paper upload/download/submission information; paper review information; and referee process information exist in digital form within the ConfiChair system. Therefore, the *Asset* element in the taxonomy is represented in the ConfiChair system scenario.

The author uploads/downloads (in this case bi-directional) papers and the reviewers reviews (in this case bi-directional) those uploaded papers using the ConfiChair system. Therefore, this creates a trust domain, Author-ConfiChairSystem-Reviewer. According to the ConfiChair system scenario shown in Figure 2, the conference chair referees the process. This creates two trust domains, Author-ConfiChairSystem-ConferenceChair as well as ConferenceChair-ConfiChairSystem-Reviewer.

Finally, the conference system administrator is responsible of administrating the ConfiChair system for all conferences where the conference chair referees the conference process. The conference system administrator does not have access to the names of authors and the names of reviewers and as well as all sensitive data (e.g. encryption of each review or score) is seen by the conference system administrator only in encrypted form. Therefore, this creates a trust domain, ConferenceChair-ConfiChairSystem-ConferenceSystemAdministrator.

4. Methodology

The study was mainly focused on a qualitative approach. Qualitative data is the main kind of data used and analyzed by interpretive and critical researchers (Oates, 2006). The study reported in this paper attempted to empirically evaluate the proposed taxonomy for trust domains through the users. This is more likely to be based on the interpretive approach because the study focuses on determining the key elements that should be incorporated into the trust domains taxonomy through the users. Furthermore, it interprets why these elements should be incorporated into the trust domains taxonomy.

4.1. Recruiting Participants

An experiment was conducted with 6 participants from the Department of Computer Science at the University of Oxford. All of them were male participants. All of them were academics and researchers in the department. Participants were invited to the Oxford University Computer Science Laboratory. All of them had the experience of being an author (more than five and a half years), reviewer (more than two years) as well as conference chair (more than a year and half). Furthermore, all of them had an experience in using a conference management system for more than five and a half years. Each participant took part in the experiment on a fully voluntarily basis. However, they were offered a cup of coffee in the end of the experiment.

4.2. Procedure

We gathered qualitative data from 6 interviews which included observations, field notes and audio recording, and that is, the period of time from the participant arrival to the study and until the participant leaves. All the interviews were conducted in-person by the researcher. First, the nature of the research was explained to each participant individually and they were asked to read and sign the consent form. Then the individual participants were explained the ConfiChair scenario and the difference between the ConfiChair system and exisiting conference management systems such as EasyChair or the Editor's Assistant (EDAS). For example, ConfiChair is a cloud-based conference management protocol developed to address a set of privacy and confidentiality requirements for existing cloud-based conference management systems. Each participant spent approximately one hour with the interview. They were also informed that they could provide any comments and feedback on both the content and format of the study had just been asked to take part.

5. Results Analysis

The data analysis of the interviews was conducted in two phrases, which were based on the Norgaard and Hornbaek's study (Nørgaard and Hornbaek, 2006). First, the current study segmented the recordings through the application of keywords to each segment. The purpose of having an interview approach was to empirically evaluate the taxonomy for trust domains through the users using the ConfiChair Scenario. The key words were taken from the elements in the proposed taxonomy as shown in the Figure 1. Donaldson and Fear (Donaldson and Fear, 2011), also stressed in their study that they developed the codeset based on the themes identified in the narratives their subjects provided. Therefore, the audio recordings were mainly segmented into six keywords: *Role, Policy, Action, Control, Evidence* and *Asset*. Second, the current study attempted to analysis and tries to form a coherent interpretation of segments that shared keywords. Therefore, the study findings were organized in six areas. Table 1 summarizes these areas and main findings within each of them.

Elements of taxonomy	Main findings	N	Example of quotes
Role	Roles such as author, reviewer, conference chair, and conference system administrator are necessary in the ConfiChair system	6	"Yes, it is natural thing that you need to have an author, reviewer, conference chair and conference system administrator in any conference management system" "I say yes, all roles are important in the conference management system" "Yes, we do need roles in any conference system" "Well, yes different roles have difference responsibilities" "Yes, I believe roles are important, because you want to prevent things like conflict of interests" "Yes, it is clear to me that the role is the most important factor, because It may probably have different requirements from the system"
Policy	Policies developed in the ConfiChair system are important for securely sharing information among others a. A reviewer doesn't see other reviewers of a paper before writing her own b. The conference system administrator does not have access to the content of papers or reviews, or the numerical scores give by the reviewers to papers c. The conference system administrator does have access to the names of authors and the names of reviewers; however, he does not have ability to tell if a particular author was reviewed by a particular reviewer	6	"I think all policies developed are important in the system" "Yes, it (reviewer sees the other reviews before writing her own) makes biased reviewers" "Conference system administrator is the one who provide the overall service and they shouldn't have the details of authors, reviewers and reviewed papers like that" "There is a potential that the conference system administrator might change course, modify things, delete things… and you don't want that" "Of course, necessary policies should be developed and maintained in order to ensure privacy, security, confidentiality and also integrity of the system" "I don't think that the conference system administrator should have access to any of them (author, reviewer, and conference chair) at all" "The issue comes down to if the work is currently unpublished, currently in review, then it's about confidentiality, it's about privacy"

			"It is a desirable thing to have developed policies in place" "No nothing, the conference system administrator should know nothing" "It is a policy that would be useful to establish an unbiased opinion" "Yes, this is something important from privacy perspective, because if I'm an author, I only like people access to my paper who does actually review my paper"
Action	Actions developed in the ConfiChair system are necessary for securely sharing information among others a. Author upload/download papers b. Reviewer reviews papers c. Conference chair referees the process d. Conference System Administrator administrates all conferences	6	"Of course, those actions are important in the ConfiChair system" "Encryption is important to consider in these actions too" "In theory, no you would expect the conference system administrator just to provide a service. However, unless if you encrypt everything on the system they would be able to see" "I suppose, when you're uploading/downloading these information (I mean papers, reviews like that) you should know that you're in a secured connection like https. It's about privacy and confidentiality as well" "First of all, any sensitive data should be encrypted in all of these actions" "All downloading/uploading should be done through https:// in order to protect academics accessing from doggy websites" "You should definitely have those actions in place, so you can cater for them. Absolutely, you should be able to cater for the worse case scenarios"
Control	Controls developed in the ConfiChair system are important for securely sharing information among others a. The login procedure implemented relies on each user having an identity id and a secret password pswid b. Secrecy of papers,	6	"It's pretty useful and of course highly important to have username and secret password" "I imagine that authors, reviewers, and conference chair are all need an unique username and password (of course, for being able to memorise) to login to the system" "From the usability prospective I know that you can have the same username and password access to different roles (such as login as author, reviewer or conference chair), but with"

	reviews and scores: Conference System Administrator does not have access to the content of papers or reviews, or the numerical scores given by reviewers to papers c. Unlinkability of author-reviewer: Conference System Administrator does not have access to the names of authors and the names of reviewers d. However, all sensitive data (e.g. encryption of each review or score) is seen by the Conference System Administrator only in encrypted form		"different levels of authentication mechanism" "That's what I said before, the conference system administrator should not have access to papers, reviews and score. He just only provides the overall service" "To be honest, there is no reason to provide the conference system administrator who the author's name, reviewer's name and etc., because those are quite important services" "If the conference system administrator can have access to the database, s/he would be able to pull out the necessary stuff" "I think it's better to encrypt all sensitive data on papers, reviewers, reviews, the link between authors and reviewers, stuff like that" "I think the only link you should have between the conference system administrator and conference chair, not conference system administrator with others" "Yes, papers, reviews and scores should also be kept secret from conference system administrator. Hypothetically, another university can forge some ideas from you" "Conference system administrator only really need to see the high level information about the conference such as when is it taking place, who is the main contact, and some technical concerns of the system" "If the encryption is done properly, that sounds fine" "It is very important authors should not be able to link to their reviewers" "The link between the people should be cut, so they can't see each other information" "Sure, that's a good practice to keep all sensitive data encrypted form"
Evidence	Evidence produced by the ConfiChair system is necessary to maintain within the system a. [Provenance] information produced by uploading/downloading papers	6	"Yes, the ones [provenance information] you mentioned are important to track within the system" "Well, you have to know when the author uploaded the paper in case they passed the deadline and so on" "Well, you're talking about the time stamp behind every action which is very important to maintain within the system, e.g. when the"

	b. [Provenance] information produced by reviewing papers c. [Provenance] information produced by refereeing the ConfiChair system process d. [Provenance] information produced by administrating all conferences through the ConfiChair system For example, provenance information – who, when (date and time), what, and where.		author uploaded his paper" "I think it is important and useful to maintain meta data within the system in case if something goes wrong" "Yes, it is important to maintain within the system, because if you're dealing with legal issues, like suddenly someone takes a legal action against the administrator of the system for stealing his/her idea" "Yes, you may need this (maintaining the evidence produced by the ConfiChair system) for digital forensic" "It actually depends on the role"

Asset	Assets are important to maintain within the ConfiChair system
	
	a. Data exist in digital form. For example:
	
	  i. Authors, reviewers, conference chairs, and conference system administrator information
	
	  ii. Paper upload/ download/ submission information
	
	  iii. Paper review information
	
	  iv. Referee process information
		6	"It's important to maintain digital back-up within the system during the conference life time. However, I don't think that you will have to maintain digital back-up after finishing the conference"
			
			"In terms of maintaining data, it's important to maintain the records of who the authors already submitted, who the reviewed panels are, who reviewed each paper, actually papers as well. But not all information necessarily be maintained in digital form"
			
			"You certainly need to keep it for the duration of the conference. After that you may probably need to destroy"
			
			"It is nice to keep the data in a back-up form and I see the purpose of it here"
			
			"During the conference, yes I will say so. If anyone has any issues, you can provide the evidence here"
			
			"From security perspective, three big letters are CIA, in terms of Integrity, yes you do need to maintain or keep tract of these assets.

Table 1: Overview of results - N refers to the number of participants (out of 6 interview sessions in total)

6. Trust Domains Taxonomy

The current study empirically investigated what key elements that should be incorporated into the trust domains taxonomy for securely sharing information among others. In addition, it interprets why these elements should be incorporated into the trust mains taxonomy. The elements of the trust domains taxonomy introduced by Arachchilage, et al. (Arachchilage *et al.* 2013), were used to empirically investigate through the ConfiChair system scenario. Therefore, a qualitative study was conducted to assess the taxonomy. The study employed 6 participants (as a pilot study) with each participant participating for an approximately one-hour session.

All participants talked about their opinions about the elements of the taxonomy through the ConfiChair scenario. All of them believed that the protocol underlying ConfiChair, a novel cloud-based conference management system, offers strong privacy and confidentiality guarantees. Furthermore, they talked about their opinions of the elements of the taxonomy as shown in Figure 1 through the ConfiChair system scenario. The taxonomy elements are *Role, Policy, Action, Control, Evidence* and *Asset*. The study revealed that *Role, Policy, Action, Control, Evidence* and *Asset* elements should be incorporated into the taxonomy. Therefore, the current study findings provided evidence of addressing the above elements in the trust domains taxonomy for securely sharing information among others.

7. Discussion

The current study empirically investigated what key elements that should be incorporated into the trust domains taxonomy for securely sharing information among others. Furthermore, it determines why these elements should be incorporated into the trust domains taxonomy.

All participants talked about their opinions of the elements of the taxonomy through the ConfiChair scenario. All of them were convinced in our pilot study that the taxonomy (shown in Figure 1) is somewhat effective in securely sharing information among others. Their common argument was that the conference system administrator should not have access to the names of authors and the names of reviewers including papers and reviews. Additionally, they argued that all sensitive data (e.g. encryption of each review or score) is seen by the conference system administrator should only be in encrypted form. One participant responded, *"No nothing, the conference system administrator should know nothing"*. Therefore, the current study conveys a simple, yet a powerful message that the proposed ConfiChair system offers strong privacy and confidentiality guarantees (Arapinis *et al.* 2012).

All participants were believed that the *Role* element is important in the taxonomy. *Roles* are used to specify the level of participation in the ConfiChair system. One participant responded, *"Yes, it is natural thing that you need to have an author, reviewer, conference chair and conference system administrator in any conference management system"*. It is true that the ConfiChair system provides the facility to different system requirements for its intended users such as an author, reviewer, conference chair, and the conference system administrator. In terms of the confidentiality and privacy perspective, it is, therefore, worth considering the conflict of interests or requirements of different user roles. One participant stressed that,

"Yes, I believe roles are important, because you want to prevent things like conflict of interests". It can therefore be argued that the *Role* element should be incorporated into the trust domains taxonomy for securely sharing information among others.

A *Role* establishes one or more *Policies* within the trust domain. *Policies* are a means of specifying the behavior of entities within the ConfiChair system. All participants believed that given *Policies* developed in the ConfiChair system are important for securely sharing information among others (in this case for strong privacy and confidentiality gurantees). For example, a reviewer doesn't see other reviewers of a paper before writing her own. All participants believed that this policy prevents the ConfiChair system from being biased reviewers. One participant commented on the above policy, *"It is a policy that would be useful to establish an unbiased opinion"*. Furthermore, the proposed ConfiChair system has another policy in place called the conference system administrator does not have access to the content of papers or reviews, or the numerical scores given by the reviewers to papers. This is imperative to offer strong privacy and confidentiality guarantees in the ConfiChair system. One participant said. *"Of course, necessary policies should be developed and maintained in order to ensure privacy, security, confidentiality and also integrity of the system"*. Another participant also stressed, *"The issue comes down to if the work is currently unpublished or in-review, then it's about confidentiality, it's about privacy"*. These statements describe how much developed policies are important in the ConfiChair system. Therefore, the *Policy* element is significantly important to incorporate into the trust domains taxonomy for securely sharing information among others.

The trust domains taxonomy describes *Actions* are performed by a given *Role* or by an agent that represents a particular *Role*. *Actions* are a series of functionalities performed by author, reviewer, conference chair, or conference system administrator in the ConfiChair system. Author uploads papers or download reviews, reviewer reviews papers, conference chair referees the process and the conference system administrator administrates all conferences are a few examples for *Actions* in the ConfiChair system. All participants believed that these actions are important in the ConfiChair system. One participant stated, *"I suppose, when you're uploading/downloading these information (I mean papers, reviews like that) you should know that you're in a secured connection like https. It's about privacy and confidentiality as well"*. It is important that the end-user should perceive the trust of his or her sensitive data such as username, password, and paper information from the proposed ConfiChair system. Another participant said, *"First of all, any sensitive data should be encrypted in all of these actions"*. These statements describe how much developed *Actions* are important in the ConfiChair system. Therefore, the *Action* element is significantly important to incorporate into the trust domains taxonomy for securely sharing information among others.

The trust domains taxonomy shown in Figure 1 describes *Controls* are a set of mechanisms, processes or procedures that enforce the *Policies* within a trust domain. These controls could be accomplished through social, e.g. penalties, or technical means e.g. trusted computing. Controls monitor activities that occur within a trust domain and produce evidence, described below, that can be used to determine the properties of a trust domain or its constituents. All participants believed that a set of controls developed in the ConfiChair system are important for securely sharing information among others. One participant commented, *"It's pretty useful and of course highly important to have username and secret password"*. Another participant backed up saying, *"From the usability prospective I know that you can have the same username and password access to different roles (such as login as author, reviewer or conference chair) but with different levels of authentication mechanism"*. It is worth understanding how these controls accomplish through technical means are important for securely sharing information among others. Another participant stated, *"I think it's better to encrypt all sensitive data on papers, reviewers, reviews, the link between authors and reviewers, stuff like that"*. This provides further evidence for these controls accomplish through technical means are necessary for securely sharing information among others. It can therefore be argued that the *Control* element is significantly important to incorporate into the trust domains taxonomy for securely sharing information among others.

The trust domains taxonomy shown in Figure 1 describes *Evidence* is data that is produced by the controls within a trust domain to indicate the kinds of activities that have occurred in a trust domain. These activities are captured by monitoring the actions that are performed by or on behalf of roles that exists within a trust domain. For example, such evidence can be provenance - records of how data came to be. All participants believed that *Evidence* produced by the ConfiChair system is necessary to maintain within the system. Examples of such evidence include; provenance information produced by uploading/downloading papers, reviewing papers, refereeing the ConfiChair system process and administrating all conferences through the ConfiChair system. One participant responded, *"Well, you have to know when the author uploaded the paper in case they passed the deadline and so on"*. On the other hand, it is very useful to maintain some evidence for digital forensic purposes. One participant said, *"Yes, it is important to maintain [provenance information] within the system, because if you're dealing with legal issues, like suddenly someone takes a legal action against the administrator of the system for stealing his/her idea"*. These statements describe how much worth of maintaining *Evidence* the ConfiChair system. Therefore, the *Evidence* element is significantly important to incorporate into the trust domains taxonomy for securely sharing information among others.

Conceptualization of a trust domain is based on the idea of enabling secure information flow among a set of entities. Such entities may each have a set of devices through which they share the data. Furthermore, these entities may provide access to the information stored on the devices or other media to other members of the domain. For this reason, Arachchilage, et al. (Arachchilage *et al.* 2013), define the concept of an *Asset* as being a fundamental element of a trust domain. An asset is something of value to the owner, but could also be valuable to other entities such as attackers or competitors. One example of an asset is data. All participants agreed that the data exist in digital form should be maintained during the period of the particular conference. They also believed if an issue arose, then you may need this information as evidence. For example, if an author made an inquiry asking to double-check the feedback of the reviewer, in case if he has received someone else's feedback. One participant responded, *"During the conference, yes I will say so. If anyone has any issues, you can provide the evidence here"*. However, all participants believed that it is not necessary to maintain data after the conference with respect to the ConfiChair system. For example, one participant said, *"You certainly need to keep it for the duration of the conference. After that you may probably need to destroy"*. It can therefore be argued that it is important to maintain data within the system during its lifetime. This is because certain data could have detrimental effects when it ends up in wrong hands like hackers. Therefore, the *Asset* element is significantly important to incorporate into the trust domains taxonomy for securely sharing information among others.

8. Conclusions and Future work

This research attempted to empirically investigate the proposed taxonomy through the ConfiChair system scenario. The study asks what elements that should be incorporated into the trust domains taxonomy for securely sharing information among others and why those elements are important. Finally, the current study results provided support to define and justify what key elements that should be addressed in the trust domains taxonomy for securely sharing information among others. The study results showed that *Role, Policy, Action, Control, Evidence* and *Asset* elements should be incorporated into the taxonomy for securely sharing information among others. Additionally, the study findings revealed that the protocol underlying ConfiChair, a novel cloud-based conference management system, offers strong privacy and confidentiality guarantees.

This study has identified some limitations. First, we interviewed 6 participants as a pilot study from the Department of Computer Science at the University of Oxford. Future research is needed to confirm our findings using different samples (relatively with a large sample size). Furthermore, it is worthwhile reporting the main study relatively with a large sample size on the quality of the taxonomy, in terms of its completeness, integrity, flexibility, understandability, correctness, simplicity, integration, and implementation as suggested by Moody and Shanks (Moody and Shanks, 2003). Second, for the purpose of empirical testing, we selected ConfiChair system scenario as the possible scenario. Therefore, research can be conducted with different scenarios to examine whether or not the findings of this study will change.

9. References

Arachchilage, N. A. G., Namiluko, C. and Martin, A. (2013). "A Taxonomy for Securely Sharing Information Among Others in a Trust Domain," *8th International Conference for Internet Technology and Secured Transactions (ICITST)*, London, IEEE, vol., no., pp.296,304.

Arapinis, M., Bursuc, S. and Ryan, M. (2012). "Privacy supporting cloud computing: ConfiChair, a case study," *Principles of Security and Trust*, Springer, pp. 89–108.

Baptista, A., Howe, B., Freire, J., Maier, D. and Silva, C. T. (2008). "Scientific exploration in the era of ocean observatories," *Comput. Sci. Eng.*, Vol. 10, No. 3, pp. 53–58.

Bizer, C. and Oldakowski, R. (2004). "Using context-and content-based trust policies on the semantic web", *Proceedings of the 13th international World Wide Web conference on Alternate track papers & posters*, pp. 228–229.

Chapman, A., Blaustein, B. and Elsaesser, C. (2010). "Provenance-based belief," In *Proceedings of the 2nd conference on Theory and practice of provenance* (TAPP'10). USENIX Association, Berkeley, CA, USA, pp. 11-11.

Donaldson, D. R. and Fear, K. (2011). "Provenance, end-user trust and reuse: An empirical investigation," in *TaPP'11: Proceedings of the third USENIX Workshop on the Theory and Practice of Provenance*, Heraklio, Crete, Greece.

Gil, Y. and Artz, D. (2007). "Towards content trust of web resources," *Web Semant. Sci. Serv. Agents World Wide Web*, Vol. 5, No. 4, pp. 227–239.

Hartig, O. and Zhao, J. (2009). "Using Web Data Provenance for Quality Assessment," *SWPM*, Vol. 526.

Kelton, K., Fleischmann, K. R. and Wallace, W. A. (2008). "Trust in digital information," *J. Am. Soc. Inf. Sci. Technol.*, Vol. 59, No. 3, pp. 363–374.

Kirkham, T. Winfield, S. Ravet, S. and Kellomaki, S. (2013). "The Personal Data Store Approach to Personal Data Security," *IEEE Secur. Priv.*, Vol. 11, No. 5, pp. 12–19.

Lauriault, T. P., Craig, B. L., Taylor, D. R. and Pulsifer, P. L. (2008). "Today's data are part of tomorrow's research: Archival issues in the sciences," *Archivaria*, Vol. 64.

Moody, D. L. and Shanks, G.G. (2003). "Improving the quality of data models: empirical validation of a quality management framework", Information Systems Journal, vol. 28, pp. 619-650.

Missier, P., Belhajjame, K., Zhao, J., Roos, M. and Goble, C. (2008). "Data lineage model for Taverna workflows with lightweight annotation requirements," *Provenance and Annotation of Data and Processes*, Springer, pp. 17–30.

Nørgaard, M. and Hornbæk, K. (2006). "What Do Usability Evaluators Do in Practice?: An Explorative Study of Think-aloud Testing," *Proceedings of the 6th Conference on Designing Interactive Systems*, New York, NY, USA, 2006, pp. 209–218.

Sexton, A. , Yeo, G., Turner, C. and Hockey, S. (2004). "User feedback: testing the LEADERS demonstrator application," *J. Soc. Arch.*, Vol l. 25, No. 2, pp. 189–208.

Wang, Y. D. and Emurian, H. H. (2005). "An overview of online trust: Concepts, elements, and implications," *Comput. Hum. Behav.*, Vol. 21, No. 1, pp. 105–125.

Weng, C., Gennari, J. H. and Fridsma, D. B. (2007). "User-centered semantic harmonization: A case study," *J. Biomed. Inform.*, Vol. 40, No. 3, pp. 353–364.

Privacy as a Secondary Goal Problem: An Experiment Examining Control

T. Hughes-Roberts

School of Science and Technology, Nottingham Trent University, Nottingham, United Kingdom
e-mail : thomas.hughesroberts@ntu.ac.uk

Abstract

Privacy is a well-documented issue for research with end-users routinely disclosing large amounts of sensitive information about themselves. The privacy paradox, for example, suggests that users are concerned about their online privacy yet behave in opposition to such stated concern. One potential reason for this paradoxical behaviour is that privacy suffers from a secondary goal problem; that is, it is often not considered in conjunction with the primary motivation for using the system. Given that the User Interface (UI) provides the stimulus for interaction this paper proposes that it is ideally placed to remind users of their privacy and motivate them to consider their behaviour with more scrutiny. An experiment is implemented asking participants to sign-up to a social network by answering a series of questions to build their profiles. A treatment is designed based on the Theory of Planned Behaviour which posits that an individual's behaviour is influenced by their perception of how easy a particular action is to inform; hence, UI elements are designed aimed at aiding users in identifying sensitive information and motivating them to consider their privacy. Specifically, participants are given the opportunity to review their submitted information and make amendments; a privacy score is dynamically altered to make the goal of privacy protection more salient. Results from the treatment group are compared to a control. Findings suggest that participants within the treatment group disclosed less than those in the control with statistically significant results and there is evidence that user behaviour is influenced by a privacy goal oriented UI.

Keywords

Privacy, Social Networks, Experiment, Human Computer Interaction (HCI), Control

1. Introduction

End-users of social networks routinely disclose sensitive information about themselves despite stating a high level of concern for their privacy in such services; a phenomenon known as the privacy paradox (Acquisti and Gross 2006). Privacy has been described as a secondary goal problem (Bonneau, Anderson et al. 2009), that it is not considered during interaction where the focus is on achieving other goals which may well be in opposition to the idea of privacy. Users within social networks may therefore forget about the impact sharing information may have when they disclose it or fail to protect it using appropriate privacy settings when it is disclosed. For example, publish on a timeline without thought of the audience or apply default privacy settings. This paper proposes that reminding users of their privacy at the point of interaction through the User Interface (UI) could produce more privacy conscious behaviour.

The paper will introduce relevant related work to define what role user interface can play in informing behaviour by utilising theories of social psychology. An experiment and methodology is proposed with a treatment designed around the Theory of Planned Behaviour; specifically, the salient property it defines as "perceived control" (Ajzen 1991). This treatment aims to make the identification and control over sensitive information clearer, making privacy a more salient part of interaction; results are compared to control group to explore the effect of psychologically informed UI's.

2. Literature Review

Literature has proposed numerous potential causes of the privacy paradox, including low level of technical skill in users (Kolter and Pernul 2009), a lack of awareness of privacy issues (Miller, Salmona et al. 2011) and the design of the social network itself (Fogg and Iizawa 2008, Livingstone 2008). Indeed, privacy itself is a highly complex issue that differs from individual to individual (Rosenblum 2007). Given that users appear to desire a level of concern for the privacy and only they can be aware of their particular privacy context at any given time, an argument can be made that user must be empowered to enact their own privacy needs.

Privacy as a secondary goal for users has also been proposed as a potential cause of poor privacy behaviour (Bonneau, Anderson et al. 2009). That is, users do not consider their privacy at the point of interaction, perhaps as it conflicts with their personal reasons for using the system (or is simply not as important). The lack of privacy salience embedded into the design of the social network has been cited as a potential reason for the lack of privacy consideration shown by users (Houghton and Joinson 2010). If the act of disclosure is considered an emergent behaviour of privacy then theories of behavioural change could provide a means of exploring it. Social networks have been described as a persuasive technology, influencing and changing users habits through their use of the system (Fogg 2009). The Theory of Planned Behaviour (Figure 1) defines three aspects of salience that influence an individual's intention and behaviour (Ajzen 1991).

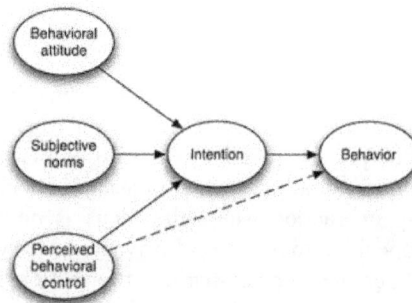

Figure 1: Theory of Planned Behaviour (Ajzen, 1991)

Each of these aspects of salience could provide a basis for altering the UI such that privacy becomes part of the behavioural intention and action and is therefore part of the goal rather than a secondary goal. Indeed, this paper proposes that the UI is ideally suited to empower users to protect their privacy by adding privacy salient information and mechanisms to it and it has been suggested that there lacks critical focus on the role of the UI (Masiello 2009). Furthermore, behavioural psychology suggests that behaviour is a reaction environmental stimulus (Breakwell 2006) and the UI in a social network is the environment with which users react and interact with. Wider research has found that the way in which information is presented to users and the control options surrounding can influence the amount of disclosure users exhibit (Brandimarte, Acquisti et al. 2012).

From the TPB, Behavioural Attitude suggests that behaviour is influenced by our knowledge and perception of the consequences associated with certain acts. Hence, the UI could provide prompts to remind users of the risks of information disclosure. Indeed, an element of persuasion has been defined as suggestion (Fogg 2003) where interventions are set to appear "at the right time" with the right information thus raising awareness of privacy issues. Subjective Norms suggests that behaviour is influenced by the thoughts and actions of those around us. The Theory of Social Capital (Portes 1998) for example, would see disclosure as the act of strengthening social ties with peers. The UI could also be used to deliver advice and guidance either from peers or expert users to aid in the decision making process of privacy behaviour. Finally, the Perceived Control aspect deals with the perception of how easy a behaviour is to perform and how easy it actually is to enact. The design of technology may make it easy to disclose private information and not so easy to protect it. Similarly, users may feel that the identification and protection of private information is simple yet this perception may not relate to reality (and hence paradox). Indeed, tunnelling has been proposed as another persuasion strategy where goal driven design is concerned to reduce uncertainty by leading users through interaction (Fogg 2003).

An experiment has been designed to test each of these salient aspects. This paper presents the findings from the Perceived Control treatment in comparison to a control group and is described in the following section.

3. Methodology

Based on the Perceived Control element of the Theory of Planned Behaviour an experimental treatment is designed to explore the following hypotheses:

H1. A User Interface that aids users in identifying and controlling sensitive information will influence user behaviour and decrease the amount of sensitive information they give.

This experiment asks users to "sign-up" to a new social network created for Nottingham Trent University Students and create their profiles on it. The experiment is designed to mimic Facebook in appearance in order to promote the ecological validity of the experiment (Lew, Nguyen et al. 2011) and place it in a clear context; see example in Figure 2. Notice the red asterisks to illustrate that the other questions asked of participants are optional and that they do not have to answer.

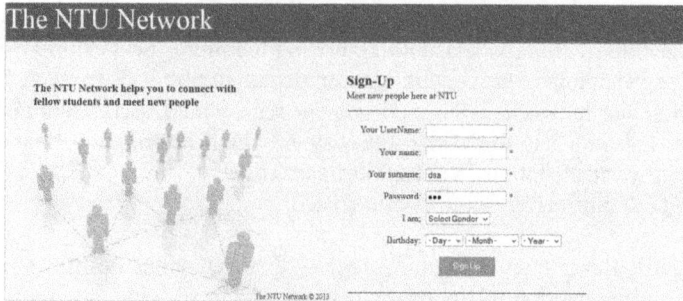

Figure 2: Experiment home page

This account creation process asks participants a series of questions that range in their potential sensitivity and privacy invasiveness similar to work by Brandimarte *et al* (2012).

In total 33 questions are asked of participants during this account creation process; the total amount of questions answered is used to test H1 by comparing the results in the treatment group to a control. These questions have a variety of input types including text boxes, drop down menus and yes/no checkboxes (e.g. have you ever pirated media?). Participants are informed that the questions are intended to populate their profile with information and create a network of like-minded individuals and the more they disclose the more accurate their resulting network will be.

The control group in total traverses three screens, the introductory screen as shown in figure 1, the question bank that "builds" their profile (see figure 3) and finally a screen to apply privacy settings to their new accounts (the purpose of this paper is to focus on the questions answered rather than the settings applied).

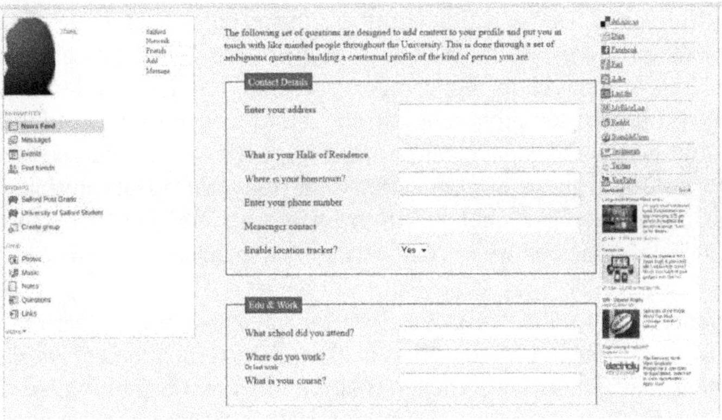

Figure 3: Profile builder page

The treatment adds a series of review screens after each from submission from the participants. This review screen is intended to provide an opportunity to examine what data they have entered outside of the context of the social network, identify potentially sensitive information they have inputted and modify where they feel is necessary. As such, two levels of disclosure were recorded for the treatment group participants: one prior to salient review and one after.

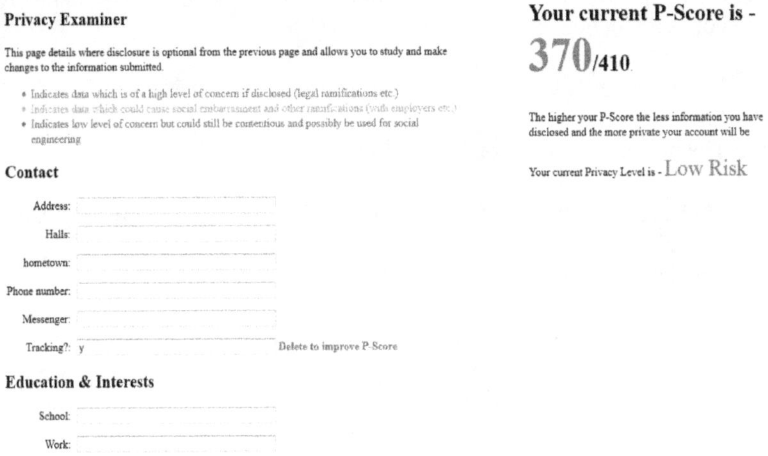

Figure 4: Salient review treatment

This screen aids in the identification of potentially sensitive information that has been submitted through a variety of dynamic UI elements. Each piece of data has a rating that is hidden if the field is blank ("Delete to improve P-Score"), should a participant remove information this rating dynamically turns off in order to emphasise the impact of the interaction and to demonstrate the tangible results of control (making risk management more obvious). This rating of sensitivity categorises the requested data into three brackets: low risk (green), medium risk (yellow) and high risk (red) (Knijnenburg, Kobsa et al. 2013). Green category data items carry little privacy risk and include such questions dealing with favourite films, music etc. Yellow data items have more potential impact and include questions dealing with political ideology, religion etc. Finally, the Red questions deal with potentially highly sensitive data items including address, drinking habits etc. It is important to note that these categorisations are not clear cut definitions of privacy invasiveness but instead are intended to provide a general guide for participants to use to inform their decisions when considering *their* privacy.

A live "P-Score" is provided to assess the level of privacy risk there potentially is based on how questions have been filled in. These dynamic elements aim to not only aid participants in identifying their sensitive information but also to promote increased control over it through a demonstration of the impact of interaction. Furthermore, the goal of privacy is made the centre of interaction to determine the degree to which participants may be affected when considering extra information during their account creation. As participants will interact with two screens in this treatment group, two measures of answered questions are provided: before and after review of information.

Following the experiment participants in the treatment group have access to an exit-survey and took part in a focus group to assess their perceptions of the treatment. This exit-survey aims to explore the degree to which participants felt the treatment was useful and specifically provides a number of statements for participants to state their level of agreement:

1. I found the privacy information helpful.

2. The privacy information helped to select what to fill in.

3. I believe the privacy information would be beneficial in the long run.

4. I acted differently due to its presence.

Participants were sampled from Nottingham Trent University's Information Systems course (convenience sampling) and were approached in scheduled lab sessions. They were asked if they would like to sign-up to a new social network specifically for the University. They were then randomly assigned to either the control or a treatment group. In total 20 (16 male and 4 female) participants were gained for the control group and 21 (17 male and 4 female) for the Perceived Control treatment group. It is noted that the participants were predominantly male as a result of the sampling technique used and as such may not be considered representative of a social network systems population as a whole.

4. Results

Table 1 provides an overview of the results from the experiment in terms of the total amount of disclosure (% of questions answered) exhibited in the experiment groups (PC1 and 2 represent the Perceived Control group before and after data review).

Group	Number of Participants	Total % of questions answered
Control	20	82%
PC1	21	74%
PC2	21	48%

Table 1: Total Disclosure in Groups

An initial review of these results shows that there is a percentage decrease when compared to the control for PC2 (after data review). Indeed, this is a statistically significant result with a Mann Whitney U $p<0.0001$. The reduction for PC1 however, is not statistically significant ($p=.244$); this would suggest that the treatment influenced participants to review and amend their submitted data. If a participant is considering their privacy then it is reasonable to assume that disclosure will be the least in more sensitive data categories as the treatment should aid in identifying which these are (a breakdown of which is in Table 2).

Group	% of "Green" questions answered	% of "Yellow" questions answered	% of "Red" questions answered
Control	83%	82%	81%
PC1	77%	73%	73%
PC2	65%	41%	37%

Table 2: Spread of disclosure across suggested sensitivities

It would appear here that upon review of their data participants did disclose less in the more sensitive data categories with statistical significance compare to the control (Table 3).

Group	Test	Green	Yellow	Red
PC1	Mann Whitney	$=.242$	$=.192$	$=.175$
PC2	Mann Whitney	$=.027$	$<.0001$	$<.0001$

Table 3: Statistical tests comparing each sensitivity category to the control group

Again, this table would suggest that the greatest effect of the treatment appeared in the more sensitive data categories; although, the green category was also reduced with statistical significance. H1, therefore, would appear to be true based on these results. However, further exploration is required to examine if participants are enacting their own privacy desires or those that they feel are persuaded by the system. Literature has noted that user do tend to forsake sub-goals in pursuit of a perceived main goal provided by the system (Jacko and Sears 2003). It could that participants are being persuaded to be more private than they desire to be.

Statement	Agreed	Neutral	Disagreed
I found the privacy information helpful	58%	32%	10%
The privacy information helped me answer	63%	32%	5%
I believe the privacy information would be beneficial in the long-run	42%	47%	12%
I acted differently due to the privacy information	42%	37%	21%

Table 4: Exit survey results summary

5. Discussion

The literature review identified that privacy can suffer from a secondary goal problem and hence is not considered during the implementation of other pre-defined goals. In this experiment, the goal was to create an account on a new social network and this is achieved through the completion of the smaller sub-goals of answering a series of questions. Certainly, disclosure within the control group seems to be fairly high with an even spread across the sensitivity categories defined in the treatment. This would suggest that their privacy is not being considered during the completion of the task set before them. Indeed, when asked post experiment about why they behaved in such a way the response was: *I don't really know, I just answered the questions* and *I didn't think, now I would have left some questions out.* These responses are similar to wider work (Strater and Lipford 2008) and are indicative of a lack of privacy thought during the interaction. Some participants described themselves as "completionists" and wanted to answer each question they could; indeed, wider research suggests that disclosing information about the self is intrinsically rewarding and potentially addictive (Tamir and Mitchell 2012).

The decreases in the more sensitive information categories in the treatment group would suggest that participants were making a selection of what to disclose based on the potential privacy invasiveness of the information asked of them. However, the question remains as to whether or not participants are enacting *their* privacy preferences or are responding the potentially persuasive goal of the treatment (that places the interaction squarely within a privacy context). From the exit-survey, the majority of participants agreed with the statements that the treatment was useful in aiding their selection. However, only 42% believed that they acted differently due to its presence; this is despite the change in disclosure when the treatment is introduced to the group (i.e. there is strong evidence that they were effected). Participants may be unwilling to admit the extent to which they were influenced by the treatment should it be persuasive in convincing them to act in accordance with strong privacy recommendations. Indeed, there is evidence in the literature that users tend to downplay the effect of perceived counterintuitive behaviour on themselves but do perceive it to be persuasive to others (Debatin, Lovejoy et al. 2009).

Interestingly, post experiment, participant's responses suggested that the dynamic "Privacy Score" was the most influential in convincing them to remove submitted information: *I wanted to get a low score, it was like a game.* Also, when asked if they changed response: *yes, it seemed to want me to.* The score would therefore seem to provide participants with a real-time reaction to their interaction that gave them something to aim for with a real and tangible goal. However, the main reason for removing information may be attributed to gaining a low score and not as a result of thinking about their own privacy needs; although, disclosure was lessened in the more sensitive categories. Privacy would therefore seem to be a more prevalent goal of the interaction where the treatment is present. However, the treatment may have made privacy the *primary* goal of interaction and therefore was persuasive in the same vein as a social network may be with gathering participant information.

6. Conclusions and Further Work

This paper has presented the results of an experiment based on the Perceived Control aspect of the Theory of Planned Behaviour and explored a means of including the idea of privacy as part of the interaction with social networks. This treatment aimed to introduce privacy into the goal of interaction in attempt to provide a solution to privacy as a secondary goal problem by making the identification of sensitive information more salient and the impact of control over that information more obvious. Participants in the treatment group did disclose less than the control and this disclosure was specifically reduced in the more sensitive categories of questions. Such a dynamic score could be added to real social networks through browser extensions or the use of API's to aid users in the use of such systems. However, the extent to which participant enacted their privacy preferences is unclear due to the potential persuasion the treatment may have introduced; that is, privacy may have become the *primary* goal of interaction and other goals may have suffered.

This experiment does show that one form of salience can be particularly effective in persuading users at the point of interaction through dynamic UI elements that instantly show the tangible effect of an interaction. However, the experiments took place in a controlled context and as such do not model the real world setting of privacy and social network behaviour. Hence, participants may have acted according to the perceived aim of the experiment explaining the extensive reduction in the more sensitive data categories. In order to verify the results here the UI elements should be placed in a real world setting to examine the potential effects in an actual context. For example, in Facebook, participants may disclose due their own pre-defined goals rather than goals defined by the system (account creation, reduce Privacy Score etc.). Would such UI elements influence these more personal goals?

Ultimately, this experiment has examined if privacy can be made a salient goal of interaction in an attempt to tackle the potential secondary goal problem it has. The treatment designed here placed privacy squarely into the interactive experience of the participant and made it a clear, tangible goal of system use. UI elements described demonstrate how privacy goals can be made to be a more persuasive part of end-user needs.

7. References

Acquisti, A. and R. Gross (2006). "Imagined Communities: Awareness, Information Sharing, and Privacy on the Facebook." Proceedings of the 6th Workshop on Privacy Enhancing Technologies.

Ajzen, I. (1991). "The Theory of Planned Behaviour." Organizational Behaviour and Human Decision Processes 50: 179-211.

Bonneau, J., J. Anderson and L. Church (2009). "Privacy Suites: Shared Privacy for Social Networks." 5th Symposium on Usable Privacy and Security.

Brandimarte, M., A. Acquisti and G. Loewenstien (2012). Misplaced Confidences: Privacy and the Control Paradox. Workshop on the Economics of Information Security, Harvard.

Breakwell, G. M. (2006). Research Methods in Psychology. Oxford, Sage Publications Ltd.

Debatin, B., J. P. Lovejoy, A. K. Horn and B. N. Hughes (2009). "Facebook and online privacy: Attitudes, behaviors, and unintended consequences." Journal of Computer-Mediated Communication 15(1): 83-108.

Fogg, B. J. (2003). Persuasive Technology: Using Computers to Change what We Think and Do. San Francisco, Morgan Kaufmann.

Fogg, B. J. (2009). The Behaviour Grid: 35 Ways Behaviour Can Change. PERSUASIVE. Clairemont, California.

Fogg, B. J. and D. Iizawa (2008). Online Persuasion in Facebook and Mixi: A Cross-Cultural Comparison. PERSUASIVE. O.-K. e. al. Berlin: 35-46.

Houghton, D. J. and A. Joinson (2010). "Privacy, Social Network Sites, and Social Relations." Journal of Technology in Human Services 28(1-2): 74-94.

Jacko, J. A. and A. Sears (2003). The Human-Computer Interaction Handbook: Fundamentals, Evolving Technologies, and Emerging Applications Mahwah, NJ, USA, Lawrence Erlbaum and Associates.

Knijnenburg, B. P., A. Kobsa and H. Jin (2013). "Dimensionality of information disclosure behavior." International Journal of Human-Computer Studies 71(12): 1144-1162.

Kolter, J. and G. Pernul (2009). "Generating User-Understandable Privacy Preferences." International Conference on Availability, Reliability and Security: 299-306.

Lew, L., T. Nguyen, S. Messing and S. Westwood (2011). "Of Course I Wouldn't Do That in Real Life: Advancing the Arguments for Increasing Realism in HCI Experiments." Computer Human Interaction.

Livingstone, S. (2008). "Taking risky opportunities in youthful content creation: teenagers' use of social networking sites for intimacy, privacy and self-expression." New Media and Society 10(3): 393-411.

Masiello, B. (2009). "Deconstructing the Privacy Experience." IEEE Security and Privacy 7(4): 68-70.

Miller, R. E., M. Salmona and J. Melton (2011). Students and Social Networking Site: A Model of Inappropriate Posting. Proceedings of the Southern Association for Information Systems Conference, Atlanta.

Portes, A. (1998). "Social Capital: Its Origins and Applications in Modern Sociology." Annu. Rev. Sociol. 24: 1-24.

Rosenblum, D. (2007). "What Anyone Can Know: The Privacy Risks of Social Networking." IEEE Security and Privacy 5(3): 40-49.

Strater, K. and H. R. Lipford (2008). Strategies and Struggles with Privacy in an Online Social Networking Community. Proceedings of the 22nd British HCI Group Annual Conference on People and Computers: Culture, Creativity, Interaction, British Computing Society.

Tamir, D. I. and J. P. Mitchell (2012). "Disclosing information about the self is intrinsically rewarding." Proceedings of the National Academy of Sciences 109(21): 8038-8043.

Reengineering the User: Privacy Concerns about Personal Data on Smartphones

M. Tsavli[1], P.S. Efraimidis[2] and V. Katos[2]

[1]Dept. Digital Systems, University of Piraeus
[2]Dept. Electrical and Computer Engineering, Democritus University of Thrace
e-mail: matina.tsavli@gmail.com; {pefraimi, vkatos}@ee.duth.gr

Abstract

Smart mobile devices carry an enormous amount of sensitive personal data of their owners. The access to this data by mobile operating systems and mobile applications is regulated by a corresponding security and permissions framework. In this paper we discuss the privacy and security concerns that have risen from the permissions model in the Android operating system, along with two shortcomings that have not yet been addressed up to date. We focus on personal data and propose a smartphone data taxonomy as a tool to highlight these concerns. Additionally, we study the impact of the applications' evolutionary increment of permission requests from both the user's and the developer's point of view and finally, we propose a series of remedies to the privacy and security corrosion.

Keywords

Personal data, privacy concerns, smartphone data taxonomy, user awareness, user's un-training, security issues

1. Motivation

As smartphone usage and capabilities grow rapidly, more complex operating systems and applications are developed in order to meet the user's ever increasing needs. Apart from the traditional mobile phone functionalities such as voice calls and text messaging, smartphones offer a variety of capabilities such as GPS services, email services, video recording, web-browsing and third-party apps (throughout this document we will use the term "app" as an abbreviation for mobile applications). Huge amounts of personal data are generated and stored on the smartphones such as location traces, usage logs, contacts, photos, documents, calls and messages. Each data type serves a series of purposes ranging from the enrichment of its functionalities in order to improve the user experience, to formatting, publishing or just safe-keeping of the data. Even when the smartphone is not used, it produces personal information about the user such as location traces, date-time logs of smartphone activation or shutdown. These potentially sensitive pieces of data are often collected from the operating system or the apps in order to support their functionality requirements. This requires the user giving his consent to these apps to access his personal data as dictated by the permissions model. As there is currently no unified applicable security policy to consolidate the data flows, which data can be accessed, by whom and for what purpose, many privacy and security concerns arise. Additionally, the users are becoming conscious of this matter and a number of tools have already started to appear on the market. A representative tool is TaintDroid, which examines thoroughly the personal data flows by analysing the operations of the underlying app (Enck et al., 2010). An approach to assess the risks of installing an app based on the category and the permission requests of the app is presented in (Sarma et al., 2012).

Our motivation is to address the necessity for effective and in-depth control of the user's personal data flows. More specifically, due to the diversity of the data sources and the value of personal information, we suggest a data taxonomy based on the actors that have or request access to the user's personal data. Additionally, there seems to be currently a considerable amount of obscurity on the permission requests by the apps as well as the way these apps manipulate user's personal data albeit the fact that legal frameworks exist in many countries that specify how the personal data are supposed to be handled. Finally, there is a tendency of users and developers to unsubscribe from security awareness related actions; the former could be due to fatigue of the consecutive acceptance of more and more permission requests and the latter due to the high complexity of the permissions model. In (Felt et al., 2012), the authors describe an approach of users' attention, comprehension and behaviour as "warning fatigue" for gradually losing their privacy concerns, while in (Balebako et al., 2014) the authors conclude that developers lack awareness of privacy measures and make decisions in ad hoc manner.

This research is organized as follows. In Section 2 we provide a smartphone data taxonomy according to the entities that have or request access to user's private data. Section 3 discusses the privacy and security concerns that have risen from the permissions model in the Android operating system, along with two shortcomings that have not been addressed before. In Section 4 we study the impact of the apps' evolutionary increment of permission requests from both the user's and the developer's view. Finally, in Section 5 we critically reflect upon the ways that personal data have been manipulated and we provide suggestions to address the current state of privacy and security issues.

2. Data taxonomy on smartphone devices

Every smartphone consists of a multitude of components and structures that combined provide a series of functionalities offered to the user. These components are hardware resources, network services, informational data and application services and constitute the assets of the smartphone. These assets can be classified in four distinct categories: i) Device, ii) Connectivity, iii) Applications and iv) Data (Theoharidou et al., 2012).

The Device asset encompasses all the hardware components of the device. These are the physical device and its resources (processor, memory, storage, sensors, display, battery, camera etc.).

The Connectivity asset refers to the technologies used in order to provide mobile network connectivity services. These are the i. GSM services (Global System for

Mobile communications), ii. WPAN services (Wireless Personal Area Networks), iii. WLAN (Wireless Local Area Networks) and WMAN (Wireless Metropolitan Area Networks) services, iv. Cellular network services, and v. NFC interface services (Near Field Communication).

The Applications assets refer to all apps that are installed on the smartphone. These apps can be preinstalled by the manufacturer or the carrier or can be third party apps that have been installed by the user.

The Data assets are all the information stored and used in a smartphone. This information can be contacts, financial data, calling history, location information, usage history, pictures etc. and can be categorized into personal, financial, business, health, authentication or connectivity data types.

The data taxonomy according to their source is (Mylonas, 2008):

- *Messaging data*: data derived from the carrier's messaging services (SMS, EMS and MMS) or instant and e-mail messages. This category includes messaging logs as the receiver, the sender, the time and date of delivery, attachments etc.

- *Device data*: all the data of the device and the operating system that are not related to third party apps (contacts, images, IMEI, Wi-Fi MAC address, device serial number etc.).

- *(U)SIM card data*: these data include specific information of the user to be uniquely identified by the telecommunication carrier, such as the IMSI (International Mobile Subscriber Identity), the MSIN (Mobile Subscriber Identification Number) and the ICCID (Integrated Circuit Card Id). The SIM card contains the mechanisms for the operating system work flow, user authentication, data encryption algorithm, and it's file system resides in persistent memory and stores data as names and phone number entries, text messages, and network service settings.

- *Application data*: all the necessary data accessible by apps and necessary for their execution. These can be configuration files, logs or temporal data.

- *Usage history data*: all the log data relating to the usage of the smartphone. These can be the call logs, the browsing history logs, the network connection history logs and the event logs of the operating system.

- *Sensor data*: all the data relating to the sensors of the smartphone. These can be location data, temperature data, direction data, vibration data etc. The most significant sensors that exist in almost every smartphone are the camera, the microphone, the GPS, the compass and the accelerometer sensors.

■ *User Input data*: these data are produced from the interaction of the user with the smartphone. For example, in this category we have the keystrokes, the button presses and the user gestures. As gestures we can characterize the drags, swipes, taps, double taps, touch-n-holds and shakes, that is all the interactions a user can make in order to complete a specific task.

These data sources can handle many information types, such as personal, business, authentication, financial, health and connectivity data. According to the information type these data sources handle, some can be more critical than others. For example, the apps can handle all types of data, including sensitive data, such as health information.

Different parties can have access to different data on the smartphones. A list of entities that can or/and have access to user information on smartphones is presented below:

■ *Mobile device*: can have access to the device data and the sensor data.

■ *Operating System*: can have access to the messaging data, the device data, the application data, the usage history data, the sensors data, the user input data and some of the U(SIM) card data.

■ *Applications*: the app's functionalities define which data can be accessed. According to the functionalities, a certain categorization applies. These types of applications can be:

    A. Games → can access sensor data and user input data.
    B. Content and media consumption apps (music, photo & video, sound recordings, books etc.) → can access device data, sensor data and user input data.
    C. Core functionality and utility (phone tools, mapping, navigation etc.) → can access sensor data.
    D. Social networking, communication & lifestyle (VoIP, micro blogging, instant messaging, social media, shopping, news, ad networks etc.) → can access messaging data, device data, some of the (U)SIM card data, usage history data, sensor data and user input data.
    E. Business and productivity apps (mobile banking, translation, office, calendar etc.) → can access usage history data and sensor data.

Browsing apps combine C and E type functionalities. These hybrid functionalities can apply because even if most popular operating systems have a pre-installed web-browsing app, it is possible to install third party web-browsing apps. These functionalities allow access to browsing history data, GPS sensor data and application execution data. All apps have access to the application data related to their usage, such as logs and configuration files, but cannot access the application data of other apps.

- *Mobile telecommunication carrier*: service providers collect incoming and outgoing calls and text messages, location data and data concerning the Internet usage (the frequency the email is checked, the frequency and the duration of the internet access). They can have access to the messaging data, the (U)SIM card data, the usage history data and the sensor data.

Data Sources / Entities	Messaging Data	Device Data	(U)SIM Card Data	Application Data	Usage History Data	Sensor Data	User Input Data
Mobile Device		✓				✓	
Operating System	✓	✓	~	✓	✓	✓	✓
Application Type: A. Games				*		✓	✓
B. Content & media consumption		✓		*		✓	✓
C. Core functionality & utility				*		✓	
D. Social networking & communication	✓	✓	~	*	✓	✓	✓
E. Business & productivity				*	✓	✓	
Mobile T/C carrier	✓		✓		✓	✓	

Table 1: Smartphone data taxonomy based on the entities that can gain access (✓ depicts access to the specified data, ~ depicts partial access, * depicts access only to the data related to their usage)

3. Contemporary privacy issues

Popular operating systems for smart devices offer a large number of permissions to handle the access of apps to the vast set of personal data items. For example the Android operating system version 4.4 supports over 140 different app level permissions to control the access of apps to the resources of the smart device. However, the permissions handling framework of modern operating systems for smart devices is far from adequate. There are noteworthy shortcomings both in the way the current features are implemented and most importantly, due to the fact that several fundamental services for handling personal data are not supported at all. We will focus on the Android operating system, but similar issues exist in other operating systems like iOS and Windows Mobile. We start with a brief description of representative known issues of the permissions model of Android and then discuss in detail two shortcomings, which, to our knowledge, have not been discussed before.

In Android, when an app is installed the user is prompted to approve the permissions that the app requests. Unfortunately, the user has no option to "negotiate". For example, if a "compass" app requests access to read the specific sensors but also the identity and the contacts of the user, the user cannot grant access only to the permissions that are related to the functionality of the app.

Certain permissions would be much more effective if they could support a more fine-grained access control. In (Jeon et al., 2012) the authors evaluate a fine-grained approach for app permissions. For example, an app that needs to connect to a specific Internet address should be granted this permission and not full access to the Internet.

In (Wei et al., 2012) the authors study the permission evolution and usage in the Android ecosystem since its inception in 2008. A key finding is that the permission model of Android is becoming more complex and hard for users and even developers to understand. A further observation is that permissions are not becoming more fine-grained and that the whole platform is not becoming more secure from the user's point of view.

A technical detail with important consequences on the effectiveness of the security model is that certain permissions are grouped in a way that makes the fair agreement between users and apps hard, if not impossible. Harmless data items are grouped together with critical PII (Personal Identifying Information) fields. For example, an application that needs to know if the phone is currently in a call, must be granted the "read phone state" permission. However, the same permission provides access to critical PII information, like the IMEI of the device, the subscriber ID, the serial number of the SIM, etc. The situation with this particular permission is even worse. For backwards compatibility reasons, any app that supports older versions of Android must request this permission because in early versions of Android this was granted by default to the apps. The app developers have no other option if they intend to support the early versions of Android. Thus, several applications are requesting the particular permission without actually needing any of the granted personal data items. From the users' point of view, it is not possible to distinguish if and how apps will make use of this permission.

The permissions have become so complex that in (Vidas et al., 2011) the authors address the complexity of the permissions framework and propose a utility to support developers in aligning their permission requests with the needs of their apps.

There are more known issues such as the above.

We would like to emphasize two additional shortcomings of the security models of mobile operating systems as follows:

1. Smart mobile devices carry an enormous amount of (sensitive) personal data of their owners. The fair access and treatment of personal data is defined in the Data Protection Directive 96/46/EC (European Parliament, 1995). In the current permissions framework of Android, the app simply

requests permissions without specifying the purpose of accessing the personal data and terms of using these data. A fundamental right of any citizen when he is asked to disclose a personal data item is to be informed about the exact usage of this data item, as well as the exact terms and conditions of this usage (where and how long will the data be stored, etc.)

2. A key issue for the protection of personal data on smart devices is whether the requesting app has the right to send the accessed data items outside of the smart device. This permission is related to the terms and conditions discussed above (bullet 1), but, in our view, deserves to be discussed separately. An app requesting a personal data item on a smart device differs from web or client desktop applications in that the app is running on a platform owned by the end user. More precisely, when an app requests a personal data item it should be clearly stated if this information is used only within computations on the device or if this personal information can be transferred outside the device. For example, if an app requests information about the age and the gender of the user simply to adjust the user interface to the corresponding age class, then there is no reason for the app to send this information anywhere outside the smart device, and the privacy of the user is not seriously threatened. If, however, the app plans to send these personal data items to some database servers of the app provider or somewhere else, then there is disclosure of personal data and this should be clearly stated in the request.

4. Un-training the user and the developer

The progressive corrosion of privacy caused by the increasing permission requests on each and every app update, may have adverse effects on the user's attitude toward security. (West, 2008) enumerated a series of psychological attributes involved in security depriving actions and the lack of user motivation is one of the main traits a user may exhibit. As the user may be predisposed towards not performing security enhancing actions - such as software updates in this case - it is reasonable to expect that the privacy degenerative app updates will further fuel such lack of motivation or even provide the user with an alibi not to perform updates.

Not performing software updates is particularly problematic for smartphones that are part of a corporate network. According to the Bring Your Own Device (BYOD) trend where an employee prefers to use his personal devices (laptops or smartphones) in order to carry out work related tasks, the security risks of an organization may rise significantly. With BYOD the traditional network (firewalled) perimeter does not exist, as user devices can "freely" enter and leave the corporate network, bypassing the perimeter controls. This situation has triggered a significant amount of research on risk analysis, security policy requirements and security controls for managing BYOD insecurity. In addition, when the device is a smartphone and also an employee's property, the risk of introducing malware in the corporate environment is high, as the administrator will not have adequate control over the device.

Therefore the software app provider's appetite to unreservedly collect and consume user personal data may be done at the expense of the security of the organization the user works as an employee. Furthermore, the increased complexity of the permissions may also cause similar effects to the app developer. A developer may not fully understand the different permissions, or may not appreciate the need for requesting the minimum set of permissions - he may in fact prefer to "play it safe" by requesting more permissions in order to avoid time consuming troubleshooting and debugging in case of software failures due to restrictive policies.

5. Discussion and outlook

It is highly worrisome that today's smartphone operating systems do not provide an adequate level of security for the user's personal data and it is possible that they are consciously developed with vulnerabilities. As depicted in Table 1, sensor data are the most critical, because they can be read by any entity that has access on the smartphone device. Moreover, the entity that seems to be the most threatening is the operating system, which has access to all personal data and yet has security vulnerabilities.

As discussed earlier, several interesting ideas such as fine grained permissions and a better grouping of the permissions have been proposed in the recent literature. If applied, such ideas can significantly improve the situation and mitigate privacy concerns of users of smart devices. In this work we make the following additional suggestions:

- First, the permissions framework should be extended to comply with the Data Protection Directive (European Parliament, 1995) by covering also the purpose and the usage terms for each personal data item. For example, when an app requests the "Read Phone State" permission it should at least clearly state how it will use each of the affected data items, for how long, that it will be securely stored during this period and that it will be securely deleted afterward.

- Second, for each data item requested by an app (and, in general, any applications running on the user-side), it should be clearly stated if this data item will be transferred outside the smart device (the data item as it is or results obtained from this data item) or if it will only be used inside the smart device. If the item will be sent outside the smart device, then its transfer, storage and usage should comply with the requirements specified in the Data Protection Directive.

Both suggestions are technically feasible and would strongly enhance the control of users over their personal data without damaging the legitimate app providers. Moreover, such measures would improve the users' ability to distinguish legitimate apps from malware or grayware (apps that carry out questionable actions without sufficient user notification or approval (Sarma et al., 2012)). Even though there are some tools, such as TaintDroid mentioned earlier, that a skilled user can use to try to figure out the risks of using an app, there is no established way for apps and other entities of the mobile computing ecosystem to commit to responsible and transparent practices on mobile users' privacy. Our proposal is an inherent way of supporting this functionality into the operating system, along with the obligation of the apps to state why and how the users' personal data will be manipulated.

Another suggestion for limiting the rich list of permissions set by the app vendor is to leverage market attitudes and consumer behaviour that will demonstrate susceptibility on unjustified permission requests. More specifically, a reputation system based on the evolution of permissions during version updates that is made public could allow a user to make an informed decision on the privacy respecting attitude of an app vendor. As with most community networks, their value follows Metcalfe's Law and in order for this recommendation to have impact, it requires commitment and subscription from a significant number of end users.

Our future intention is to conduct a user study to measure the user's awareness and concepts around privacy concerns in order to validate the above mentioned suggestions.

6. References

Balebako, R., Marsh, A., Lin, J., Hong, J. and Cranor, L. F. (2014), "The Privacy and Security Behaviors of Smartphone App Developers", *Workshop on Usable Security* (USEC 2014), San Diego, CA.

Enck, W., Gilbert, P., Chun, B., Cox, L.P., Jung, J., McDaniel, P. and, Sheth, A.N. (2010), "TaintDroid - An Information Flow Tracking System for Real-Time Privacy Monitoring on Smartphones", *Proceedings of the 9th USENIX conference on Operating systems design and implementation*, p.1-6, Vancouver, BC, Canada.

European Parliament (1995), "Directive 95/46/EC of the European Parliament and of the Council of 24 October 1995 on the protection of individuals with regard to the processing of personal data and on the free movement of such data", *Official Journal of the EC, 23*, 6.

Felt, A. P., Ha, E., Egelman, S., Haney, A., Chin, E. and Wagner, D. (2012), "Android permissions: User attention, comprehension, and behavior", In *Proceedings of the Eighth Symposium on Usable Privacy and Security,* ACM, p. 3.

Jeon, J., Micinski, K.K., Vaughan, J.A., Fogel, A., Reddy, N., Foster, J.S. and Millstein, T. (2012), "Dr. Android and Mr. Hide: fine-grained permissions in android applications", *In Proceedings of the second ACM workshop on Security and privacy in smartphones and mobile devices (SPSM '12),* ACM, New York, NY, USA, 3-14.

Mylonas, A. (2008), "Smartphone spying tools", *MSc Thesis, Royal Holloway*, University of London.

Sarma, B. P., Li, N., Gates, C., Potharaju, R., Nita-Rotaru, C., and& Molloy, I. (2012), "Android permissions: a perspective combining risks and benefits", In *Proceedings of the 17th ACM symposium on Access Control Models and Technologies*, ACM, New York, USA, pp. 13-22.

Theoharidou, M., Mylonas, A. and Gritzalis, D. (2012), "A risk assessment method for smartphones", *In Proc. of the 27th IFIP Information Security and Privacy Conference*, Springer (AICT 376), p.443-456.

Vidas, T., Christin, N. and Cranor, L. (2011), "Curbing android permission creep", *In Proceedings of the Web*, Vol. 2.

Wei, X., Gomez, L., Neamtiu, I., and& Faloutsos, M. (2012), "Permission evolution in the android ecosystem", In *Proceedings of the 28th Annual Computer Security Applications Conference*, ACM, New York, NY, USA, pp. 31-40.

West, R. (2008), "The Psychology of Security", *Communications of the ACM*, Vol. 51, No. 4, pp. 34-41.

Shake Hands to Bedevil:
Securing Email with Wearable Technology

A. Renkema-Padmos[1], J. Baum[2], K. Renaud[3] and M. Volkamer[1]

[1] SecUSo, CASED / TU Darmstadt, Germany
[2] Independent researcher, Germany
[3] School of Computer Science, University of Glasgow, UK
e-mail:arne@secuso.org; jerome@jeromebaum.com; karen.renaud@glasgow.ac.uk;
melanie.volkamer@cased.de

Abstract

Email users rarely use end-to-end encryption. It takes effort and requires explicit action. Users may not see the need for this, have access to the technology, possess the know-how, or may be faced with complex interfaces. To enable effortless exchange of encrypted emails we propose KeyRing, a design for a wearable device that builds on in-person trust establishment through device pairing. This pairing can be used to make the exchange of secure emails between the wearers easier. We discuss how the corresponding interactions of *handshake*, *seal*, and *unseal* can be implemented, and find that the most promising approaches are a ring communicating over infrared and a wristband communicating over Bluetooth. Issues around the human-device interface, user acceptance, feasibility, and deployment are discussed, but need further work.

Keywords

Tangible interaction, wearables, communications security

1. Introduction

Encryption can help prevent casual snooping and dragnet surveillance. After the Snowden leaks on the extent of NSA surveillance (Greenwald *et al.*, 2013), the public should know their emails are being monitored. Yet, few people use end-to-end email encryption. This may be due to users not seeing the need for this, not having access to the technology, not possessing the know how (Renaud *et al.*, 2014), or being faced with complex interfaces (Whitten and Tygar, 1999). Availability is especially problematic in webmail where simplicity and advertising income are key. If encryption is to be more widely used, all of the issues mentioned need to be taken care of. We address the usability aspect of end-to-end email encryption.

Our approach is tangible security, inspired by the historical use of seal rings in securing letters with wax, the modern practice of cryptographic handshakes, and people wearing cryptographic dongles around their neck, as well as the philosophy of industrial designer Naoto Fukusawa: "design dissolving into behaviour". Bødker *et al.* (2012) identified tangible security as a fruitful area for security research. We look at the possibility of integrating secure email into existing social activities through wear- able technology, applying human-human interaction principles to security interactions.

The contributions of our paper are:

- an overview of the research into wearable security tokens;
- identifying handshakes and sealing as interactions to support email security;
- suggestions for realising the proposed interactions in reality.

2. Related work

Given the increased interest in wearable technology in recent years, as well as the shift to mobile technologies, the area of wearable security is a interesting research area. A broad range of different wearable authentication technologies has been published, with application domains ranging from health to fashion, in form factors like pills (Fried, 2013), handbags (Yan *et al.*, 2012), and rings (Roth *et al.*, 2010). We are not aware of any work that uses wearables to make email security more usable for end-users.

Early work in the area of wearable user identification is that of contactless radio-frequency identification (RFID). Contact wearable user identification work was done by Matsushita *et al.* (2000), showing that capacitative touch (explored by Post *et al.*, 1997) can be used to signal a user's identify to the devices that they handle.

Various application areas for these kinds of technologies were explored. Ebringer *et al.* (2001) secured devices by connecting them to a secondary device with a virtual leash: if the leash breaks the primary device is locked. Another concept is the use of a wearable token for providing transparent encryption by Noble and Corner (2002; 2005). Using wearable technology for carrying messages and contraband was explored by Glance *et al.* (2001), and Schneider *et al.* (2000) and Satyanarayanan (2000) used wearables for transporting trust to replace the transport of content.

Different prototypes and products have been built based on the idea of wearable authentication. WearableKey (Matsushita *et al.*, 2000) prototyped user identification through physical contact, based on capacitive touch and a wristwatch. Contactless authentication was prototype by Motorola as an electronic tattoo (Arora and Ghaffari, 2013; Fried, 2013), and token for quickly unlocking phones (Motorola, 2014). Cryptographic tokens in the form factor of a bracelet were explored by the Singapore government (Gratzer and Naccache, 2007).

The form factor of rings has also been proposed and tested for identity applications. The Java Ring is an early example of a contact token in the form factor of a ring (Surendran, 2014). A concept for a contactless (Bluetooth) ring enbodying a social media contact was proposed by Labrune and Mackay (2006). Roth *et al.* (2010) prototyped a ring that can identify a user to an infrared touch table, and Vu *et al.* (2012; 2013) did the same for devices with a touch screen. A crowdsourced project succeeded in funding the production of a device that can authenticate the wearer via contactless (NFC) communication (Kickstarter, 2014).

Intellectual property rights are a potential issue for wearables. Various patents have been filed such as US 20030046228 A1, WO 2005117527 A2, and US 20090146947 A1. These describe ways of using wearable devices for authentication, how to build a trust network using such devices, and possible form factors such as bracelets, rings, and earrings. Whether these patents will hamper adoption remains to be seen.

3. Proposed interactions

To make secure email more usable we propose three interactions to support secure communications: *handshake*, *seal*, and *unseal*. The intention is to ease secure email communication by building on familiarity with in-person trust establishment and the centuries-old practice of sealing letters.

3.1. Handshake

This is the key exchange stage. Instead of having to find a way to securely exchange keys online, this protocol requires people to meet in person, in order to establish trust.

Two prospective email users will exchange an encryption key through a metaphorical or genuine handshake. In essence, their KeyRings will have to be in close enough proximity to each other, having been instructed by their owner to agree on a bespoke key for future email interactions. The wearable device will store the key for use in subsequent "Seal" and "Unseal" steps. Exchange of keys could happen automatically, but may be user directed to prevent malicious deception.

The protocol is as follows, when Tamara and Ted wish to send encrypted emails:

- Tamara and Ted meet in person;
- They activate their KeyRings and bring them close enough to each other so that the devices can communicate;
- The KeyRings generate a key *for this relationship* and store the key together with the other KeyRing's identifier and the email address of the other person.

3.2. Seal

Once users have paired their devices and successfully agreed a key, the aim is to make subsequent communications as simple as possible. The presence of the KeyRing indicates that encryption should be enabled. Alternatively, sealing can be made an explicit act through a physical sealing motion, involving gestures, another device, or clicking on an icon. The metaphor of sealing does not translate one-to-one to cryptographically secured communication, but it should be understandable enough for most users. It is thought to prevent confusion about the use of signing versus encryption, as the default setting for "sealing" would be to encrypt and sign.

When Tamara wishes to send an encrypted email to Ted, she:

1. Opens the KeyRing-Enabled Email Client;

2. Selects Ted's name as the email recipient;

3. Composes the email;

4. Seals the email either with a gesture, by clicking on an icon, or has KeyRing encryption enabled by default;

5. Clicks on the "Send" button.

3.3. Unseal

When the user receives an encrypted message he/she will be notified, and asked to signal that decryption should occur. The unsealing motion of traditional wax based seals can be employed. Optionally, all decryption and verification of email can be done automatically. Additionally, to represent the sender, an icon/symbol could be displayed on a trusted display.

When Ted receives an encrypted email from Tamara he:

1. Opens the KeyRing-enabled Email Client;

2. Clicks on the email in the inbox;

3. Clicks on the "unseal" icon or uses a gesture to signal that unsealing is required;

4. Opens and reads the plaintext email.

4. Physical realisation

Grosse and Upadhyay (2013) already identified the need for more appealing form-factors for authentication tokens, and highlighted jewellery as one potential candidate, possibly powered by RFCOMM/Bluetooth or NFC. In this section we propose a device that supports key exchange for bootstrapping trust for usable secure email communication. We do not know precisely how feasible the design is with current technology, or whether the protocols and algorithms are available to fully support the proposed interactions, but we provide preliminary ideas in this section.

4.1. Design considerations

The design space and solution space for such a device is large, and includes many aspects: communication design (e.g. antenna, body, light, sound), computational power, timing, algorithms, power, storage, cost, desirability, demand, safety, size, management. In a real-world implementation of the interaction patterns, trade-offs between all of these aspects will have to be made depending on where and how the device will be used. Here we discuss these aspects in more detail, before describing concrete implementations proposals in the next section. While the full design space is likely to be intractable, general comments about promising directions can be made.

Model of the context of use. The threat model for the device is that the Internet backbone is monitored, hardware random number generators might be backdoored, and end-points could be compromised. The initial key exchange might be observed, but we see this as less of an issue. The utility model is that the device makes email encryption easier and safer by performing encryption on the wearable device, by making trust verification easier, and by allowing keys to be used across end-nodes (such as phones, tablets, and laptops). The usability model is a device that should make encrypted email as easy to use as non-encrypted email for a large class of use cases.

Form factor. The size of the device can be something like a ring, a wristband (i.e. KeyChain), or a smartwatch. When the handshaking motion is not directly observed by the device, form factors like a pendant or smart glasses are also possible. We think that a hand-worn device is best due to communication range considerations, and for preventing observability of the handshake.

Given the size of current microprocessors (e.g. low power ARM or ARV architectures) the patterns should be realisable in a ring-shaped device, although power constrains will be a real concern. A wristband will be more feasible, especially for a prototype version.

Key exchange. The key exchange and encryption can build on both public key cryptography and on symmetric encryption. If a secure way of sharing keys can be implemented, then public key encryption might not be necessary. Due to key sizes, power constraints, and ease of protecting the implementation against side-channel attacks, the use of symmetric keys seems most appropriate. A remaining issue is how to transfer keys securely. We propose transmitting them directly through some covert physical channel, possibly enhanced with input from sensors that are in similar physical locations, e.g. building on the speed with which hands are shaken. Due to privacy considerations it is important that the device not broadcast continuously, which is also important for battery savings.

Key management. Because the keys might be compromised through loss of the device or through theft, it is important that appropriate key management is in place. One approach that can limit the impact of key compromise is the use of ephemeral keys, although this is difficult to implement in existing email encryption solutions. Additionally, traditional techniques such as revocation certificates can be used, which could be provided as a third-party service to the user to increase usability. A remaining issue is how to protect against misuse of key material in case of theft of the device. Protection via a PIN, backed by a tamper-resistant smart card is one possible approach.

Communication channel. The communication between the two (or more) devices could take the form of ultrasound, infrared light, visible light, radio-frequency communication, capacitive sensing, haptics (vibrations), etcetera. Physical channels that seem fit for private transfer of information are ultrasound or infrared in the cupped hands of a handshake. Another option that seems appropriate is the use of capacitive touch, although a proper way of doing multiplexing within such an application would have to be developed and tested. Besides taking a contact or contactless approach, it is also possible to take a hybrid approach. An issue with any channel is the data rate that could be supported. Additionally, there may be issues with the availability of an interface between the PC and the KeyRing. Generally, different ways of communicating will have different security vulnerabilities, cost, accuracy, and power requirements.

Protocol. For the communication protocol we propose a simple tag-length-value protocol, along with a checksum, running over a serial line. It could be that different channels are needed for PC to ring communication. For half-duplex communication some form of collision detection is necessary. It is deemed important that the protocols are standardised, easy to implement (to reduce security holes), and freely available.

Device security. Securing the device against theft is not the primary goal, although this would certainly be possible by using something like a smart card combined with a PIN mechanism. Alternative mechanisms for user authentication may be fingerprints or other biometrics, device unlocking with the help of external input devices such as a laptop, or a trusted secondary device that is paired with the KeyRing.

End-user interaction. The interaction between the device and the user can work through different channels. One logical way of providing feedback to the user is through haptic feedback, i.e. vibrations. Another low-cost and visible way would be the use of LEDs for (colour) coding, which can also support crude animation. Alternatives are sound, smell, electrical signals, and shape-shifting interfaces.

Input from the user to the device can also take place in many different ways. The use of gesture recognition for the handshake, and automation for the decryption seems reasonable to us. To prevent decryption of messages forwarded by a malicious device, a simple pairing mechanism through a button press seems sufficient. Activation of the device might occur through an authenticated sequence from a PC, phone, or tablet, or maybe even be based on a gesture by the user.

Feasibility. Given current technology and the above considerations, it seems feasible to implement the proposed interaction patterns. A concrete description of how such a system might be implemented is given below. Note that an important aspect of the feasibility of the system is cost. We present both a system that might be built on top of existing devices as a software feature, as well as an approach that involves custom hardware design. The former may be cheaper, but can entail decreased flexibility.

4.2. Proposal for the System Design

Here we present and discuss a proposal for a high-level and low-level system design that implements the handshake, seal, and unseal interactions. Ideally we will reuse existing projects and infrastructure as much as possible. We can build the system on top of existing libraries that implement cryptographic standards such as AES (Advanced Encryption Standard) and SHA (Secure Hashing Algorithm), which can be used for key derivation and message authentication codes. From a high-level perspective, two KeyRings will create key material, which they exchange and use to derive a shared secret. This will be the basis for sessions keys used for encryption and authentication of email. Ideally, the KeyRing will provide a trusted cryptographic platform that can be used by a wide variety of services (e.g. PGP, TexSecure, Pond, etc) and support many identity providers (e.g. CAs, keybase.io, PGP key servers, etc).

The low-level view involves specific communication methods for transferring keys between the KeyRings, as well as for enabling KeyRing to PC and PC to KeyRing communication. For communication between the KeyRings the observability aspect is important, while for communication with the PC interoperability is paramount. We think there are several possible candidates that can serve as implementation of the KeyRing concept. A *smartwatch with Bluetooth* would have easy communication with PCs and phones, although observability of the key exchange might be a problem. *Rings with infrared* are better at hiding the key exchange, but the channel to and from a PC will be more difficult. Additionally data rates might be an issue. In order to communicate with the PC the use of ultrasound is a possibility. In either case, a hybrid scheme may be the most appropriate.

5. Discussion

Like all devices, our solution is not perfect, and there are several limitations and open questions related to the feasibility and usability of the protocols described in this paper. There are several specific aspects that need to be taken into account to make the tangible security patterns feasible. These can be summarised as the following questions: do users want it, can it be made, and will users buy it? We will pay special attention to these aspects in future work.

User acceptance. The acceptance of our proposed key management protocol and implementation is of vital importance if it is to be adopted by end-users. Various facets are likely to influence the acceptance of the device. Firstly, the device needs to be considered wearable, being comfortable and stylish/unobtrusive. Secondly, it needs to be socially acceptable: the handshake is an interaction pattern specific to Western cultures, and other cultures may not want to adopt it because of social norms (e.g. bowing is the norm in Japan, and shaking hands with the opposite sex is not the norm in many parts of the world). Thirdly, some way of dealing with lost or discharged devices may be needed, e.g. a backup solution. Users are prone to losing keys, and there is a risk that they will lose the KeyRing. Additionally, a fallback may be needed when the device has no power and urgent email need to be read or sent. Lastly, the impact on anonymity needs to be considered.

Technical feasibility. A big question is whether current technology allows for the interactions and form factors described in previous section, and if not, when we can expect the technology to be available. Major issues in a lot of wearable technologies are processing power and battery lifetime, the upgrading of devices, and their user interface. This is related to user acceptance: the device needs to be technically feasible from a power management perspective while at the same time falling within a comfortable size for the user. As we have described in the realisability section, a wristband form factor should be feasible for a prototype that will run for an average working day, and that can store an adequate number of contacts. With further improvements in technology and engineering, a ring form factor also seems feasible.

Besides the issue of manufacturing, there are other technical issues that are just as important. For a security device that stores keys for long-term communication with other users, compatibility is a major concern. Additionally, given a changing security landscape, some sort of upgrade potential seems wise. Balancing these may be difficult.

Deployment. Academic research is generally not directly interested in the economic viability of the research, or the ability of end-users to deploy the solution themselves. While the interactions might be applied in a limited contexts by individuals, for the interactions to have a bigger impact they will need to see widespread adoption. We have discussed the issue of people not using end-to-end email encryption in the introduction, and this remains a major open problem.

We see this paper as one step in the direction of enabling easier secure communication. We plan to further explore the barriers towards the adoption of encrypted communication in the future. Preliminary directions include the raising of awareness, finding a "killer application" for the device, and dealing with network effects.

Technology in use. There are various issues that come up when the device would be implemented in the field. As the device would be worn on the body, there is the risk of violence linked to theft of the KeyRing. Liveness detection is one possible way of decreasing the effectiveness of stealing the device. This is also the approach applied by Google Glass, which can be secured by a PIN code, while the device automatically locks when it is taken from the head of the wearer.

Related to user acceptance, the impact of ubiquitous authentication needs to be investigated. While the outcome might be hard to predict, a reasonable approach seems to be adding an element of user control.

6. Conclusions

We have presented an overview of prior work in wearable encryption and authentication technologies, showing that it is a promising research area. We have extended this work with our proposed interactions for making email encryption easier to use (hand-shake, seal, and unseal), and have provided thoughts on how these protocols may be implemented (e.g. a ring communicating over infrared, or a wristband communicating over Bluetooth). Our proposal is a call for the usable security community to investigate contextualised interventions, and to review their practicality.

As described in the previous sections, we intend to build a prototype that supports the interactions, in order to make email security easier for the end-user. We plan to fine-tune and test it through participatory design and enactment (e.g. through Wizard of Oz experiments), inspired by Mathiasen and Bødker (2011). The expected miniaturisation of technology in the coming years should make the device easier to realise.

Additionally, we are looking to explore the kinds of interactions that could be supported when users wear multiple rings, as well as looking at the associated technical challenges. Also, interactions with the device itself need to be further explored, e.g. through gesture elicitation techniques. Another interesting avenue would be interacting with the device itself through, for example, deforming or combining rings. Other future work may look at extending the concepts to other situations and applications, for example cognitive augmentation by making the web of trust between people tangible, or tackling the problem of ATM security.

7. Acknowledgements

We would like to thank the anonymous reviewers of TEI 2014 and HAISA 2014. We would also like to thank the Horst Görtz Stiftung (horst-goertz.de) for funding this research through CASED (cased.de).

8. References

Arora, W. J. and Ghaffari, R. (2013), 'Extremely stretchable electronics'. US Patent 8,389,862.

Bødker, S., Mathiasen, N. R. and Petersen, M. G. (2012), 'Modeling is not the answer!: Designing for usable security', *Interactions* 19(5), 54–57.

Corner, M. and Noble, B. (2005), 'Protecting file systems with transient authentica- tion', *Wireless Networks* 11(1-2), 7–19.

Ebringer, T., Zheng, Y. and Thorne, P. (2001), Parasitic authentication, *in* 'Proc. Work- ing Conference on Smart Card Research and Advanced Applications', Kluwer Aca- demic Publishers, Norwell, MA, USA, pp. 307–326.

Fried, I. (2013), 'Motorola's Dennis Woodside and Regina Dugan'. URL: *http://allthingsd.com/20130529/motorolas-dennis-woodside-and-regina-   dugan-talk-moto-x-tattoos-and-taking-big-risks-at-d11-full-video/*

Glance, N., Snowdon, D. and Meunier, J.-L. (2001), 'Pollen: Using people as a com- munication medium', *Computer Networks* 35(4), 429 – 442.

Gratzer, V. and Naccache, D. (2007), 'Trust on a nationwide scale', *Security Privacy, IEEE* 5(5), 69–71.

Greenwald, G., MacAskill, E. and Poitras, L. (2013), 'Edward Snowden: The whistle- blower behind the NSA surveillance revelations', *The Guardian* 9.

Grosse, E. and Upadhyay, M. (2013), 'Authentication at scale', *IEEE Security and Privacy* 11, 15–22.

Kickstarter (2014), 'NFC Ring by John McLear'. Accessed 2 June 2014. URL: *http://www.kickstarter.com/projects/mclear/nfc-ring*

Labrune, J.-B. and Mackay, W. (2006), Telebeads: Social network mnemonics for teenagers, *in* 'Proceedings of the 2006 Conference on Interaction Design and Chil- dren', IDC '06, ACM, New York, NY, USA, pp. 57–64.

Mathiasen, N. R. and Bødker, S. (2011), Experiencing security in interaction design, *in* 'Proc. CHI', CHI '11, ACM, New York, NY, USA, pp. 2325–2334.

Matsushita, N., Tajima, S., Ayatsuka, Y. and Rekimoto, J. (2000), Wearable key: De- vice for personalizing nearby environment, *in* 'Proc. ISWC', ISWC '00, IEEE Com- puter Society, Washington, DC, USA, pp. 119–.

Motorola (2014), 'Motorola Skip: Pins are for fashion not for phones'. Accessed 2 June 2014. URL: *http://www.motorola.com/us/motorola-skip-moto-x/Motorola-Skip-for-Moto-X/motorola-skip-moto-x.html*

Noble, B. D. and Corner, M. D. (2002), The case for transient authentication, *in* 'ACM SIGOPS European Workshop', EW 10, ACM, New York, NY, USA, pp. 24–29.

Post, E., Reynolds, M., Gray, M., Paradiso, J. and Gershenfeld, N. (1997), Intrabody buses for data and power, *in* 'Wearable Computers, 1997', pp. 52–55.

Renaud, K., Volkamer, M. and Renkema-Padmos, A. (2014), Why doesn't Jane protect her privacy?, *in* '14th Privacy Enhancing Technologies Symposium'.

Roth, V., Schmidt, P. and Güldenring, B. (2010), The IR ring: Authenticating users' touches on a multi-touch display, *in* 'Proceedings of the 23nd Annual ACM Sym- posium on User Interface Software and Technology', UIST '10, ACM, New York, NY, USA, pp. 259–262.

Satyanarayanan, M. (2000), Caching trust rather than content, *in* 'ACM SIGOPS Eu- ropean Workshop', EW 9, ACM, New York, NY, USA, pp. 245–246.

Schneider, J., Kortuem, G., Jager, J., Fickas, S. and Segall, Z. (2000), 'Dissemi- nating trust information in wearable communities', *Personal Ubiquitous Comput.* 4(4), 245–248.

Surendran, D. (2014), 'Knuckletop computing: The Java Ring'. Accessed 2 June 2014. URL: *http://people.cs.uchicago.edu/ dinoj/smartcard/javaring.html*

Vu, T., Baid, A., Gao, S., Gruteser, M., Howard, R., Lindqvist, J., Spasojevic, P. and Walling, J. (2012), Distinguishing users with capacitive touch communication, *in* 'Proc. Mobicom', Mobicom '12, ACM, New York, NY, USA, pp. 197–208.

Vu, T. and Gruteser, M. (2013), 'Personal touch-identification tokens', *Pervasive Computing, IEEE* 12(2), 10–13.

Whitten, A. and Tygar, J. D. (1999), Why Johnny can't encrypt: A usability evaluation of PGP 5.0, *in* 'Proc. USENIX Sec', Vol. 99, McGraw-Hill.

Yan, Z., Chen, Y. and Zhang, P. (2012), An approach of secure and fashionable recognition for pervasive face-to-face social communications, *in* 'WiMob', pp. 853–860.

You Have Three Tries Before Lockout - Why Three?

K. Renaud, R. English, T. Wynne and F. Weber

School of Computing Science, University of Glasgow
e-mail: {karen.renaud, 2rosanne.english}@glasgow.ac.uk; 3t.o.wynne@gmail.com;
40802085W@student.gla.ac.uk

Abstract

It is considered good practice to lock users out if they enter the wrong password three times. This is applied almost universally by systems across the globe. Three tries was probably considered a good balance originally between allowing the legitimate user to make some genuine errors and foiling an attacker. This rule makes sense intuitively yet there is no empirical evidence that three tries is the most efficacious number. It is entirely possible that the number should not be three, but some other number, such as two, five or even seven. It is very hard to test this since attempts could be either a legitimate user attempting to recall his/her password, or an intruder trying to breach the account. If an attacker is allowed more attempts one could imagine the system's security being compromised. Here we argue for the use of a simulation engine to test the effects of such password-related security measures on the security of the entire eco-system. A simulation approach expedites no-risk empirical testing. We use a simulator called SimPass, which models both user password-related behaviour and potential password-based attacks from within and outside an organization. We provide evidence of the expected security impact of increasing the prevalence of password sharing. That is it will lead to increased use of others' credentials and a lack of accountability. We then test different settings for locking of accounts after a certain number of failed authentication attempts to determine a potentially optimal setting. We find that a three times lockout policy might well be too stringent and deserves further investigation.

Keywords

Simulation, Passwords, Security Policies

1. Introduction

Companies increasingly rely on digital systems to run their businesses effectively. The digitisation of the work environment requires that efforts be made to protect such records from unauthorised access. Every user has to be identified and such an identity verified for the system to grant access to protected information. Most organisations deploy passwords. Due to forgetting, insecure coping behaviours which compromise the potential security of the mechanism are employed (Adams & Sasse, 1999; Gehringer, 2002; Herley, 2009; Inglesant & Sasse, 2010). Organisations respond to these insecure behaviours in two ways:

1) *Policing the Human*: Organisations write and enforce security policies which include sections forbidding a variety of insecure password behaviours and providing guidelines for good password practice (Lubbe & Klopper, 2005).

2) *Implementing Technical Controls*: to strengthen the security of the system. An example is to force users to provide a password that satisfies strength metrics (Grainger, 2002) or forcing regular password changes.

Composing and enforcing information security policies can be challenging for organisations (Mandajuno & Sota, 2004; Posthumus and Von Solms, 2004). One can obtain a generic policy but these need to be tailored to the requirements of the organisation (Da Veiga & Eloff, 2007). Policies have to be reviewed on a regular basis (Williams, 2001), but the real impact and potential side effects of policy changes, made in good faith, are hard to pin down and often only emerge later. Thus changes could unwittingly have a detrimental effect on the security of an eco-system.

It is almost impossible to test the effects of policy rules in a real life environment since causatives and behaviours are so complicated and the effects often difficult to detect. Von Solms and Von Solms (2006) argue that one should not include any directive in a security policy that cannot be measured. Yet some of the most commonly included password-related directives have their roots in legacy practices. For example, password sharing is forbidden yet how can one measure the incidence of this activity? The user of a shared password leaves no trace since the access manifests as legitimate use. Finally, it is a brave security officer who adjusts well-established mechanisms. If a security breach occurs subsequently, fingers might well be pointed in his/her direction. Moreover, he or she will have no evidence to prove that the change did not cause the breach. Hence in security many play it safe, adopting approved mechanism in order to ensure their own job security.

An alternative to testing policy changes in the wild is the use of a simulation engine. Simulation is a well-established approach (Simon, 1996) whereby a software model is abstracted from knowledge garnered from a set of observed real systems and then run with a range of input parameters of interest. A validated model will be able to test predictions across a generalised subset of the parameter space where conditions are similar to the validation points. Simulations are helpful in two ways: they can explain (in the sense of identifying a unifying model) retrospectively what has already been observed; more importantly, they can give insight into the functioning of systems of the modelled type, in particular, exploring possible side-effects in previously unexplored regions of the parameter space. The findings produced by a simulation must be confirmed by means of observation in a real environment. However, it does present a no-risk mechanism for testing changes and can help to predict the possible riskiness thereof.

2. Testing Security Controls

Organisations cannot realistically experiment with the relaxation of password control techniques in case the security of the organisation's systems becomes compromised. A simulation environment offers the opportunity to experiment safely and gain insights into the potential side effects of a relaxation, or adjustment, of a policy or technique.

Simulation has been used to good effect in other contexts (Scalese & Issenberg, 2005; Vaughn, 1995; Vickery et al., 2000; Reinhart & Fitz, 2006). The common theme in these usages is that simulations provide a quasi-environment that attempts to mirror the real-life environment in all its essential features. This environment supports no-risk testing and experimentation and can support knowledge discovery.

Technical security has benefitted from the use of simulations (Lee et al., 2005) but we have not been able to find evidence of simulations being used to inform design of secure socio-technical systems. The SimPass simulation engine was developed to emulate the behaviour of agents (employees both malicious and non-malicious, and hackers) in an organisation with a number of systems which the agents attempt to access over a period of time using a username and password combination (Renaud & McKenzie, 2013). On commencing the simulation, a number of agents and systems are generated. Each SimPass entity has a number of configurable attributes informing their behaviours, such as whether the agent is dishonest, malicious, or likely to share passwords. Systems can either issue passwords or allow users to choose their own, for example. Depending on the settings, the agent reacts in different ways when asked to authenticate at random intervals. Well-established forgetting statistics (Ebbinghaus, 1964) are used to make an agent forget passwords. Agents will also engage in particular coping behaviours to deal with the load that passwords impose on them, such as writing them down, reusing, recycling, using weak common passwords, sharing and stealing passwords. Further detail of SimPass (including the default configurations as used in this work) can be found in Renaud & McKenzie (2013).

By configuring the SimPass engine, we can examine the impact of a particular behaviour or policy setting. The outputs we are interested in for the purpose of this paper are the percentage of "bad logins" (an agent using another agent's credentials), and the number of lock-out events (caused when an agent forgets a password).

We will test two commonly utilized techniques/policies for enhancing security, one from each of the categories mentioned in the introduction. The first appears in most organizational security policies (forbidding password sharing). The second is almost the default policy in most password implementations (locking accounts if a person enters an incorrect password a certain number of times, usually 3).

- *Password Sharing:* Evidence of password sharing abounds (Adams & Sasse, 1999). Sharing is frowned upon by security aficionados (Mandajuno & Sota, 2004; Lubbe & Klopper, 2005). Moreover, banks increasingly implement policies that free them of any liability should the password or PIN for a bank account be disclosed (Murdoch et al., 2010).

  On the other hand sharing has the potential to reduce wasted time. Moreover, it seems reasonable for departments to have a common password since they share roles and responsibilities. Singh et al. (2007) explored password sharing in banking. They concluded that there are good reasons to share passwords, such as if someone is suffering from a disability that does not allow them to go shopping for themselves or when the access to an ATM is restricted. The reasoning behind barring of sharing could be the ability to link transactions to individual employees (achieving non-repudiation). Hence this is essentially a risk mitigation technique.

- *Three times lock out*: Most systems allow people to make three faulty authentication attempts before locking them out of the system, and requiring them to contact system support to be granted access again. This policy allows the user to make a limited number of errors but resists the efforts of hackers. There is very little in the literature questioning this default setting. Brostoff and Sasse (2003), however, did investigate the widely used "3 strikes and you're out" policy. They conclude by advocating the use of 10 login attempts instead of 3 to reduce the workload for systems administrators and help desks. What their study does not investigate is the security impact of such an increase. Since this, too, is a risk mitigation technique, we would have to show a negligible risk increase if this limit were to be relaxed.

In both these cases the spirit of the security control is to reduce the number of "**bad logins**". These are system accesses where person A uses person B's credentials to access the system. This can happen if B willingly shares his or her credentials with A, or where A obtains them fraudulently or manages to guess them.

Hypotheses

The hypotheses for the effects of sharing are as follows:

> **H1:** As password sharing increases the number of lockout events will decrease.

> **H2:** As password sharing increases, there will be a significant increase in the percentage of bad logins.

The hypotheses for the effects of authentication attempt restrictions are as follows:

> **H3:** Allowing a larger number of authentication attempts before lock out reduces the number of users being locked out

> **H4:** Allowing a larger number of authentication attempts before lock out does not increase the number of bad logins

Hypotheses H1 is expected to be supported since if more people know a password, it is likely if one user forgets it they can ask their trusted colleague. We also anticipate H2 to be supported as a bad login is where a user B logs in as user A; if B is given a password it is assumed they will use it. We anticipate H3 will be supported as a user will have more attempts if they have forgotten their password, and H4 not to be supported as allowing more legitimate attempts could allow more illegitimate attempts (and hence successes).

3. Simulations

3.1. Effects of Sharing

To test the impact of sharing on system security we ran a number of simulations with a 0%, 25%, 50%, 75% and 100% sharing prevalence. (Independent variable: % sharing, dependent variables: number of lockout events & number of bad logins.). Actual sharing rates are hard to gauge but some studies suggest it in some contexts as many as two thirds of employees share passwords (Renaud, 2013).

We constructed histograms and Q-Q plots for both dependent variables at each level of sharing. Normality was demonstrated by approximate bell curves with no apparent skew in the histograms and an approximately straight line in the QQ plots. Figure 1 shows that increasing the prevalence of sharing does indeed reduce the number of accounts locked (ANOVA < 0.000; F=7649.9). This allows us to reject the null hypotheses for H1. There is also a statistically significant difference in terms of the number of bad logins (ANOVA < 0.000; F=2232.723) with increased sharing prevalence, the corresponding boxplot is shown in Figure. This allows us to reject the null hypothesis for H2 also.

The first two hypotheses are supported as expected. We will now test how increasing the number of tries before lockout would impact on system security and on end-users.

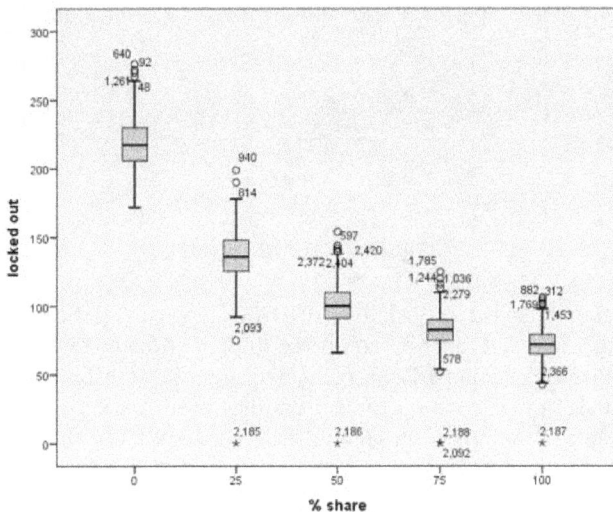

Figure 1: H1 Boxplot

3.2. Lockout after how many Tries?

We ran 500 simulations for each of 3, 5, 7, 9, 11 and 13 tries until lockout. (Independent variable: number of authentication attempts permitted before lock out; dependent variables: number of accounts locked for H3 and the number of bad logins for H4.)

Normality was established by examining the histograms and normal Q-Q plots for each level of attempts before lock out. The data follows the expected normal distribution well with the exception of one obvious outlier. The ANOVA results for H3 are presented in Table 1. Since the significance level is less than 0.05 we can deduce that there is a significant difference in the means of at least one group. The Levene statistic was calculated and the significance value was 0.173, meaning the homogeneity of variance is not violated and it is acceptable to use the Tukey HSD test to establish which groups have significant differences.

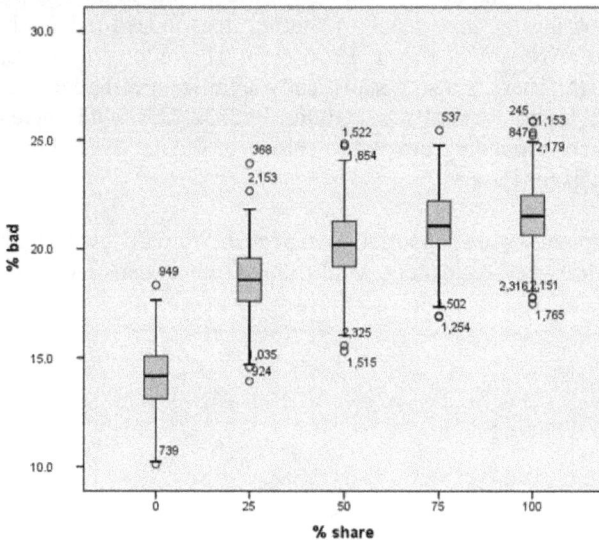

Figure 2: H2 Boxplot

The multiple comparisons tests using Tukey HSD showed significant differences in the group using a lock out rate of 3 compared to each of the other levels (5, 7, 9, 11, and 13). All other group comparisons showed no significant difference. The multiple comparisons table is presented in Table 1 and has been restricted to show only the significant groups. Examining the boxplot in Figure 3 we can see that the median number of locked out accounts is higher for 3 attempts than for each of the other levels of attempts. We can conclude from this that a value of three does not appear optimal and increasing this number to 5 provides a significantly lower number of accounts locked out but increasing this to a value higher than 5 appears to have no significant affect on the number of accounts locked out. The next step is to examine

H4 i.e. the impact of this increase on the number of bad logins to establish if there is an acceptable level of authentication attempts that do not result in a significant increase in the number of bad logins.

(I) Tries till lockout	(J) Tries till lockout	Mean Difference (I-J)	Std Error	Sig	95%	
					Lower Bound	Upper Bound
3	5	6.124**	1.001	0.000	3.27	8.98
	7	5.814*	1.001	0.000	2.96	8.67
	9	6.532*	1.001	0.000	3.68	9.39
	11	6.566*	1.001	0.000	3.71	9.42
	13	7.074*	1.001	0.000	4.22	9.93

Table 1: H3 Multiple Comparisons

The first step for testing H4 was to establish the normality of the data for the simulations before applying parametric tests. Satisfied with the normality of the data, it was possible to progress to the ANOVA, Levene, and Tukey HD tests. The number of bad logins was the independent variable and the number of authentication attempts before lock out was the dependent variable. The multiple comparisons were completed using Tukey HSD as the Levene statistic was 0.137, larger than the value of 0.005 required for non-violation of the homogeneity of variance assumption. As with H3, the only groups which resulted in a significant difference were at the level of 3 attempts compared to each other level (7, 9, 11, and 13) and in addition 5 attempts compared to 11 is also significantly different. All other group comparisons showed no significant difference. The resulting multiple comparisons for the significant groups are shown in Table 2.

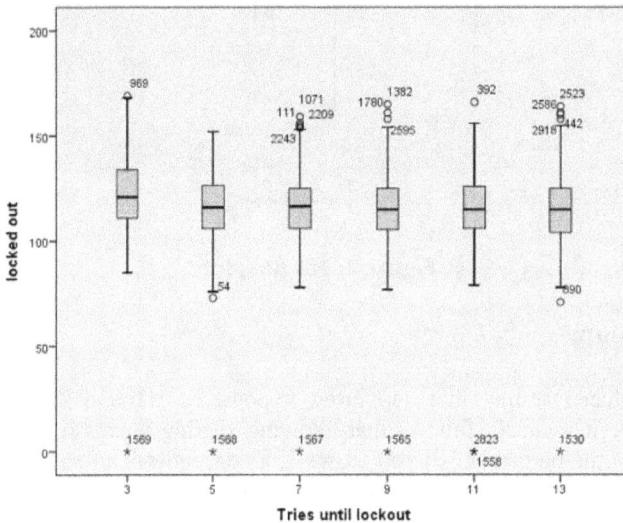

Figure 3: H3 Boxplot

(I) Tries till lockout	(J) Tries till lockout	Mean Difference (I-J)	Std Error	Sig	95%	
					Lower Bound	Upper Bound
3	5	.651*	.094	.000	.38	.92
	7	.699*	.094	.000	.43	.97
	9	.816*	.094	.000	.55	1.08
	11	.953*	.094	.000	.69	1.22
	13	.906*	.094	.000	.64	1.17
5	11	.302*	.094	.017	.03	.57

Table 2: H4 Multiple Comparisons

The corresponding boxplot is shown in Figure 4 where it can be seen that a level of three attempts before lock out results in a higher median percentage of bad logins for group 7, 9, 11, and 13 whilst 5 provides a comparable result. The conclusion we can draw from this is that a higher value than 3 (5, 7, 9, 11, and 13) for the number of attempts before being locked out provides a similar or lower median number of bad logins. Thus 3 attempts appear potentially less optimal in the lockout values which were examined here. A higher number of attempts before lockout could potentially reduce lockouts as well as reducing the percentage of bad logins. We will suggest an explanation for this non-intuitive result in the next section.

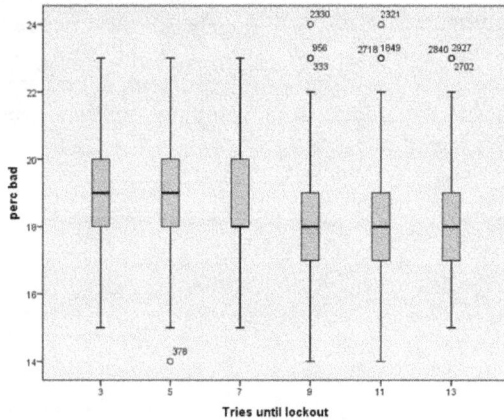

Figure 4: H4 Boxplot

4. Discussion

SimPass produced results that supported hypotheses H1 and H2. This was as expected since it logically follows that allowing sharing means less forgetting and the increase in the percentage of bad logins is a consequence of sharing. For H3 we provided evidence that increasing the number of permitted authentication attempts before lock out reduced the number of lock out events, as expected. Specifically, we found significant evidence that the mean number of locked accounts decreased significantly for attempt values of 5, 7, 9, 11, and 13 when compared to a value of 3 attempts before lock out. This contributes evidence to the hypothesis that whilst increasing the number of attempts helps to reduce the number of locked accounts, there may be a limit to the impact. Thus, selecting a value such as 5 may provide a sufficient significant reduction in the number of accounts locked out.

For H4 we provided evidence that there were a higher percentage of bad logins with 3 permitted attempts before lock out than with a greater number. This was a somewhat unexpected finding since the motivation behind locking out is that it deters potential intruders from carrying out attacks and continuing to try passwords until the correct password is provided. The flip side of this coin, however, is that legitimate users may borrow and steal passwords if they are locked out. This, too, increases the number of bad logins.

The data shows that a larger number of attempts did not necessarily have a significant impact on the percentage of bad logins. A higher value than 3 (5, 7, 9, 11, and 13) for the number of attempts before being locked out actually provides a lower mean percentage of bad logins, because bad logins include use of other employees' credentials both with and without their knowledge. Hence it seems that the number of attempts before lockout could be increased to five without compromising the security of the system, this making it easier for end users without increasing risk significantly.

The simulation suggests that system security, *per se*, would not be compromised, which would be a positive outcome for legitimate users. The reality is that most computer users have 5-6 distinct passwords, and allowing them a few more attempts might help them to fix on the one they used for the system in question. If the number of allowed tries was increased to 5, this would allow hackers two more attempts. When a lockout policy is implemented hackers will often start off with the most commonly used passwords, so if the relaxation in number of tries were accompanied by a strength requirement it might make the effects of the extra two tries negligible.

5. Conclusion

In this paper we use a simulation engine, SimPass, to test potential information security control mechanisms, specifically with respect to passwords. We tested the impact of password sharing and locking users out of their accounts after too many wrong password attempts. The engine produced predictable results in the first instance, demonstrating the negative effects of sharing on system security. In the second case, the simulation showed that the best number of tries to allow before lockout is five, not the de facto three so commonly used in industry.

It is undeniably challenging to carry out this kind of study in industry. There is a level of risk involved in increasing the number of tries before lockout which organisations are understandably reluctant to embrace. However, this will have to be done in order to validate these findings. What SimPass does do is to suggest potentially viable changes and give some indication as to the impact thereof.

6. Acknowledgements

The authors thank Theresa Omoronyia for help with the statistical analysis.

7. References

Adams, A. and Sasse, M.A. (1999) 'Users are not the enemy', Communications of the ACM, vol. 42, no. 12, pp. 40–46.

Brostoff, S. and Sasse, M. (2003) 'Ten strikes and you're out: Increasing the number of login attempts can improve password usability', in CHI 2003 Workshop on Human-Computer Interaction and Security Systems, Ft. Lauderdale, Florida.

Da Veiga, A. and Eloff, J. (2007) 'An information security governance frame- work', Information Systems Management, vol. 24, no. 4, pp. 361–372.

Ebbinghaus, H. (1964) 'Memory: A contribution to experimental psychology', H. A. Ruger & C. E. Bussenius, Trans. (Ed.). New York: Dover. (Original work published 1885)

Gehringer, E. F. (2002) 'Choosing passwords: security and human factors', In (ISTAS'02). International Symposium on Technology and Society. IEEE, pp. 369–373.

Herley, C. (2009) 'So long, and no thanks for the externalities: the rational rejection of security advice by users', in Proceedings of the 2009 workshop on New security paradigms workshop. ACM, pp. 133–144.

Inglesant, P. and Sasse, M. (2010) 'The true cost of unusable password policies: password use in the wild', in Proceedings of the 28th International conference on Human factors in computing systems. ACM, pp. 383–392.

Lee, J.-S. Kim, D. S. Park, J. S. & Chi, S.-D. (2005) 'Design of intelligent security management system using simulation-based analysis', in Proceedings of the 18th Australian Joint conference on Advances in Artificial Intelligence, ser. AI'05. Berlin, Heidelberg: Springer-Verlag, pp. 766–775.

Lubbe, S. & Klopper, R. (2005) 'The problem with passwords', Alternation. Themes in Management and Informatics, vol. 12, no. 2, pp. 53–78.

Mandujano, S. & Soto, R. (2004) 'Deterring password sharing: User authentication via fuzzy c-means clustering applied to keystroke biometric data', in ENC 2004. Proceedings of the Fifth Mexican International Conference. IEEE, pp. 181–187.

Murdoch, S., Drimer, S., Anderson, R. & Bond, M. (2010) 'Chip and PIN is broken', in Security and Privacy (SP), 2010 IEEE Symposium on. IEEE, pp. 433–446.

Posthumus, S and Von Solms, R. (2004) 'A framework for the governance of information security', Computers & Security, vol. 23, no. 8, pp. 638–646.

Reinhart, C. & Fitz, A. (2006) 'Findings from a survey on the current use of daylight simulations in building design', Energy and Buildings, vol. 38, no. 7, pp. 824–835.

Renaud, K. & Mackenzie, L. (2013) 'SimPass: Quantifying the impact of password behaviours and policy directives on an organisation's systems', Journal of Artificial Societies and Simulation, vol. 16, no 3.

Renaud, K. (2012) 'Blaming Noncompliance Is Too Convenient. What Really Causes Information Breaches?', IEEE Security & Privacy, May, vol. 10, no 3, pp. 57–63.

Scalese, R. J. & Issenberg, S. B. (2005) 'Effective use of simulations for the teaching and acquisition of veterinary professional and clinical skills', Journal of Veterinary Medical Education, vol. 32, no. 4, pp. 461.

Simon, H. A. (1996) The sciences of the artificial. MIT press, Cambridge, Massachussets.

Singh, S., Cabraal, A., Demosthenous, C., Astbrink, G. & Furlong, M. (2007) 'Password sharing: implications for security design based on social practice', in Proceedings of the SIGCHI conference on Human factors in computing systems. ACM, pp. 895–904.

Vaughn, R. G. (1995) 'Use of simulations in a first-year civil procedure class', J. Legal Educ., vol. 45, pp. 480.

Vickery, P., Skerlj, P., Steckley, A. & Twisdale, L. (2000) 'Hurricane wind field model for use in hurricane simulations', Journal of Structural Engineering, vol. 126, no. 10, pp. 1203–1221.

Von Solms, R. & Von Solms, S. (2006) 'Information security governance: A model based on the direct–control cycle', Computers & Security, vol. 25, no. 6, pp. 408–412.

Williams, P. (2001) 'Information security governance', Information security technical report, vol. 6, no. 3, pp. 60–70.

Modelling the Security of
Recognition-Based Graphical Passwords

R. English

University of Glasgow, United Kingdom
e-mail: Rosanne.English@glasgow.ac.uk

Abstract

Recognition-based graphical passwords have received attention in recent research as an alternative authentication mechanism. The research often presents new schemes, usability studies or proposes countermeasures for specific attacks. Whilst this is beneficial, it does not allow for consistent comparison of the security of recognition-based graphical password schemes. This paper contributes a proposed solution to this problem. Presented here are mathematical models for estimating the number of attacks required before success for four attack types. These models combine to provide an overall metric of the security of recognition-based graphical password schemes. The metric presented provides a consistent, repeatable, and quantitative method for comparing recognition-based graphical password schemes which was previously not possible.

Keywords

Recognition-based graphical passwords, metrics, security

1. Introduction

A recognition-based graphical password (RBGP) scheme is an alternative authentication mechanism where the user selects a number of images called passimages (Charrau *et al.*, 2005) to be used to authenticate. In this paper the collection of the user's passimages will be called their passimage set. When the user attempts authentication they are presented with a number of challenge screens that present at least one of their passimages and a number of alternative images, called distractor images. To successfully authenticate, the user must identify and select their passimage from the distractor images on each screen. Further information on graphical passwords can be found in literature, for example reviews by Biddle *et al.* (2011) and Suo *et. al* (2006).

In addition to RBGPs, there are two further categories of graphical passwords - recall and cued recall. The security of recall and cued-recall graphical passwords have been considered in terms of the ease of guessing in a consistent manner by examining potential password space and bias in user selections. In contrast, analysis of the security of RBGPs has been arguably inconsistent. For example, one approach to calculating the entropy (hence guessability) of a RBGP is proposed by Hlywa *et al.* (2011), whilst a different approach to measuring guessability is reported by DeAngeli *et al.* (2005) and Dhamija and Perrig (2000). In addition, consideration of the security of RBGPs often focuses on countermeasures for a specific attack (e.g.

shoulder surfing is the focus of Wiedenbeck *et al.* (2006) and Sasamoto *et al.* (2008)). Whilst this is useful, it remains unclear how to compare proposed RBGP schemes in terms of their security. There remains no standardised method of measuring the level of security of a RBGP scheme. This paper contributes to the measurement of RBGP security by proposing a metric that allows the security to be assessed and compared in terms of resistance to four identified attacks.

The approach taken is to construct a tuple that consists of individual metrics for each attack type considered. Each metric is presented as a mathematical model, which uses the configuration of the RBGP scheme to estimate the number of attacks required before the attacker is successful. Models for four attacks: random guessing, guessing based on category bias, frequency attacks, and shoulder surfing attacks are presented. These are combined into the overall security metric tuple which is applied to a number of examples and evaluated.

The remainder of this paper is structured as follows. The scope of the work by considering the variables to be used in the metric models (the configuration of the RBGP schemes) and the attacks under consideration are presented in Section 2. The individual mathematical models which combine to give the overall metric are presented in Section 3. A summary of how to apply the metric and examples are presented in Section 4, and the conclusion is presented in Section 5.

2. RBGP Scope

To clearly identify the scope of the work it was necessary to establish the attributes of a RBGP scheme which contribute to their configuration and identify the attacks to be considered in the metric. These are presented in this section.

2.1. RBGP Configurations

A list of variables which contribute to the configuration of RBGP schemes is established here to identify aspects of the configuration which may have an impact on the success rate of different attacks. The different aspects contributing to the configuration of RBGPs were established from current literature as the number of passimages (denoted p for this work), the number of challenge screens (s), the number of distractors per challenge screen (d), the number of constant distractors per passimage (c), and whether the passimages were assigned to the user or not.

A review of RBGP schemes in literature identified 17 RBGP schemes with sufficient information regarding configuration. These schemes can be split into two groups. One group consists of a single challenge screen with multiple passimages presented on this screen. Nine of the 17 RBGP schemes identified presented only one challenge screen. The remaining eight schemes presented represent the group of schemes which present a single passimage on multiple challenge screens, thus the metric considers this configuration.

Using a single image on multiple screens can be further refined by the passimage selection being restricted to a specific order, or order being irrelevant. No schemes which had multiple challenge screens with one passimage per screen where order was important. Thus, the metric assumes unordered selection. Images can also be assigned to the user, selected by the user from a provided set of images, or uploaded by the user. These options were approximately equally distributed in the schemes identified, however it was felt that allowing users to upload their own image was potentially too guessable (see Tullis and Tedesco, 2005) and conversely using an assigned set of images may impact memorability. Thus it was decided to examine user selected images from a pre-defined set.

2.2. Attacks Considered

Once these configurations were established, it was necessary to identify areas of potential threats to identify the attacks to be considered. DeAngeli *et al.* (2005) propose that security of authentication mechanisms can be judged in terms of three aspects; guessability (the probability an attacker can guess the user's password), observability (the probability of an attacker being able to observe the authentication process), and recordability (the ease with which a user can record the user's password). Recordability was defined as outside the scope as it relates to how easily the password can be recorded. It is unclear to what extent users may record their passimages and how easily an attacker may gain access to this information. This is not an aspect which could feasibly be modelled.

A total of four attacks were considered - two guessing attacks and two observation attacks. These were random guessing, semantic ordered guessing, shoulder surfing, and frequency attacks. Random guessing, shoulder surfing, and intersection/frequency attacks were identified as attacks which are often identified in literature and hence deserved consideration for the proposed metric.

A semantic ordered guessing attack is an attack where guessing is prioritised based on the semantic category of the images (assuming the common approach of using semantically themed images such as faces, objects etc.). Studies exploring the feasibility of these semantic ordered guessing attacks in which the attacker selects the "most probable" image given the challenge screen presented are reported in English and Poet (2011). Results showed that bias in user choice could decrease the estimated guessability by varying degrees dependent on how distractors are selected for a given challenge screen. On average, guessing using a prioritised attack was 13 times more likely to succeed than random guessing for a passimages scheme. The work by Davis *et al.* (2004) and the prior related work both indicate the feasibility of prioritised guessing attacks. There may be a number of different approaches to prioritising images for guessing attacks. A SOGA was included to represent a prioritised guessing attack similar to that proposed by Davis *et al.* (2004) where the information required to construct the model was readily available.

At this stage the variables relating to the configuration of a RBGP have been identified, and the attacks under consideration have been selected. Thus, the next step is to construct the metric. The approach taken is to establish a tuple that consists of an estimated number of attacks required before successful authentication for each type of attack considered. A tuple approach was considered appropriate instead of combining values (e.g. by summing the scores) or using a Euclidean metric since the interpretation of security is context sensitive. For example, in the context of authentication in a home environment where no other individual is present, a negative shoulder surfing value would not be a concern. Thus, it would not be appropriate to reduce the overall security score due to this. Another approach could have been to weight the individual values before combining them. However, the weighting could be different depending on context. The resulting tuple represents the security of a RBGP scheme in terms of the attacks identified. Presented here is a 4-tuple metric consisting of four estimated values of the number of attacks required before successful authentication. There is one estimate for each of the attacks; random guessing, semantic ordered guessing, shoulder surfing and frequency attacks. The calculation of each of the component parts is summarised in the following four subsections.

3. Establishing the Metric

3.1. Models for Guessing

3.1.1. Random Guessing

The estimate of the number of random guessing attacks required before success is obtained from the calculation of the probability of success. This is commonly reported as $\frac{1}{x^s}$ where x is the number of images shown on a challenge screen (the number of distractors plus one passimage, $d+1$) and s is the number of challenge screens. The denominator of this calculation is used to provide an estimate of the number of random guessing attacks required before success, thus the RG value is calculated as shown in Equation 1.

$$RG=(d+1)^s \qquad (1)$$

3.1.2. Semantic Ordered Guessing

The calculation of the number of semantic ordered guessing attacks (SOGA) required before success relies on an estimate of the number of attacks which are successful for a given potential passimage set. This is calculated by performing simulations of SOGAs based on the category distribution of real user choices. Further details of such simulations are presented in English and Poet (2011) where the following percentages of success were achieved: 21% of passimage screens were successfully attacked where distractors were selected randomly (ignoring the semantic categories), 23% of passimage screens were successfully attacked where distractors were selected from distinct passimage categories (excluding the passimage category), and 20% of screens were successfully attacked where distractors were selected from passimage categories (excluding the passimage category). These success rates can be used as estimates for user selected passimage schemes where the images can be split into semantic categories.

Once the percentage of success has been estimated, one can calculate the estimated number of attacks as shown in Equation 2 where s denotes the number of challenge screens. If the passimages are assigned to the user, then this attack is not applicable and this is denoted by *.

$$\left(\frac{100}{successPercentage}\right)^s \tag{2}$$

3.2. Models for Observability

To establish the models for observability simulation software was built, the purpose of which was to represent a RBGP scheme with a given configuration, construct a user's passimage set and allow frequency and shoulder surfing attacks to be emulated against that set. The RBGP scheme can have a varied configuration, in addition if a shoulder surfing attack is being simulated an attacker has a percentage of recall, which reflects their ability to recall the passimages observed. After construction of the simulation software it was possible to simulate each attack type to establish which variables of the configuration of a RBGP scheme had a significant impact on the success rate of the attacks. These variables were then used to run 500 simulations at a variety of configurations for each variable. This resulted in a collection of data which could be used as the basis for mathematical modelling. The modelling process was repeated multiple times to obtain more accurate (better fitted) models. Due to space restrictions further information cannot be included, but is available in detail in Chapters 6 and 7 in http://www.dcs.gla.ac.uk/~rose/2012EnglishPhd.pdf. The following sections present the final models for shoulder surfing attacks and for frequency attacks.

3.2.1. Shoulder Surfing Value

As for the semantic ordered guessing value, one must estimate the percentage of recall rate or success rate of an attacker given a specific shoulder surfing countermeasure. This can be done by performing an experiment to establish how successful shoulder surfing attacks are for the countermeasure implemented. Alternatively an estimated value of successful recall between 1 and 100% can be chosen. Once the recall value has been established, the shoulder surfing value can be calculated as shown in Equation 3 where p denotes the number of passimages in a user's passimage set, s is the number of challenge screens in a session, and r is the percentage of recall. The modelling was based on log_2 of the median number of attacks and so the final equation includes a power of 2.

$$SS = 2^{1.3852p - 0.0824p^2 - 0.2143s - 0.0472r + 0.0002r^2} \tag{3}$$

3.2.2. Frequency Value

An intersection attack, as defined by Dhamija and Perrig (2000) is an attack in which the attacker records multiple challenge screens and notes the images which are constant between two screens. Assuming all distractor images change this would result in the passimage being identified. Takada *et al.* (2006) identify a similar attack which they call a frequency attack. In a frequency attack, the attacker notes multiple challenge screens and notes the frequency with which each image appears then selects the image which occurs most frequently for any given screen. For this work a frequency attack will considered primarily since an intersection attack can be thought of as a special case of a frequency attack.

Unlike the previous two calculations, the frequency model relies primarily on the configuration of the RBGP scheme (and not user choice distribution or attacker recall). This includes the number of distractors kept constant per passimage (denoted by c) in addition to the number of screens (s), the number of distractors per screen (d), and the passimage set size (p). The frequency value can be calculated as shown in Equation 4. The modelling was based on log_2 of the median number of attacks and so the final equation includes a power of 2.

$$FREQ = 2^{0.0156p + 1.6655s + 0.9497c - 0.5575d + 0.018p^2 + 0.0132s^2 - 0.0344c^2 + 0.0309d^2} \quad (4)$$

This equation should only be used if the number of distractors kept constant per passimage is less than the number of distractors per challenge screen. If the challenge screens are constant then a frequency attack will be reduced to a random guessing attack. In this case, * denotes the attack is not applicable.

3.3. Overall Metric

Now each individual model has been determined, it is possible to combine these into the final metric. The metric is denoted as shown in Equation 5 where RG denotes the random guessing value, SOGA denotes the semantic ordered guessing attack value, SS denotes shoulder surfing value and FREQ denotes frequency attacks value. If for any of the attacks a countermeasure is implemented which means the attack is not possible, then a * is used to denote this.

$$(RG, SOGA, SS, FREQ) \quad (5)$$

There are a number of limitations of the metric which should be considered. The final metric models are based primarily on simulations, and so the reality of attacks may be different. This approach provided a flexible and controlled alternative to a large scale user study which was attempted but was unsuccessful in recruitment of sufficient participants. Also, the work primarily considers RBGP schemes with a predetermined set of images (which was constant for the duration of the work) and does not consider user provided images. It is necessary to be careful not to use the models for prediction, i.e. applying configuration values outside the values used in the simulations. This is because the model was based on the configurations used in the simulations, and values outside this could deviate substantially from the models. The models could be used outside the ranges, but care must be taken in interpretation of the prediction. Note that a prediction arises from the metric where configurations outside those upon which the models are based are used. An estimation is provided where configurations used were incorporated into the model. To minimise the need to apply values outside the configurations used, the simulations used configurations from literature to date and values either side. For example, 4 challenge screens are common, and simulations were run with 1 through to 10 screens.

Another potential issue is with the interpretation of the values resulting from these models. One must not consider the values reported as a concrete value of the number of attacks required in any given case. The values reported are estimates based on simulations, in reality other factors such as a combination of shoulder surfing, frequency and guessing attacks could be used which cannot be represented by these models. However, the purpose of this work was not 100% accuracy, but to provide an estimate which could be used to achieve a comparison of the security of different RBGP configurations.

4. Using the Metric and Example Application and Comparison

Now the metric has been established it is appropriate to discuss how to apply the metric and use it in decision making. This section aims to discuss these aspects.

To calculate the component values for the tuple the following approach is taken. First examine the RBGP scheme to establish values for the configuration (as previously indicated, p, s, d, c, r and *successPercentage*). Next, establish if any of the attacks are not feasible for the scheme being examined. For any such attack, use a * in the appropriate place in the metric tuple to denote the attack is not applicable to the scheme. For each of the attack types remaining use the appropriate configuration values (identified in step one) in the appropriate mathematical model described in Section 3. Next, round each of the model values to the nearest whole integer. Finally, combine the values in the order (RG, SOGA, SS, FREQ) to obtain the final metric as applied to the scheme under consideration.

The metric as applied to the scheme under consideration can now be examined in terms of the security either individually or against other schemes. For simplicity, this paper considers the comparison between two schemes as an example. This could be easily extrapolated to examine more than two schemes. To compare two schemes, scheme 1 and scheme 2, one should consider the values for each of the models within the tuple. Let us call the constituent tuple values of each scheme RG1, SOGA1, SS1, and FREQ1 for scheme 1 and RG2, SOGA2, SS2, FREQ2 for scheme 2. It is then possible to compare the values for each of the attacks e.g. RG1 can be compared to RG2 and so forth. Thus, if for example RG1 is larger than RG2 then we can deduce that scheme 1 is more resistant to random guessing attacks. Follow a similar approach for the remaining attacks.

In using this for decision making, for example to select an appropriate scheme, one should consider the context in which the scheme will be deployed. For example if observability is a key concern, but guessability less so then particular attention should be paid to the observability values. This may result in a situation where one scheme has a higher resistance for one attack and a lower resistance for the other whilst the scheme it is being compared to has the opposite resistance. In this situation it is down to judgement of the decision maker to consider what is most important in the context. Having now discussed how to use the metric, the next section aims to provide some example applications. Due to space restrictions only two schemes are included, but more applications of the metric are available in Chapter 8 of http://www.dcs.gla.ac.uk/~rose/2012EnglishPhd.pdf together with further discussion of benefits and limitations of the approach.

4.1. Application to PassFaces

The application of the final metric to the PassFaces scheme is presented here. From reviewing the PassFaces white paper (available from PassFaces (2005)) the following information on the configuration of the scheme was extracted $s=p=4$, $d=8$, $c=8$. Images are assigned and so a SOGA is not applicable, represented by *. Images appear highlighted upon selection potentially making shoulder surfing more successful as shown by Tari *et al.* (2006) where approximately 60% of attacks were successful, thus this value is used for the recall rate of PassFaces. The resulting metric for PassFaces is then calculated as (6561,*,2,*) where * represents that a frequency attack will be no better than random guessing since the number of distractors kept constant is equal to the number of distractors per screen.

From this result the weakest aspect of the security is shoulder surfing. If one were authenticating where the process could be viewed, then this could be an issue. The number of attacks required could be increased by doubling the number of passimages to 8, which results in a SS value of 7. It could be further increased by allowing keyboard entry, which results in a success rate of approximately 11% (again, shown by Tari *et al.* (2006)) which results in a shoulder surfing value of 22.

4.2. Application to Adapted VIP

Whilst the VIP scheme proposed by DeAngeli *et al.* (2002) has only one screen, it is adapted here to multiple challenge screens. This allows the metric to be applied to the scheme and provides an additional example. The metric is now applied to the adapted VIP1 scheme. Since there are four passimages in a session $s=4$ is used. From the defining paper, the configurations were as follows; with four passimages in a challenge session, $p=10$, $d=9$, $c=0$. The shoulder surfing recall was estimated at 60% (as assumed for the PassFaces scheme) since there was no details on highlighting the images upon selection, but the images were selected on a touchscreen. A SOGA was not applicable to the adapted VIP1 since the images were randomly assigned to the users. There was no mention of maintaining constant distractors for passimages and so this was assumed to be 0. It should be noted that the random guessability value may underestimate the resistance as the calculations do not account for sequence, which is incorporated into the adapted VIP1 scheme. Also, location was maintained and thus there is potential for the shoulder surfing value to be overestimated as could be arguably easier to shoulder surf a passimage which stays in one position. The resulting metric is (10000,*, 6, 80).

4.3. Comparison

The purpose of this metric is to allow consistent comparison of the security of RBGP schemes. Using the metric to demonstrate this it is now possible to compare the security of the PassFaces scheme with the security of the adapted VIP1 scheme. It can be seen from the metrics reported in the previous section that the PassFaces scheme is more secure in terms of frequency attacks, but the adapted VIP1 scheme is more secure against random guessing and marginally more secure against shoulder surfing attacks due to the increased passimage set size. Both schemes are equally secure against SOGAs since passimages are assigned to users. In selecting an appropriate scheme, one would need to consider the context under which the mechanism would be used. For example, if shoulder surfing is not a concern then the PassFaces scheme may be a better choice.

5. Conclusions

This work aimed to present a model for the security of recognition-based graphical passwords. The overall model consisted of four smaller models which allow an estimation of the number of attacks required for the following attack types; random guessing, semantic ordered guessing, shoulder surfing, and frequency attacks. This was an important topic to research since alternatives to alphanumerical authentication are arising more but analysis of security can be limited where recognition-based mechanisms are considered. In particular, it was difficult to compare two schemes in terms of their respective levels of resistance to attack. This work has contributed to a resolution of this issue by proposing a metric which can be used for RBGP schemes where multiple challenge screens are presented with one passimage per screen. The consistent, objective, and quantitative approach now allows schemes to be readily compared in terms of resistance to the guessing and observation attacks discussed here. Previously this was not possible. The work provides an estimated number of attacks before success for each of the following attack types: random guessing, semantic ordered guessing, frequency, and shoulder surfing attacks. This metric can be used to establish the more appropriate scheme given a selection, or as a method of deciding which configuration is most appropriate for a particular context.

6. References

PassFaces Corp., 2005, Two Factor Authentication, http://www.realuser.com/ Last accessed 05/30/2014.

Biddle, R., Chiasson, S., and van Oorschot, P.C., 2011. Graphical passwords: Learning from the first twelve years, *ACM Computing Surveys*, 44(4)

Charrau, D., Furnell, S., and Dowland, P., 2005. PassImages: An alternative method of user authentication, *Proceedings of 4th Annual ISOneWorld Conference and Convention, Las Vegas, USA*

Davis, D., Monrose, F., and Reiter, M., 2004. On User Choice in Graphical Password Schemes, *Proceedings of the 13th conference on USENIX Security Symposium-Volume 13*, page 11

De Angeli, A., Coutts, M., Coventry, L., Johnson, G., Cameron, D. and Fischer, M. 2002. VIP: a visual approach to user authentication. In *Proceedings of the Working Conference on Advanced Visual Interfaces*, pages 316–323

De Angeli, A., Coventry, C., Johnson, G. and Renaud, K., 2005. Is a picture really worth a thousand words? Exploring the feasibility of graphical authentication systems. *International Journal of Human-Computer Studies*, 63(1-2), pp128–152

Dhamija, R., and Perrig, A., 2000. Deja vu: A User Study Using Images for Authentication. In *Proceedings of the 9th conference on USENIX Security Symposium-Volume 9*, pp 45–48

English, R. and Poet, R. 2011. Measuring the Revised Guessability of Graphical Passwords, *5th International Conference on Network and System Security*, pp.364-368

Hlywa, M., Biddle, R., and Patrick, A. 2011. Facing the facts about image type in recognition-based graphical passwords. *Proceedings of the 27th Annual Computer Security Applications Conference*, volume 36, pages 149–158

Sasamoto, H., Christin, N., Hayashi, E. 2008. Undercover: authentication usable in front of prying eyes. In *Proceeding of the twenty-sixth annual SIGCHI conference on Human factors in computing systems*, pages 183–19

Suo, X., Zhu, Y., and Owen, G. 2006. Analysis and Design of Graphical Password Techniques. *Advances in Visual Computing*, pages 741–749

Takada, T., Onuki, T., and Koike, H. 2006. Awase-e: Recognition-based image authentication scheme using users' personal photographs. In *Innovations in Information Technology*, pages 1–5

Tari, F., Ozok, A., and Holden, S. 2006. A Comparison of Perceived and Real Shoulder-surfing Risks between Alphanumeric and Graphical Passwords. In *Proceedings of the second symposium on Usable privacy and security - SOUPS '06*, page 56

Tullis, T., and Tedesco, D. 2005. Using personal photos as pictorial passwords. *CHI '05 extended abstracts on Human factors in computing systems*, page 1841

Wiedenbeck, S., Waters, J., Sobrado, L., and Birget, J. 2006. Design and Evaluation of a Shoulder-surfing Resistant Graphical Password Scheme, *Proceedings of the working conference on Advanced visual interfaces*, page 177

Alternative Graphical Authentication for Online Banking Environments

H. Alsaiari[1], M. Papadaki[1], P.S. Dowland[1] and S.M. Furnell[1,2]

[1]Centre for Security, Communications and Network Research, Plymouth University, Plymouth, United Kingdom
[2]Security Research Institute, Edith Cowan University, Perth, Western Australia
e-mail: info@cscan.org

Abstract

Many financial institutes tend to implement a secure authentication mechanism through the utilization of the One-Time-Password (OTP) technique. The use of a hardware security token to generate the required OTP has been widespread. Despite the fact that this method provides a fairly high level of security, many systems have not taken into consideration the need for a secure alternative login method whenever the hardware token is unavailable. This paper discusses the authentication issues associated with current e-banking login implementations when the hardware security token is unavailable. The study was supported by a user survey to realize the constraints confronting the user while logging in to their online banking system. The result showed that many online banking users had multiple accounts and found carrying around several security tokens is inconvenient. Moreover, high proportion of the users had confidently accepted the concept of one-time graphical password as an alternative means of authentication. Therefore, a potential solution has been introduced along with a conceptual discussion. The proposal aims to consolidate several authentication mechanisms to unite their various advantages into one robust authentication system with consideration of usability. The composite mechanism comprises of a One-Time-Password combined with graphic-based authentication techniques.

Keywords

Alternative authentication, User authentication security, Online banking authentication, Graphical password, One-Time-Password

1. Introduction

Online banking, also known as Internet banking, is a means of delivering banking services electronically to customers. Online banking services include accessing account information, the transfer of funds between different accounts and making electronic payments and settlements (Dube & Gulati, 2005; FFIEC, 2003). The popularity of online banking is growing, but it is now faced with major challenges, one of which is the high risk of data compromise. Thus, in order to minimize the threats to online banking and at the same time increase customer security, confidence and acceptance of this electronic service channel, the online accounts of customers must be securely protected via enhancing user authentication without adversely impacting upon the users' experience (Williamson & Money–America's, 2006).

As reported by Verizon (2013), 37% of breaches in 2013 affected financial organizations, which increased by about 10% compared with the previous year's report. Crime against the finance industry involved various type of common attacks such as tampering (physical), brute force (hacking), and spyware (malware). The target of such breaches was mostly payment cards, credentials, and bank account info. Basically, gaining unauthorized access in an easy and less-detectable way is possible through leveraging other's authorization access. Moreover, an earlier report (2012) showed that about four of every five breaches involving hacking was factored by authentication-based attacks (guessing, cracking, or reusing valid credentials). Authentication credentials theft presented a high value of loss as a result of espionage-related breaches. About 80% of these attacks can be forced to adapt or die whenever the idea of a suitable authentication replacement is collectively accepted.

The critical importance of securing the wide range of banking services being deployed over the Internet is a major concern for both service providers and customers. Thus, extreme caution is always paid to safeguarding the e-banking system as well as customer information. The first line of defence is protecting the authentication system from fraud and identity theft. Currently, the traditional text-based password is the foremost knowledge-based authentication and the primary form of user authentication (De Angeli et al., 2005; Fu et al., 2001) and while there are many techniques to secure passwords (Pinkas & Sander, 2002), most are insufficient in the face of attackers' tools (Chakrabarti & Singbal, 2007; AuthenticationWorld.com, 2012). The deficiencies of the textual password is well-known and affects both aspects of usability and security (Dhamija & Perrig, 2000; Suo, Zhu & Owen, 2005). Therefore, the need for alternative methods has emerged where various alternative knowledge-based techniques have been proposed, such as graphic-based passwords (recognising graphical elements – e.g. images, iconography, grids) (Gyorffy, Tappenden & Miller, 2011; Kuber & Yu, 2010) or associative/cognitive questions (Zhao, Dong & Wang, 2006; Alexander, 2008). Each approach has different aspects of strengths and weaknesses.

In crucial systems such as in financial organizations, robust security is constantly demanded. One of the solutions to meet that goal is the One-Time-Password approach. The idea of OTPs is to encode the password for a single use only; producing a unique password for each login session or transaction. In other words, the user will end up using different dynamic password for each login. Illegitimately obtaining an OTP should be useless and helpless for attackers to generate any further encoded passwords. Thus, managing to record or steal a used OTP would be totally unusable for further login attempts since an OTP loses its validity (expire and discard) after first use. This means that OTP systems are protected against replay attacks (Yampolskiy, 2007; McDonald, Atkinson & Metz, 1995).

This paper aims to point out limitations in some authentication cases within the online banking system and propose a potential solution to securely fill-in this gap using the same web browser without the need for any additional devices. The remainder of the paper proceeds with a brief review of some authentication features provided by leading financial institutes. Section 3 then discusses the authentication problems in online banking. Section 4 presents the preliminary survey results that investigate the authentication issues in online banking and gauge perceptions towards alternative authentication methods. Section 5 gives a general introduction to our proposed prototype of OTGP and conclusions and future work are addressed in Section 6.

2. The provided authentication by leading banking institutes

We conducted a review of the authentication approaches offered by banking services providers. We assessed the practices of the top four banks as ranked by relbanks.com (relbanks.com, 2012) in the UK and Saudi Arabia on the basis that respondents from these countries would form the basis for later survey data collection. The purpose was to gain tangible results from a field review that investigate and compare different authentication experiences within the electronic banking domain.

The comparison data was collected by visiting each online banking service of these banks to explore the provided authentication features. The services were compared on the basis of the following factors:

- **Authentication options**: when more than one authentication method is available for the user to choose from (e.g. OTP hardware-token or subset digits of textual password). Combining more than one form of authentication mechanism is called **Two-factor authentication**.
- **Static password**: The conventional password approach.
- **Subset digits of password**: challenges the user by requesting to submit different digit locations of the full password (e.g. 2nd, 4th, 7th digit of your password).
- **Memorable information**: a type of personal questions that can be easy and short to answer by legitimate user.
- **OTP (SMS)**: a One Time Password sent to mobile phones through carrier short messages.
- **OTP (Soft-Token)**: a type of One Time Password that is generated by software application usually installed on smart phones.
- **OTP (Hard-Token)**: a special hardware device that directly generates a One Time Password.
- **PIN-dependent token**: an additional feature to the hard-token device where a PIN is needed to generate One Time Password.
- **Card-dependent token**: Another additional feature to the hard-token device where a smart-card is required to generate One Time Password.
- **Authorization site image**: a feature that allows the selection of a picture that will indicate a correct access to the official online banking website at every login time (and not a phishing website).
- **Authorization personal image**: allows uploading a personal picture that will be shown at every login to ensure accessing the official online banking website.

- **Designation of safe computer**: a computer that typically being used to access online banking accounts can be designated to be recognised as a Trusted Computer, any access from any other PCs will be denied.

	Bank	Authentication options	Two-factor authentication	Static password	Subset digits of password	Memorable information	OTP (SMS)	OTP (Soft-Token)	OTP (Hard-Token)	Token needs PIN	Token needs Card	Other
								Authentication features				
UK Banks	HSBC	✗	✓	✗	✗	✓	✗	✗	✓	✓	✗	
	Barclays	✓	✓	✗	✓	✗	✗	✗	✓	✓	✓	
	Royal Bank of Scotland	✗	✗	✗	✓	✗	✗	✗	✗	✗	✗	
	Lloyds	✗	✗	✓	✓	✓	✗	✗	✗	✗	✗	
Saudi Arabian Banks	National Commercial Bank	✓	✓	✓	✗	✗	✓	✓	✓	✗	✗	-Authorization Site Image
	Al-Rajhi Bank	✓	✓	✓	✗	✗	✓	✓	✓	✓	✗	
	Samba Financial	✓	✓	✓	✗	✗	✓	✗	✓	✗	✗	-Authorization personal Image -Designation of safe computer
	Riyad Bank	✓	✓	✓	✗	✓	✓	✗	✓	✗	✗	

Table 1: Authentication technologies used by leading banking institutes

The comparative Table 1 reveals that various authentication techniques to secure access to the systems have been applied. The text-based password is still the most common method used, appearing in different forms, such as static password, subset digits or memorable information. Usually, text passwords are used in conjunction with other authentication methods such as One-Time-Password (OTP) which also forms a two-factor authentication. In addition, the majority of banking systems have fortified their systems by implementing two-factor authentication instead of relying on a single factor. A number of banking systems have offered a variety of One-Time-Password (OTP) implementation methods using hardware tokens, short messages (SMS) or software tokens with the support of some additional security features.

Furthermore, it can be inferred that some authentication features are applied in one country but not the other. For instance, while some UK online banking systems utilise subset digits of password and memorable information, Saudi Arabian banks mostly do not. Whereas, soft-token OTP is implemented in Saudi Arabia but not commonly used in the UK. Notably, this part of the study was focused solely on the login authentication service which means that it does not cover any further authentication like transaction-based authentication or adding a new payee.

3. Limitations of online banking authentication

Giving the option for the user to choose the appropriate authentication method is a fundamental usability feature that adds flexibility to the system. Despite the fact that this feature does exist in some current systems, it is realized that the available options depend mainly on phone banking services providing the required access or on giving the customer the choice of selecting between the use of a hardware token or SMS. That means that there is still potential for encountering some of the usability problems, such as that of being reliant on hardware devices like mobile phones or OTP tokens, which are vulnerable to theft and loss or in the case of mobile phones may suffer an interruption in the service coverage (Weir et al., 2010). In addition, other systems may offer the traditional passcode option or allow authentication via a series of Q&A challenges in case the user is unwilling/unable to use the recommended secure authentication options which potentially fall back into the weaknesses of the traditional textual password. However, none of the discussed authentication options other than the text-based password offer in-session authentication which uses the web browser to process any extra login task. That in turn emphasizes the dependence on an additional out-of-band means (e.g. token/mobile) to secure the authentication task.

More recently, many banks have adopted OTP authentication using hardware tokens that are supplied to each client as part of a multi-factor authentication scheme. Although this method is effective, it has a fundamental downside due to the reliance of the applied OTP authentication being mostly on a single OTP delivery method. Thus, many online banking systems are not equipped with a supplementary authentication method to back up the primary hardware-based OTP authentication. In other words, lost/stolen/forgotten/damaged hardware tokens will prevent clients from gaining access to the online banking system due to the absence of an operative alternative means of logging in under such critical circumstances. However, some online banking systems utilize an out-of-band method, such as mobile SMS messaging, as a parallel means of obtaining the OTP. Still, this service can encounter several problems, such as message delivery delay, weak signalling, roaming availability and charges (Weir et al., 2010; RBS, 2014). Therefore, the need for a secure, usable secondary authentication method to play an alternative role alongside the primary hardware-based OTP scheme has emerged in cases where the hardware token is unavailable.

Graphic-based authentication is among the promising alternative proposals, which occupies an important position within user authentication research area (Ray, 2012).

According to classic cognitive science experiments, humans have a vast, almost limitless memory especially for pictures (Dhamija & Perrig, 2000). Thus, authentication types that depends on graphics are likely to tackle the memorability problems that negatively affect text-based authentication since remembering complex passwords as well as multiple passwords for different systems are claimed to be a difficult task (Furnell, 2005; Furnell & Zekri, 2006), while at the same time, humans find it easier to recognise images even after a period of time (Anderson, 2001).

4. Research survey

A structured online questionnaire was designed and delivered to investigate the authentication issues associated with online banking in addition to gauging the participants' perceptions and attitudes towards alternative authentication methods for online banking. The main purpose of the survey was to find answers for some research-related questions such as whether users manage multiple online accounts, are using security tokens for that purpose, the user perception regarding carrying around several tokens, have they ever encountered login problems when using these tokens, and finally their acceptance of alternative authentication methods. The survey was comprised of a total of twenty nine questions encompassing demographic information, experiences of user authentication schemes and security-related techniques, usage of the banking system, experiences of authentication within the online banking system and lastly the users' opinions and acceptance level of the alternative authentication mechanisms.

4.1. Results interpretation and analysis

A total of 250 respondents participated in this online survey over a period of 3 weeks. All participants were volunteers, participants were recruited from students and staff in the authors' university, and colleagues/friends of the author who were invited via email and text messages. Two thirds of the respondents were males and the remaining third were females. The age group between 30 and 39 years comprised the majority of the sample and represented 43% of the total number of participants. The residential location shows that almost 90% of the respondents resided either in the UK (46%) or Saudi Arabia (44%). Regarding the educational background, the highest percentage of participants (44%) had studied at Higher education level, while 39% were Postgraduates. As for the employment status, the highest percentage of participants (67%) were employed followed by 24% being students. Regarding the level of computer experience, most participants (48%) considered themselves to be at advanced level followed closely by 47% at intermediate level with only a small percent (4%) having a basic level of computer skills.

The results revealed that 57% of the participants have used OTP as an alternative authentication method. Regarding the importance of multiple levels of authentication where various authentication approaches from the same category (usually knowledge-based) are combined, 90% of the participants were supportive of this kind of technique, agreeing that it was important.

An important question was asked aiming to measure the users' opinions on carrying around multiple security devices to fulfil the authentication requirements of multiple online accounts. Table 2 demonstrates that most respondents opposed the idea with 69% feeling that carrying multiple tokens is not convenient and 38% thinking it is unnecessary. However, 38% of the participants said it is acceptable on balance.

	Convenient		Necessary		Acceptable	
	Frequency	Percent	Frequency	Percent	Frequency	Percent
Agree	44	17.6	90	36.0	96	38.4
Neutral	34	13.6	64	25.6	71	28.4
Disagree	172	68.8	96	38.4	83	33.2

Table 2: Participants' opinion about carrying multiple tokens

The participants were also asked some banking-related questions. As per the survey results shown in Figure 1, the vast majority of respondents (93%) were online banking users. Amongst these, 65% were managing more than one online account with 56% having between 2 and 5 online accounts. Noticeably, 9% of the respondents had more than five online accounts, while approximately a quarter of the participants had only a single online account. Around two thirds of the online banking respondents stated that they access their online banking accounts on a regular basis, while nearly a quarter of the respondents accessed their accounts occasionally. The final part of this section investigated the purpose of using online banking services. The results shows that 40% of the participants were utilizing this service to conduct a variety of online payment services, such as paying bills or transferring funds, while 36% of them used the service for checking bank account information/transactions.

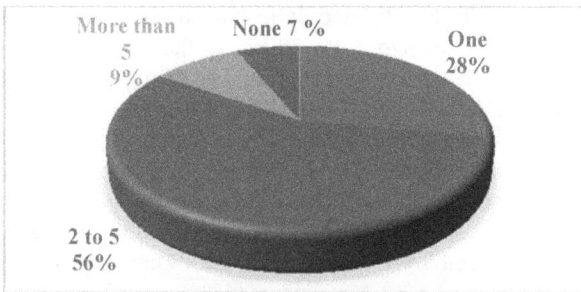

Figure 1: Number of online banking accounts

With regards to the online banking experience, more than 85% of the participants' online banking systems require multi-factor authentication. Remarkably, OTP authentication was offered by the banks of 90% of the participants, as shown in Table 3. Furthermore, since most of the participants were from the UK and Saudi Arabia, a further analysis was carried out to assess the popularity of certain types of OTP techniques in these countries. The findings indicated that the most used technique in the UK was the security token device whereas SMS text messages were the most common in Saudi Arabia. It should be noted here that the responses to some questions were open to multiple choices which explain why the responses count in Table 3 exceeded the number of participants.

Type of OTP	Count	Responses %
None - the online banking system does not facilitate a One-Time-Password	32	10.4%
SMS text message	136	44.2%
Security token device (Hardware)	114	37.0%
Soft token (Software)	26	8.4%

Table 3: The offered types of One-Time-Password

Table 4 illustrates that 76% of the responses indicated that they were satisfied with the use of One-Time-Password authentication, while in contrast a very small portion were dissatisfied with this type of technique.

OTP experience	Frequency	Percent
Satisfied	160	76.2
Neutral	38	18.1
Dissatisfied	12	5.7

Table 4: Participants experience with OTP technique

As part of multi-factor and OTP authentication, the participants were asked if they had failed to login using these methods before. The result shows that 64% had experienced failure in fulfilling the login requirements for several reasons (Figure 2), such as mistyping the code which comes first with (48%), the lack of mobile services (21%) and lost token/mobile (9%). However, 43% of these incidents occurred only rarely, while less than 3% happened frequently.

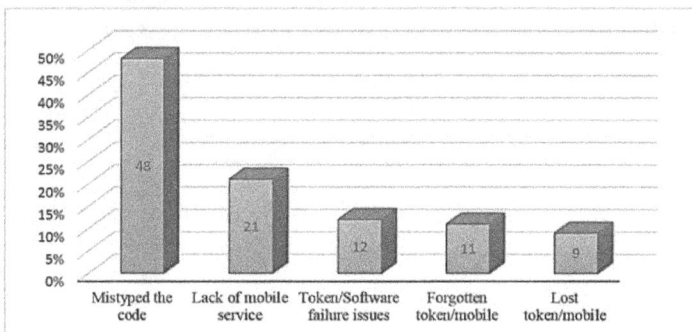

Figure 2: Reasons of experienced login failure

Table 5 shows that 73% of the participants who had login problems were still expressing themselves to be 'satisfied' overall when using one-time-password. However, only less than 5% of the participants with multiple online accounts had dissatisfaction experience using one-time-password and approximately 18% of the responses were 'neutral' as presented in Table 6.

	Frequency of login failure using multi-factor or One-Time-Password authentication			
	Rarely	Sometimes	Frequently	Percentage%
Experience of using One-Time-Password Satisfied	103	22	4	73
Neutral	31	10	2	22
Dissatisfied	7	4	0	5
Percentage %	70.2	25.5	4.3	

Table 5: Satisfaction of the participants who experienced login failure

	Multiple online banking accounts %
Experience of using One-Time-Password Satisfied	77.7
Neutral	17.6
Dissatisfied	4.7

Table 6: Satisfaction of the participants with multiple accounts

The last section presented a conceptual model (Figure 3) about the prospective solution with a concern about participants' opinions towards alternative authentication mechanisms. In terms of accepting the idea of replacing or supplementing the existing one-time-password method with a one-time graphical password technique, responses showed that almost half of the participants (49%) accepted the idea, while in contrast, less than a quarter (23%) rejected it. Another question in this regard was about the participants' confidence in the alternative graphical authentication method for online banking. 49% of the participants responded with "confident" and 26% with "un-confident".

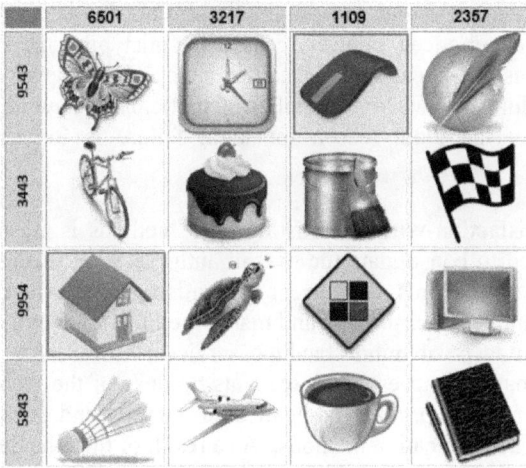

Figure 3: One-time graphical password conceptual model

4.2. Discussion of research survey

The collected data showed diversity in the participants' experiences and knowledge of authentication and online banking. It appears that plenty of the participants had a reasonable understanding of authentication enhancement in the online banking environment; nevertheless, a small percentage of participants had little knowledge of online banking authentication. The positive record of participants' computer experiences indicates the development of users' computing skills and their competency to perform more complex computer tasks.

As per the survey results, it was found that a high percentage of respondents hold and manage several online banking accounts. This demonstrates a trend towards the utilization of the online channel to simplify performing banking transactions as well as other account management tasks. Moreover, the results also emphasize the difficulty of using multiple security tokens to manage these accounts; many participants disagreed with the idea of carrying around multiple devices for login purposes, describing it as inconvenient and unnecessary. Additionally, the survey showed that a high proportion of the total sample number access their accounts on a daily or weekly basis, which obviously proves the increasing popularity of and demand for online banking services.

One of the interesting results of the survey was the high percentage of responses indicating that the online systems of the participants' banks require multi-factor authentication. Furthermore, many of those systems make use of the OTP authentication method. More than half of the participants had already been using One-Time-Password as an alternative method of authentication. That in turn reveals the importance and feasibility of both techniques for the online banking environment. Interestingly, the result shows that the majority of respondents have had satisfactory experiences using OTP techniques. In spite of this positive statistic, the survey recorded a relatively high ratio of failing to satisfy the login requirements for multi-

131

factor or OTP authentication but these failures were not frequent. By excluding half of the incidents (experienced failures) caused by mistyping the code, which is a common human mistake, it can be inferred that a lack of mobile services is the cause of many login failures. However, a number of participants have different views on this, believing that the main reason for login failure is forgetting or losing a token/mobile.

Although user satisfaction with the existing OTP methods is reasonable, that does not negate the need to consolidate the overall authentication mechanism for such a crucial system. In other words, the current system is to some extent able to fulfil the needs of a large number of customers and match the functional expectations of many customers and providers of online banking services; however, at times customers find themselves unable to access their accounts because of the inability to fulfil the login requirements of the primary authentication method and at the same time the lack of alternative authentication methods. As a result of this, the demand for further investigation and consideration of this issue has emerged. The authentication system should cover most possible login scenarios to ensure high availability and less restriction.

The aim of the final section of the survey was to determine participants' views towards alternative authentication mechanisms. Specific questions were asked about graphics utilisation for authentication purposes, which were positively answered with acceptance to such technique's implementation. In addition, the participants were asked about how acceptable it would be to replace or supplement the existing one-time-password system with one-time graphical password system. The result presented that a large number (nearly half) of participants were open to the idea of using such graphical authentication in the context of online banking system with confidence.

5. Overview of the proposed solution

The conducted review of the current state of graphical techniques along with the outcome of the survey study has pointed to the need for an enhanced authentication method to fulfil the security and usability requirements. This research aims to contribute in overcoming the major issues in the existing graphical schemes to obtain an enhanced scheme that can be utilised for filling-in the authentication shortage in the online banking systems. Therefore, a hybrid secure solution is proposed – a One-Time-Graphical-Password "OTGP" which intends to leverage a multi-level authentication to ensure a robust and secure authentication. For which purpose, a combination of multiple authentication mechanisms will be employed which are a One-Time-Password along with a Graphical password. In addition, various graphical password methods have been merged to form a new mixture of Recall and Recognition-based techniques. The final component of this integrated authentication system will involve a determination task of OTP input formats. More precisely, the method will be established by solving the lock-pattern (Draw-based), followed by identifying password images (Image-recognition) and last step will be entering the corresponding OTP code according to the pre-chosen format (Knowledge-based).

Table 7 illustrates a breakdown of the hybrid scheme characteristics. For better clarification, this study suggests the addition of some distinguishing details in a manner that involves several design aspects. Firstly, the input approach, for instance, is what the user needs to submit as the login information for the authentication session. This input approach includes the following: Draw, Click, Choice or Typing. The second aspect is the display style, which means the presentation mode that forms the password challenge, such as: Grid, Image, Icon.

		Category	Approach	Style
1	**Pattern unlock**	Recall	Draw	Grid
2	**Image recognition**	Recognition	Choice	Multi-images
3	**OTP formation**	Recall	Typing Entry	Keyboard

Table 7: Categorisation and characteristic breakdown

The main expected technical advantages of the proposed scheme are summarised as follows:

- Combination of multiple authentication mechanisms (Graphical password and One-Time-Password).
- Combination of multiple graphical password categories (Recall-based [Draw] and Recognition-based [Choice]).
- System assigned themes with user chosen images.
- Various OTP formats.

The proposed scheme involves two phases; enrolment and authentication. The steps of the process flow for these phases are shown in more detail in Table 8.

General Process Flow	Enrolment Phase	Authentication Phase
Secret Knowledge (Username)	Select a unique username	Enter correct username
Pattern Unlock Graphical Password (Recall-based, Draw-based)	A 4x4 Pattern grid will be displayed. The user needs to draw a pattern as minimum of 4 points (strokes)	Unlock pattern grid by redrawing the pre-chosen pattern
Image Recognition Graphical Password (Recognition-based, Choice-based)	The system will assign 4 random themes for the user. A panel of images from each of the assigned themes will be presented for the user to make his/her own selection	The system displays a 4x4 panel of images containing (2 random pass-images out of the 4 previously chosen pass-images + 14 other decoy images). The user needs to identify the two pass-images
One-Time-Password Formation of the final password entry	Since the edge side of each row and column of the panel will be assigned 4 random digits, user can choose from a number of different OTP format combinations such as: (1st pass-image = Top axis code + 2nd pass-image = Left axis code)	Enter the associated OTP with each image in the same OTP format chosen previously
Confirmation / Authentication	Confirming the entire password process (Pattern redrawing, choosing pass-images, OTP format selection	Access is granted when all provided information is correct

Table 8: Process flow for the enrolment and authentication phases

6. Conclusion and Future Work

An overview of various authentication features provided by some of the leading banks has been presented and discussed. It was found that the adoption of multi-factor authentication using hardware token OTPs has increased. However, the study has shown that there are some failures in fulfilling the login requirement using the OTP method, even though the user experience with such a technique has been found to be satisfactory. Furthermore, carrying around multiple security tokens to manage several online accounts has been described as inconvenient and unnecessary. In this paper, the issue of the absence of an alternative authentication method when the main hardware OTP token is not present has been discussed. To overcome this issue, a general conceptual structure of the proposed solution has been introduced involving several authentication mechanisms such as graphic-based and One-Time-Password that aim to meet the main objective of having a usable secure authentication mechanism that is available anytime and anywhere without the need for additional devices. The initial features and advantages of the OTGP scheme were briefly presented. The next phase will look at system implementation with initial user trials and lab experiments. Statistical data such as time, security level, and password memorability over time intervals will be some of the outputs of the experiment. Upon the assumption of positive results from the initial trials, the final phase of the OTGP project will then expand the study through a field experiment to obtain a wider range of participants for more accurate results.

7.   References

Alexander, C. (2008) 'Two Factor Authentication That Doesn't Use Chips'. *Card Technology Today*, 20 (5). pp 9.

Anderson, R. J. (2001) 'Access Control'. *Security Engineering: A guide to building dependable distributed systems*. 1st edn.: Wiley, pp 51-71.

AuthenticationWorld.com (2012) *Password Authentication*. Available at: http://authenticationworld.com/Password-Authentication/index.html (Accessed: 02/04/2014).

Chakrabarti, S. & Singbal, M. (2007) 'Password-Based Authentication: Preventing Dictionary Attacks'. *Computer*, 40 (6). pp 68-74.

De Angeli, A., Coventry, L., Johnson, G. & Renaud, K. (2005) 'Is a Picture Really Worth a Thousand Words? Exploring the Feasibility of Graphical Authentication Systems'. *International Journal of Human-Computer Studies*, 63 (1–2). pp 128-152.

Dhamija, R. & Perrig, A. (2000) 'Déjà vu: A User Study Using Images for Authentication', *the 9th USENIX Security Symposium*. pp. 45-58.

Dube, D. & Gulati, V. P. (2005) 'Information System Audit and Assurance'. (Appendix B). pp 594.

FFIEC (2003) 'FFIEC E-Banking Booklet'. [Online]. Federal Financial Institutions Examination Council. Available at: http://www.isaca.org/Groups/Professional-English/it-audit-tools-and-techniques/GroupDocuments/e_banking.pdf (Accessed: 02/04/2014).

Fu, K., Sit, E., Smith, K. & Feamster, N. (2001) 'Dos and Don'ts of Client Authentication on The Web', *Proceedings of the 10th conference on USENIX Security Symposium*. Washington, D.C. USENIX Association, pp. 19-19.

Furnell, S. (2005) 'Authenticating Ourselves: Will We Ever Escape the Password?'. *Network Security*, 2005 (3). pp 8-13.

Furnell, S. & Zekri, L. (2006) 'Replacing Passwords: In Search of the Secret Remedy'. *Network Security*, 2006 (1). pp 4-8.

Gyorffy, J. C., Tappenden, A. F. & Miller, J. (2011) 'Token-based Graphical Password Authentication'. *International Journal of Information Security*, pp 1-16.

Kuber, R. & Yu, W. (2010) 'Feasibility Study of Tactile-based Authentication'. *International Journal of Human-Computer Studies*, 68 (3). pp 158-181.

McDonald, D. L., Atkinson, R. J. & Metz, C. (1995) 'One Time Passwords in Everything (OPIE): Experiences with Building and Using Stronger Authentication', *the   Proceedings of the 5th USENIX Security Symposium*. Salt Lake City, Utah.

Pinkas, B. & Sander, T. (2002) 'Securing Passwords Against Dictionary Attacks', *Proceedings of the 9th ACM conference on Computer and communications security*. ACM, pp. 161-170.

Ray, P. P. (2012) 'Ray's Scheme: Graphical Password Based Hybrid Authentication System for Smart Hand Held Devices'. *Journal of Information Engineering and Applications*, 2 (2). pp 1-11.

relbanks.com (2012) *Banks Around the World*. Available at: http://www.relbanks.com (Accessed: 02/4/2014).

RBS (2014) Will I be charged for any mobile phone text alert messages I may get? - Ask a Question. The Royal Bank of Scotland ©. Available at: http://supportcentre-rbs.custhelp.com/app/answers/detail/a_id/745/kw/network%20operator (Accessed: 12/4/2014).

Suo, X., Zhu, Y. & Owen, G. S. (2005) 'Graphical Passwords: A Survey', *Computer Security Applications Conference, 21st Annual*. 5-9 Dec. 2005. pp. 10 pp.-472.

Verizon (2013) *2013 Data Breach Investigations Report*. Verizon Enterprise Security Solutions. Available at: http://www.verizonenterprise.com/resources/reports/rp_data-breach-investigations-report-2013_en_xg.pdf (Accessed: 02/04/2014).

Weir, C. S., Douglas, G., Richardson, T. & Jack, M. (2010) 'Usable Security: User Preferences for Authentication Methods in eBanking and the Effects of Experience'. *Interacting with Computers*, 22 (3). pp 153-164.

Williamson, G. D. & Money–America's, G. (2006) 'Enhanced Authentication in online Banking'. *Journal of Economic Crime Management*, 4 (2).

Yampolskiy, R. V. (2007) 'User Authentication via Behavior Based Passwords', *Systems, Applications and Technology Conference, 2007. LISAT 2007. IEEE Long Island*. 4-4 May 2007. pp. 1-8.

Zhao, Z., Dong, Z. & Wang, Y. (2006) 'Security Analysis of a Password-based Authentication Protocol Proposed to IEEE 1363'. *Theoretical Computer Science*, 352 (1–3). pp 280-287.

Improving Internet Banking Security by using Differentiated Authentication based on Risk Profiling

M.J. Butler and R. Butler

Stellenbosch University, South Africa
email: martin.butler@usb.ac.za; rbutler@sun.ac.za

Abstract

Online security remains a challenge to ensure safe transacting on the internet. User authentication, a human-centric process, is regarded as the basis of computer security and hence secure access to online banking services. The increased use of technology to enforce additional actions has the ability to improve the quality of authentication and hence online security, but often at the expense of usability. The objective of this study was to determine if there are factors that could be used to create different authentication requirements for different users. That is, could internet banking users, for example, be directed to different authentication regimes after classifying their potential safety profile based on the browser that they are using? A web-based survey was designed to determine online consumers' perceptions of their skills and competence in respect of passwords creation and management practices, and capture demographical data as well as choices in browsers used. After using a construct for password performance, derived from previous research on the same dataset, the browser used was compared with use of poor password practices. Based on the results a case could be made to have different authentication methods for consumers based on their browser selected to ensure a safer online environment.

Keywords

Online banking, User authentication, Differentiated authentication, Risk profiling

1. Introduction

The phenomenal growth of online banking has transformed the way in which consumers interact with their financial services provider. The majority of clients' interaction with their service providers occurs online via their preferred browser and is increasingly moving towards mobile platforms. User authentication remains a foundation for computer security (Conklin, Dietrich and Walz, 2004:1) and passwords, in combination with other measures, remains critical to identify and authenticate online banking users.

Computer users remain a weak link in online security since user password practices has a direct effect on the level of security of a system (Gehringer, 2002:369). Not selecting and managing passwords with care may make those passwords more susceptible to potential abuse and misuse (Furnell, 2005:10). Accordingly, even the most sophisticated security systems are compromised if users do not select and manage their passwords properly (Tam, Glassman and Vandenwauver, 2010:233). Despite problems relating to password security remaining 'conspicuously unsolved', passwords as a means to identify users, whether in isolation or combination, remains the most common method of authentication (Furnell, 2005:9 and 11).

Newer technology supported authentication systems like biometrics and One-time-Pin are becoming popular (Tam *et al.* 2010:233) and do contribute to a safer online environment. However, the use of these technologies is uniformly applied to all users. That is, the attributes of users are not used to create differentiated authentication. All users, irrespective of any additional knowledge that may be known, or inferred at the point of authentication, are treated equally when verified.

2. Online banking

As the user of online banking increases security issues relating to confidentiality, integrity, and privacy have become a progressively greater concern to both banks and customers. Banks recognise the benefits, like increased efficiency and customer convenience, of this new medium. Despite this growing ubiquity of online banking services, security and privacy concerns and fears are still foremost in the minds of users and are indeed well founded.

Almost inevitably, this exponential growth in internet banking has been paralleled with an equally swift and altogether more disturbing rise in sector fraud. With the amount of money at stake, today's so-called cyber criminals have greater resources and enhanced technological capability to conduct online fraud. As banking transactions have moved from physical bank locations with vaults protecting their clients' assets to the online world, so have the criminals (Rice, 2012:441).

User authentication, including those for online banking services, employs something a user knows, a user has, or something the user does (refer Table 1). With the increasingly diverse risks in online environments, user authentication methods are also becoming more diversified, and in online banking more often than not it is based on a combination of two or more of such factors.

3. The technological contributions

It is well documented that traditional personal identification methods, like passwords, suffer from a number of drawbacks and are unable to satisfy the security requirement of the highly inter-connected information society. As a result a number of different technologies have been developed and implemented in online authentication.

- Biometrics refers to identification of an individual based on his/her physiological or behavioural traits. This ranges from the use of physical features including voiceprints, fingerprints and iris recognition, to behavioural features including gait and handwriting recognition. Biometrics is inherently difficult to copy, share and distribute; difficult to forge; and importantly cannot be lost or forgotten because the individual has to be physically present (Kaman, Swetha, Akram and Varaprasad, 2013; Tassabehji and Kamala, 2012).

- Out-of-band authentication is a method of verifying a 'user's identity using a channel other than the one being used to facilitate the transaction' in order to improve online security (Feig, 2007:23). By using a second communication channel that should also be unique to the same user, the level of security is greatly improved and this is fast becoming a standard in online banking.
- Graphical passwords have been proposed as alternatives to text-based **password** authentication. Biddle, Chiasson and Van Orschot (2012) provided a comprehensive overview of published research in the area, covering both usability and security aspects as well as system evaluation.
- One-time-pin (OTP) is a system where text messages are sent to phones with one-time use codes to verify a login. This popular method is a subset of Out-of-band authentication. Some of the newer applications of the One-time PIN place a digital certificate on the user's phone to authenticate future transactions. The system does not rely at all on the mobile phone's phone number but rather on the actual digital certificate placed on the phone (Wolfe, 2011:10).
- Key stroke dynamics is a technology to ensure that the user, post-authentication, is indeed the user authenticated (Pisani and Lorena, 2013). The benefit of key stroke dynamics, although rather complex and processing intensive to implement, is the non-intrusive nature and continuous monitoring post-authentication.

Amid increasing pressure to protect customers online, some of the major global banks are turning towards two-factor and multi-channel authentication. However, to date all measures are uniformly applied to all users, irrespective of any information that may be known at instance of authentication, or even after authentication when the user and attributes associated with the user is known. An important departure point to address poor password performance is recognising that proper password security systems involve both human and technological aspects (Brostoff and Sasse, 2002:41). Technical measures incorporated into security systems are of little value if users do not understand the measures, risks or consequences associated with poor password practices.

4. The user challenge

Conklin *et al.* (2004:5) regards an untrained user as one of the weakest links in a security system. While certain password users may be very proficient in applying proper password practices, proper security measures and guidelines are often 'unknown, neglected, or avoided' by other computer users (Notoatmodjo and Thomborson, 2009:71). However, institutions use the same method of authentication for all users. For example, creating a complex authentication regime fitted to the 'least secure' user to ensure fail safe authentication in spite of very limited knowledge of online security, raises unnecessary entrance barriers for authentication of users that behave in a secure manner. Differentiating levels of knowledge and application among users is a concern, but also an opportunity to increase online safety were it is needed most.

In principle, there are only three authentication categories that can be used to secure the online environment as indicated in Table 1.

Authentication Types	Validating	Examples
Proof-of-Knowledge	Something the user knows – tacit knowledge or knowledge shared by the service provider	Passwords, PIN, Mother's maiden name, Telephone number
Proof-of-Possession	Something the user possess	Smartcards, Tokens, Hardware devices, Digital certificates
Proof-of-Characteristics	Something physical or behavioural attribute	Fingerprints, Wrist vein patterns, Iris/ Retina scan, Facial/Voice recognition

Table 1: Types of Authentication

Choubey and Choubey (2013) reviewed a number of security features used by different banks globally. The measures employed ranged from simple password only systems to rather complex structures involving an OTP generated through external hardware. Somewhere in between are systems involving additional information based of memorable words or other user information.

According to Choubey and Choubey institutions have a predicament in introducing more layers of security since it leads to more difficulty for end-users in accessing and utilising their financial information. In addition, the spread in security features leads to difficulty in the security testing of different banks as well as inconveniencing users when they move from one institution to another. They even argued that the "learning curve associated with different types of security features could become a bottleneck in market diversity in future" (Choubey and Choubey, 2013:202).

5. The cost, convenience and security conundrum

An important contributor to online security is selecting 'strong' passwords that are hard to guess (secure) but still memorable (convenient) (Conklin *et al.* 2004:5). However, when dealing with passwords users are confronted with a 'security-convenience trade-off' (Tam *et al.* 2010:242), which causes a conflict between the convenience of remembering and the security of passwords (Weber, Guster, Safanov and Schmidt, 2008:46). Depending on whether security or convenience is the foremost concern for users, password practices will either be secure or not.

Yan, Blackwell, Anderson and Grant (2004:25) determined that users rarely choose passwords that are both hard to guess and easy to remember. Factors that contribute to this 'password overload' are the increasing number of password-protected systems, enforced password lifetime and composition rules and human memory limitations (Chiasson and Biddle, 2007:1; Yan *et al.* 2004:25; Furnell, 2005:10). This results in users developing their own methods to remember their passwords. When the security motivation is secondary to convenience it leads to weak password practices, which include using short and weak passwords that are easy to remember, sharing passwords, writing down passwords, re-using passwords and not changing
140

passwords regularly (Campbell, Kleeman and Ma, 2007:3; Furnell, 2005:10; Notoatmodjo and Thomborson, 2009:71).

Unfortunately the usability of security technologies is often neglected by designers (Brostoff and Sasse, 2002:41). Furnell, Bryant and Phippen (2007:416) recommend improving the usability of security features as users often don't apply these features because they have problems to find, understand and use these security features. Inglesant and Sasse (2010) advise greater emphasis on human computer interface (HCI) principles to increase password security.

6. Differentiated authentication

Furnell (2007:445) remarks that one of the reasons why many computer users do not apply safe password practices is because 'they may not know any better' due to a lack of appropriate knowledge, guidance and support. To date all instances of authentication are uniformly applied to users. Irrespective of any knowledge known about the user and their potential online behaviour, the same methods (and hence security levels) of authentication is required for all users.

According to Ciampa, Mark and Enamait (2013) research indicated that 'consumers are willing to take extra steps to protect their identities, but they do not necessarily want to pay extra for these services'. The proposition of this paper is then that due to the different strengths in passwords selected, and the different measures taken to keep passwords secure, it may perhaps be a better idea to rather differentiate between 'more secure' and 'less secure' users and define a differentiated authentication regime. Such a differentiated authentication regime would take cognisance of all known information (inferred at the point of authentication) or associated with the user immediately after 'First level authentication' (refer to Figure 1).

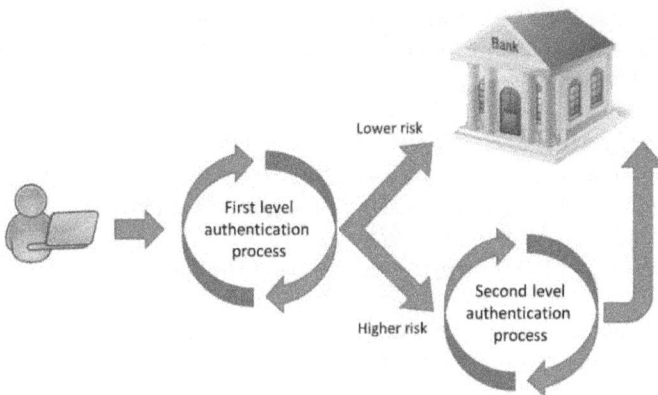

Figure 1: Proposed authentication process

More than nine out of every 10 people surveyed by Ciampa *et al.* (2013) indicated their willingness to deal with more than just the usual user name/password authentication if it meant stronger security. Consumers indicated a high degree of acceptance of 'risk-based' authentication, with 73% indicating a positive inclination towards an institutional-side assessment of the user's identity based on such things as log-on location, IP address, and transaction behaviour.

7. Research problem and objective

Proposing a differentiated authentication regime is dependent on (1) the ability to actually differentiate between users security practices and (2) being able to uniquely identify the user, or use group, to impose the additional measures. Raising additional entrance requirements after initial identification is not complex since the identification action provides user specific attributes that could be used to infer a potential risk profile. More interesting is the use of information known at, or even before, authentication. That is, if it is possible to identify user group attributes that correlate to security practices. This lead to questioning if browser preference could potentially indicate an underlying disposition towards online security, or not.

The objective of this study was to:

- Create a performance metric of online banking consumers' password practices.
- Correlate their practices with their browser of preference and analyse if there are any difference in performance, based on the browser of choice.

If there are a difference in behaviour, it provides an opportunity to raise different authentication regimes based on the risk profiling associated with the browser used.

8. Methodology

8.1. Survey

The data was gathered by the distribution of an online survey. The instrument was designed and refined via two iterations of pilot testing. The survey contained questions to determine:

- Password performance: By testing the respondents' knowledge, capability and motivation a measure of potential performance could be constructed.
- Demographic information: Gathering demographic information that could be correlated with password performance.
- Browser usage: Determining the browser used by the respondents.

The survey was distributed via email to a database of online South African users from the authors' tertiary institution and also via snowball method by the researchers.

8.2. Sample of respondents

Out of a total of 914 attempts 791 responses were received. A further 54 respondents did not use internet banking which left a sample of 737 valid responses. Demographical information was analysed to determine a potential bias within the sample and it was determined that there was an acceptable alignment between the known South African online consumer demographics and the sample demographics.

8.3. Performance construct

A function for performance used by McCloy, Campbell and Cudeck (1994) was used as primary construct to create a measure of potential performance. McCloy *et al.* (1994) defined performance (PC) is a function of the declarative knowledge (DK), relating to a task, the user's capability to perform the task (PKS) and motivation (M): PC = f (DK, PKS, M). The computer user's password performance was thus defined as a function of the following three components:

- Knowledge : the user's knowledge, education, skills and competencies relating to password practices;
- Capability: the user's aptitude to apply password-related knowledge properly when creating and managing passwords; and
- Motivation (M): the underlying desire behind the user's password behaviour.

The respondents' **knowledge** was tested in the questionnaire by means of a set of questions that tested their knowledge about strong and secure passwords as well as good practice in terms of safekeeping and not sharing passwords.

The respondents' **capability** was tested by asking them to rank different combinations of passwords from the most to the least secure. In ranking the passwords they needed to display their ability to understand the factors such as password length, complexity, different character sets, as well as common words. Although the sets of five different passwords were selected by the researchers to have different levels of security, it was also verified by different password strength meters. Users were also asked about the sharing of passwords and the last time that they changed their internet banking password to get an indication of practice, i.e. knowing about regular changes constitute knowledge, having changed the password in the last 12 months constitute capability.

In terms of **motivation** respondents were tested about prioritising security using the security-convenience trade-off. It was decided that security as a top priority is an acceptable predictor of motivation to behave securely. A second set of questions prompted users about factors that will lead to a change in password practices. In this instance the construct defined different prompts and used action, based on the event as an indicator of motivation. Finally, the desire to use additional knowledge, such as getting access to information from the survey and guidelines for online security, was used as an element of motivation.

8.4. Data analysis

Users' perceptions about their password performance was analysed based on the perceptions and practices applied and a metric calculated for each respondents' Knowledge, Capability and Motivation. It was decided to not infer the browser use from that of the respondents' choice to complete the survey, but rather to ask which browser they mostly used. Figure 2 shows the frequency distribution for the performance by preferred browser.

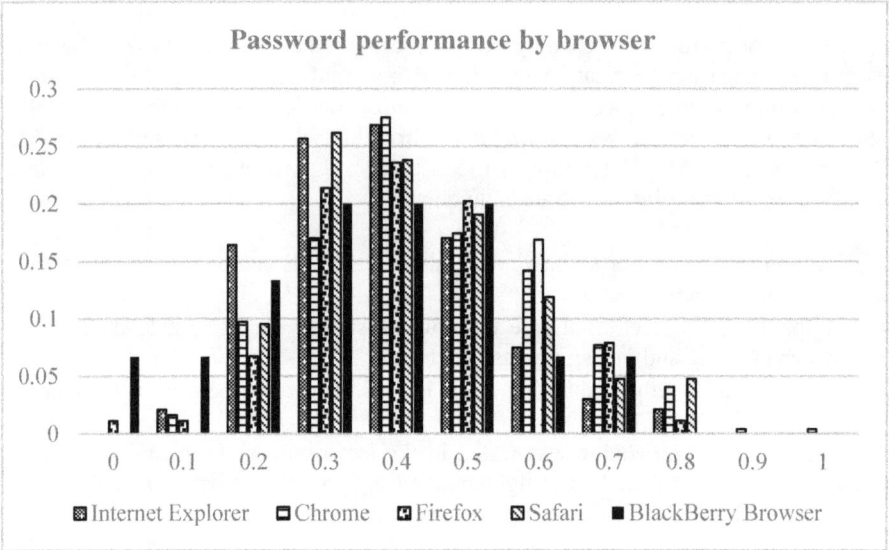

Figure 2: Password performance by survey results

From the sample of 737 valid responses the following were excluded as being too small a sample to infer any usable results, BlackBerry Browser (15), Opera (5), Other / No idea (4) which left a total sample of 708 responses. The mean level of Password Performance measured for Internet Explorer (0.336) is lower than that of either Chrome (0.394), Firefox (0.391) or Safari (0.381). But are these differences statistically significant?

9. Password performance and browser selection

A one-way Analysis of Variance (ANOVA) was used to examine differences between two or more groups created from a single independent variable, in this instance password performance, on a single dependent variable, in this instance, browser used. The test is used to decide whether the differences in the samples average scores are large enough to conclude that the groups' average scores are unequal.

The ANOVA is proven to be reliable under the following assumptions:

- the values in each of the groups (as a whole) follow the normal curve,
- with possibly different population averages
- equal population standard deviations.

In terms of normality, Figure 2 indicates sufficient normality in the data for each browser to conduct the test. In terms of variance, the rule of thumb is that the largest sample (Internet Explorer) is not larger than twice the smallest sample (Opera), which is indeed the case as indicated in Table 2.

The zero hypothesis was defined as no significant variance between sample means, i.e. H_0: $\mu_1 = \mu_2 = \mu_3 = \mu_4$ and the alternate hypothesis as a significant difference between the means, i.e. H_1: $\mu_1 \neq \mu_2 \neq \mu_3 \neq \mu_4$. If the zero hypothesis is true, then the 'between group variance' will be equal to the 'within group variance.' Table 2 shows the results of the statistical test for variance in sample means for a confidence interval of 95%.

Anova: Single Factor (0.05)

SUMMARY

Groups	Count	Sum	Average	Variance
Internet Explorer	335	112.6109	0.336152	0.020634
Chrome	247	97.33837	0.394082	0.027622
Firefox	88	34.41523	0.391082	0.021622
Safari	42	15.98869	0.380683	0.023587

ANOVA

Source of Variation	SS	df	MS	F	P-value	F crit
Between Groups	0.55758	3	0.18586	7.958215	3.1803E-05	**2.61748**
Within Groups	16.53497	708	0.023354			
Total	17.09255	711				

Table 2: One-way ANOVA test for difference between sample means

Because F (7.96) > F crit (2.62) the null hypothesis was rejected showing a significant variance between sample means and thus inferring a differentiated level of password performance based on users' browser most often used. By merely inferring which browser an online banking consumer is using, it is thus conceivable to perform risk-based authentication as suggested by Ciampa *et al.* (2013).

10. A differentiated model of user interaction

While some computer users may apply poor password practices due to ignorance, studies by Furnell *et al.* (2007), Riley (2006) and Tam *et al.* (2010) found that although users do possess the knowledge to distinguish between secure and insure practices, their practical application thereof often lacks. There exists an opportunity for financial services institutions to create differentiated authentication based on the risk profile of the client. Although the test performed here was for a single factor known at the point of authentication, it is conceivable to extend this beyond the initial authentication (see Figure 1) and also differentiate after identification by using factors that could be inferred from demographical information known by the financial services institution.

A common remedy to improve password performance is security education, training and awareness programs (Riley, 2006; Furnell *et al.* 2007:417). To date this education could be voluntary for all users, or ideally, targeted at the necessary users. It is further conceivable, in fact highly desirable, that this 'targeted training' could also be directed at users that are in 'critical need' for education. Rather than a blanket one size fits all training, it is possible to direct a user to a 'how to create a strong password' session only when the password is deemed to be 'weak'.

A final recommendation considers the uniform warnings often present on Internet banking sites. Even after authentication, users are uniformly warned about the latest online scam as part of their education. It is possible to, for example, infer how the user accessed the URL and warn about clicking on links rather than typing in the URL. By tailoring the communications with the user through the use of risk profiling not only are the message more appropriate, but conceivably the attention of the consumer that notices a tailored message.

11. Limitations of the research and recommendations

The following two limitations of the recommendations and hence research has been noted:

- Differentiated authentication and subsequent communication could be construed as discrimination. The concept of risk profiling is not new, but is mostly not as "in your face" as what could be experienced by users if applied during and immediately after online authentication.
- In spite of the observed difference in security practices it has not been proven in this research to be material in nature. Further research is required to establish the extent and impact of the difference.
- A negative effect on online privacy for online users.

12. Conclusion

Continued technological innovation and competition among existing banks and new market entrants has led to a growing array of banking products and services. These include traditional activities such as accessing financial information, obtaining loans and opening deposit accounts, as well as relatively new products and services such as electronic account payment services, personalised financial 'portals', account aggregation and business-to-business market exchanges. The dependence on technology for the provision of these services ensuring the necessary security present additional risks for banks and new challenges for banking regulators.

The online world is the embodiment of paradoxes where great effort goes into firewalls, security audits and virus checkers, and yet at the same time, the access given to a web browser often makes these defences futile. Multiple authors (Gaur, Patel and Saini, 2013; Wahlberg, Paakkola, Wieser, Laakso and Roning, 2013) have investigated the inherent security issues within browsers that could be exploited technically and have indicated the difference in vulnerability when using a particular browser. This research, however, uses the browser selection choice as a user attribute and does not seek to identify browser issues, but rather attempt to understand the user behaviour by using the browser selected as an user attribute. The security risks of Internet banking have always been a concern to the service providers and users. In studying factors that lead to adoption of online banking, Yap, Wong, Loh and Bak (2010) determined that 'web site features that give customers confidence are significant situation normality cues'. It is reasonable to infer that differentiated authentication could be construed as such a factor.

Passwords will remain the most common authentication method used by computer systems and the human factor remains an important consideration to ensure security. This research suggests that using 'risk-profiling' to create a system of differentiated authentication of users, using a relative unassuming attribute such as the browser used could improve online security.

13. References

Biddle, R., Chiasson, S. and Van Orschot, P.C. (2012), "Graphical Passwords: Learning from the First Twelve Years", *ACM Computing Surveys,* Vol. 44, No. 4, pp1-19.

Brostoff, S. and Sasse, M.A. (2002), "Safe and Sound: a Safety-critical approach to security", Proceedings of the New Security Paradigm Workshop 2001, http://hornbeam.cs.ucl.ac.uk/hcs/people/documents/Angela%20Publications/unsorted/p41-brostoff.pdf, (Accessed 10 April 2014).

Campbell, J., Kleeman, D. and Ma, W. (2007), "The good and not so good of enforcing passwords composition rules", *Information Systems Security*, Vol. 16, No. 1, pp2-8.

Chiasson, S. and Biddle, R. (2007), "Issues in User Authentication", CHI Workshop: Security User Studies: methodology and best practices, April.

Choubey, J. and Choubey, B. (2013). "Secure user authentication in Internet Banking: A Qualitative Survey", *International Journal of Innovation, Management and Technology*, Vol. 4 No. 2, pp198-203.

Ciampa, M., Mark, R. and Enamait, J. (2013), "A Comparison of User Preferences for Browser Password Managers", *Journal of Applied Security Research,* Vol. 8, No. 4, pp455-466.

Conklin, A., Dietrich, G. and Walz, D. (2004), "Password-based Authentication: A System Perspective", Proceedings of the 37th Annual Hawaii International Conference on System Sciences, pp1-10.

Feig, N. (2007), "Authentication goes mobile: banks look to out-of-band authentication as customers seek enhanced online banking security", *Bank Systems + Technology,* Vol. 23, p23.

Furnell, S.M. (2005), "Authenticating ourselves: will we ever escape the password?", *Network Security*, pp8-13, March.

Furnell, S.M. (2007), "An assessment of website password practices", *Computers and Security*, Vol. 26, pp445-451.

Furnell, S.M., Bryant, P. and Phippen, A.D. (2007), "Assessing the security perceptions of personal Internet users", *Computers and Security*, Vol. 26, pp410-417.

Gaur, M.S., Patel, D. and Saini, A. (2013), "Insecurities within browser: issues and challenges", In *Proceedings of the 6th International Conference on Security of Information and Networks* (SIN '13), ACM, pp 458-458.

Gehringer, E.F. (2002), "Choosing passwords: Security and human factors", *Technology and Society*, pp369-373.

Inglesant, P. and Sasse, M.A. (2010), "The true cost of unusable password policies: password use in the wild", Proceedings of CHI 2010 (ACM Conference on Human Factors in Computing Systems), 10-15 April.

Kaman, S., Swetha, K., Akram, S. and Varaprasad, G. (2013), "Remote User Authentication Using a Voice Authentication System", *Information Security Journal: A Global Perspective*, Vol. 22, No. 3, pp117-125.

McCloy, R.A., Campbell, J.P. and Cudeck, R. (1994), "A Confirmatory Test of a Model of Performance Determinants", *Journal of Applied Psychology*, Vol. 79, No. 4, pp493-505.

Notoatmodjo, G. and Thomborson, C. (2009), "Passwords and Perceptions", Proceedings of the Australasian Information Security Conference (AISC2009), Wellington, New Zealand, *Conferences in Research and Practice in Information Technology*, Vol. 98, pp71-78.

Pisani, P. H. and Lorena, A.C. (2013), "A systematic review on keystroke dynamics", *Journal of the Brazilian Computer Society*, Vol. 19, No. 4, pp573-587, November.

Rice, P. (2012), "Civil Liability Theories for Insufficient Security Authentication in Online Banking", *Depaul Business & Commercial Law Journal,* Vol. 10, No. 3, p439.

Riley, S. (2006), "Password Security: What Users Know and What They Actually Do", *Usability   News,*   Vol.   8,   No.   1,   February, http://psychology.wichita.edu/surl/usabilitynews/81/Passwords.asp, (Accessed 19 March 2013).

Tam, L., Glassman, M. and Vandenwauver, M. (2010), "The psychology of password management: a tradeoff between security and convenience", *Behaviour and Information Technology*, Vol. 29, No. 3, pp233-244, May-June.

Tassabehji, R. and Kamala, M.A. (2012), "Evaluating biometrics for online banking: The case for usability", *International Journal of Information Management*, Vol. 32, No. 5, pp489-494, October.

Wahlberg, T., Paakkola, P., Wieser, C., Laakso, M. and Roning, J., (2013), "Kepler - Raising Browser Security Awareness", *Software Testing, Verification and Validation Workshops (ICSTW), 2013 IEEE Sixth International Conference on* , pp.435-440, 18-22 March.

Weber, J.E., Guster, D., Safanov, P. and Schmidt, M.B. (2008), "Weak password security: An empirical study", *Information Security Journal: A Global Perspective*, Vol. 17, No. 1, pp45-54, January.

Wolfe, D. (2011), "Bank Sharpens Authentication", *American Banker*, Vol. 10, 22 September.

Yan, J., Blackwell, A., Anderson, R. and Grant, A. (2004), "Password memorability and Security: Empirical results", *Security and Privacy*, IEEE, Vol. 2, No. 5, pp25-31, September-October.

Yap, K. B., Wong, D.H., Loh, C. and Bak, R. (2010), "Offline and online banking – where to draw the line when building trust in e-banking?", *International Journal of Bank Marketing*, Vol. 28, No. 1, pp27 – 46.

An Assessment of the Human Factors Affecting the Password Performance of South African Online Consumers

R. Butler and M.J. Butler

Stellenbosch University, South Africa
e-mail: rbutler@sun.ac.za; martin.butler@usb.ac.za

Abstract

User identification and authentication is regarded as the basis of computer security. In spite of many new technologies to assist with authentication, passwords remain central to access control systems in most computer systems. The password practices that online consumers apply have a direct effect on the level of security and are often the target of an array of attacks. Research suggests that passwords breaches are frequently the result of poor user security behaviour. Internationally, poor password behaviour among users is common. The objective of this study was to investigate the password performance of South African online consumers and to understand the factors contributing to poor password performance. A web-based survey was designed to determine online consumers' perceptions of their password-related knowledge, measure their ability to apply safe practices and asses their motivational levels to employ secure practices. Poor password practices among South African online consumers were evident from this study. Using a construct for password performance, this analysis indicated a deficiency in the knowledge, capability and motivation of users. Ignorance, Incompetence and Indifference were apparent as causes for online consumers' poor password behaviour. It is suggested that measures aimed at improving password performance be tailored based on the underlying causes for poor password performance as indicated by this study.

Keywords

Passwords, Password Performance, Security, Human Behaviour

1. Introduction

Almost every person interacts with a computer or computer system on a daily basis. For decades, user identification and authentication has been regarded as the foundation of computer security (Zviran and Haga, 1999:162; Conklin, Dietrich and Walz, 2004:1). According to Adams and Sasse (1999:41) confidentiality is an important aspect of computer security which relies on systems (such as passwords) to identify and authenticate computer users.

Stallings (1995:213) describes the use of a password system as 'the front line of defence against intruders'. The main purpose of a password system is to prevent unauthorized persons from violating a computer system's integrity and validity by gaining unauthorised access. As the use of technology increases, having to identify oneself uniquely by way of a password before being allowed to perform certain actions has become acceptable, understandable and even expected in order to ensure a secure environment (Weber, Guster, Safonov and Schmidt, 2008:45; Chiasson and Biddle, 2007:1).

Although other user authentication systems such as biometrics (using physical characteristics), Single-Sign-on and One-time-Pin (using device ownership), are evolving, the use of passwords remain a cost effective and efficient method to control access and authenticate computer users (Conklin *et al.* 2004:1; Campbell, Kleeman and Ma, 2007:2; Gehringer, 2002:369; Tam, Glassman and Vandenwauver, 2010:233). In fact, the advent of new technologies like cloud based computing effectively removes the first barrier to access, physical presence, as more computing applications move to the Internet, increasing the importance of secure authentication.

2. Attacks to discover passwords

Computer systems are vulnerable to a wide array of security violations (Florencio and Herley, 2007:657). Zviran and Haga (1999:164) remarks that almost every penetration of a computer system at some stage relies on the attacker's ability to compromise a password. Attacks on passwords can occur at the following levels (Campbell *et al.* 2007:3; Furnell, 2005a:10; Notoatmodjo and Thomborson, 2009:71; Butler, 2007:520; Florencio and Herley, 2007:657):

- At the system-end, where attackers launch technical or brute force attacks to crack or guess the passwords of authorized users.
- Attacks on the communication channel with which passwords are transmitted, by increasingly sophisticated technologies deployed on different layers of the network infrastructure.
- Attacks aimed directly at the user to discover his or her password. Phishing and Social Engineering are increasingly popular methods of deceiving computer users into disclosing their passwords.

Yet, despite these problems relating to password security remaining 'conspicuously unsolved', passwords as a means to identify users and their access rights, whether in isolation or combination, remains the most common method of authentication (Furnell, 2005a:9 and 11; Furnell, Dowland, Illingworth and Reynolds, 2000:529). Passwords that are hacked, cracked or disclosed can be used to gain unauthorised access to systems, and may result in financial losses and fraud.

While technology can provide a level of protection against some of these attacks, the human remains a potential weak link. According to Tam *et al.* (2010:233) even the most sophisticated security systems becomes useless if computer users do not choose and manage their passwords properly. Not selecting and managing passwords with care may make that password more susceptible to potential abuse and misuse (Furnell, 2005a:10).

Since attacks can be aimed at cracking 'weak' passwords as well as gaining access to all ('strong' and 'weak') passwords, it is imperative that proper password practices encompass both (1) the creation and (2) the management of passwords, to control access to information that could be compromised, altered or even destroyed. Although the practices concerned when creating and managing of passwords are interdependent, they are for the purposes of this study viewed as distinct, yet sharing certain actions.

3. Physiological determinants of performance

User behaviour concerning passwords has a direct effect on the level of security of a computer system (Gehringer 2002:369). While certain password users may be proficient in their password practices, proper security measures and guidelines are often 'unknown, neglected, or avoided' by other computer users (Notoatmodjo and Thomborson, 2009:71). Researchers (Pfleeger and Caputo, 2012; Anderson and Agarwal, 2010) suggest a greater understanding of the behaviour of users to prevent them from being the 'weakest link' concerning password security.

Users differ in their password performance as their behaviour is influenced by a number of aspects (McCloy, Campbell and Cudeck, 1994:493). According to Heider (1958), as cited by Anderson and Butzin (1974:598), an individual's performance in a particular task is a function of the individual's ability and motivation relating to that task:

$$\text{Performance} = \text{Ability} \times \text{Motivation}$$

Ability refers to the knowledge, skills and competencies that enable a human to perform a particular task. It is associated with what people know and think, what they can do and how they behave because of how they feel. Aspects that can influence a user's ability include their personality, prior education, previous experience, etc. (McCloy *et al.* 1994:494). Motivation refers to the underlying drive behind a user's particular behaviour in performing that task. The user's desire to extend effort, the intensity of the effort, as well as the user's commitment in extending effort, all impact motivation (McCloy *et al.* 1994:494).

Heider's function for performance was refined by McCloy *et al.* (1994) who found that performance (PC) is a function of the knowledge of facts, rules, principles and procedures (declarative knowledge - DK) relating to a task, the user's capability when his/her knowledge has been successfully combined with knowing how and being able to perform that task (procedural knowledge and skills – PKS) and motivation (M).

$$PC = f(DK, PKS, M)$$

4. Password performance model

Based on the function for an individual's performance in a task, the determinants of a user's password performance can be defined as the following (refer to Figure 1):

- **Knowledge**: the user's knowledge and education relating to password practices;

152

- **Capability**: the user's competence to successfully combine password-related knowledge with knowing how and being able to apply proper password practices.
- **Motivation**: the underlying desire behind the user's password behaviour.

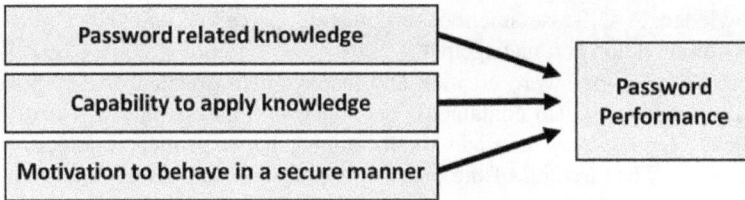

Figure 1: Password performance model

This construct for the determinants of password performance represents an opportunity to deconstruct poor password performance in a way different than most research to date. If the reasons why users do not apply proper password practices are known, then appropriate methods aimed at addressing the underlying causes for poor password behaviour can be designed and implemented to improve password security.

5. Research problem and objective

Accepting that poor password performance is common among computer users, it is not known whether all three determinants of password performance (as indicated in Figure 1) are problematic within the South African context. It is also unknown if measures aimed at improving password security are sufficient to address the particular underlying cause(s) of poor password performance that may be present among users. In order to improve password security it is necessary that any problematic areas first be identified. Any such areas can then form the essence of further research, as well as mitigation measures, to improve password security, at the very least, within the South African context.

The objective of this study was to:

1. Determine the password practices applied by South African online consumers.
2. Analyse poor password practices according to the determinants of password performance – i.e. Knowledge, Capability and Motivation.
3. Comment on known mitigation practices' ability to address the underlying causes for poor password performance and guide future research.

6. Methodology

The research instrument was a survey that contained 43 questions, both structured and open-ended. It was designed and refined via two iterations of pilot testing. In order to put users who might fear that they may be required to share potentially sensitive information at ease, care was taken to ensure respondents that their passwords would not be asked, and that the purpose of the study was to merely gather information on the practices that users apply.

The survey contained questions to determine the following three aspects:

- Knowledge: A self-assessment of respondents' perceived knowledge relating to password creation and management.
- Capability: The password creation and management practices that respondents apply. The survey also contained a section where users were provided with a number of passwords and had to distinguish between more and less secure passwords. The strength of the passwords provided was tested against various password strength meters.
- Motivation: Based on the responses it was determined whether convenience or security was the more predominant concern to users when they create and manage passwords.

The survey was distributed via email to a database of online South African users from the authors' tertiary institution as well as via snowball method by the researchers. Users' perceptions about their password practices' knowledge and application as well as motivation were analysed. Based on the perceptions and practices applied a score was calculated for each respondents' Knowledge, Capability and Motivation. Although a 100% (absolute) score in each area would represent perfect password performance a cut-off point of 70% was deemed sufficient, and used for analysis.

7. Data analyses

The responses was analysed to determine the levels of Knowledge, Capability and Motivation, independently for each respondent. Figure 2 provides a frequency distribution of the analyses.

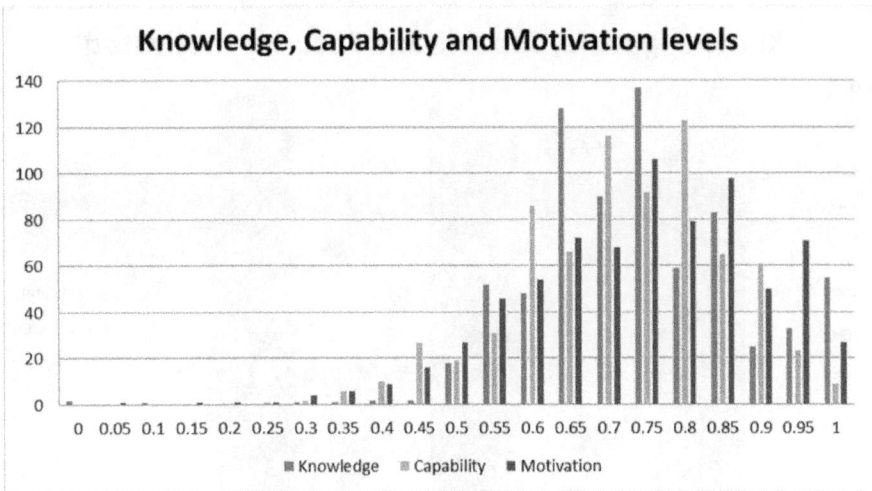

Figure 2: Knowledge, Capability and Motivation levels of respondents

When analysing the Knowledge, Capability and Motivation of the 737 respondents, 55 respondents (7,5%) perceived that they possess absolute knowledge of password practices. However, a mere 9 respondents (1,2%) demonstrated flawless capability to apply proper password practices and only 27 (3,7%) displayed a perfect 'security first' aptitude when selecting and managing passwords.

The poor password performance indicated in this study is no different from previous studies. However, it is suggested that there are three factors that contribute to these practices. The factors, based on the determinants of performance (in Figure 1) and the data analysis (Figure 2) are:

- Lack of password-related knowledge, i.e. **Ignorance**;
- Lack of capability to apply proper password practices, i.e. **Incompetence**; and
- Lack of motivation to apply secure practices, i.e. **Indifference**.

A comparison between the percentages of respondents that were knowledgeable, capable and security-motivated, as opposed to those that were not, is depicted in Figure 3. The analysis indicates the presence of all three factors contributing to poor password behaviour amongst the respondents. Although the motivation levels are slightly better than those for knowledge and capability, all three factors remain problematic and are thus drivers of poor password performance among South African online consumers.

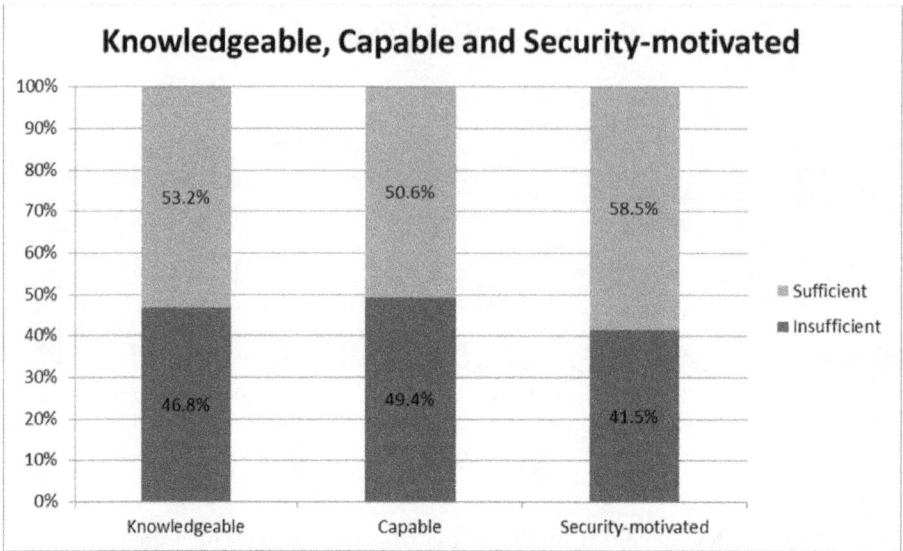

Figure 3: Respondent performance on determinant of behaviour

Although many technological mitigation measures, such as enforcing password complexity and imposing regular password changes, have been proposed to address poor password practices, the authors are interested to see if existing mitigation actions focus on the human aspects that were shown by this study to be the underlying causes for poor password performance. As deficiencies in all three determinants of password performance are evident it is essential that all three areas be addressed to improve password security.

8. Findings and discussion

8.1. Knowledge vs Ignorance

Furnell (2007:445) remarks that one of the reasons why many computer users do not apply safe password practices is because 'they may not know any better' due to a lack of appropriate knowledge, guidance and support. This was confirmed by Adams and Sasse (1999:42), who found inadequate knowledge of what constitutes secure passwords among users and as a result users tend to 'make up their own rules'. Various researchers (Riley, 2006; Conklin *et al*. 2004:5; Adams and Sasse, 1999:43 and 46; Butler, 2007:250) have found that users lack knowledge of proper password practices, security risks, users' vulnerability and possible consequences. Due to their ignorance these users apply poor password practices and/or engage in more risky behaviour.

The survey results regarding respondents' Knowledge indicate that 47% of the respondents were 'ignorant' as they perceived their knowledge of password practices as insufficient. Only 35% of the respondents indicated that they 'knew exactly' what a strong password is. Insufficient knowledge was also indicated in an open-ended question which asked respondents about any matters not specifically addressed in this survey that would potentially make them change their passwords. 128 respondents (17%) indicated that completing this survey already had them thinking about changing their password, made them realise that they are applying unsafe password practices, or that they need more information and knowledge on security and safe password practices.

8.2. Capability vs Incompetence

While some computer users may apply poor password practices due to ignorance, studies by Furnell, Bryant and Phippen (2007), Riley (2006), Tam *et al.* (2010) and Wessels and Steenkamp (2007:11) found that although users do possess the knowledge to distinguish between secure and insecure practices, their practical application thereof often lacks, indicating an incompetence among these users.

Nine questions in the survey required respondents to assess the strength of various passwords. Only 85 respondents (11%) were able to rank the strength of all of the passwords correctly. When compared with the 35% of respondents who indicated that they 'knew exactly' what a strong password was, it is clear that users may not be capable to apply their knowledge on password practices. In analysing practices it transpired that 49% of the respondents' practiced poor password behaviour, as opposed to 28% and 29% of the respondents who respectively felt that they possessed the necessary knowledge to apply proper password creation and management practices. Weak practices indicated include insecure practices in the composition of passwords, not selecting unique passwords for all accounts and purposes, re-using past passwords or variations thereof, using passwords simultaneously for more than one site, sharing passwords and not regularly changing passwords.

Possible reasons for respondents' incapability to apply proper password practices may be that users overestimate their perceived knowledge regarding password practices due to a phenomenon known as optimistic bias (Weinstein, 1980:806). Optimistic bias may lead password users to overestimate their ability to create 'strong' passwords that are properly managed and protected, and/or underestimate the potential risk associated with compromised passwords.

8.3. Motivation vs Indifference

The first step towards a proper password system is selecting 'strong' passwords (Stallings, 1995:218) that are hard to guess (secure) but still memorable (convenient) (Conklin *et al.* 2004:5). However, Yan, Blackwell, Anderson and Grant (2004:25) found that users rarely choose passwords that are both hard to guess and easy to remember as they are confronted with a 'security-convenience trade-off' (Tam *et al.* 2010:242). In addition users often perceive security measures as 'obstacles' and secondary to the primary task that they are trying to achieve, resulting in users who 'ignore or even subvert the security' (Pfleeger and Caputo, 2012:602). Studies have indicated that this conflict between convenience and the security of passwords may be present despite users' knowledge of proper password practices (Brown, Bracken, Zoccoli and Douglas, 2004:650; Carstens, McCauley-Bell, Malone and DeMara, 2004:68; Weber *et al.* 2008:46).

Other factors that intensify the strain on users' memories are the increasing number of password-protected systems, enforced password lifetime and composition rules and human memory limitations (Conklin *et al.* 2004:3; Carstens *et al.* 2004:68; Furnell, 2005a:10). Notoatmodjo and Thomborson (2009:71) refer to computer users suffering from 'password overload' and suggest that password overload is a major contributor to unsafe password practices. To deal with this memory issue users began developing their own methods to remember their passwords. When the security motivation is secondary to convenience it leads to weak password practices, which include using short and weak passwords that are easy to remember, sharing passwords, writing down passwords, re-using passwords and not changing passwords regularly (Campbell *et al.* 2007:3; Furnell, 2005a:10; Zviran and Haga, 1999:164-165; Yan *et al.* 2004:25).

The study revealed that 42% of the respondents' Motivation when choosing and managing passwords was convenience rather than security. When creating passwords more users ranked the 'ease of remembering' and passwords that are 'short and easy to enter' more important than the 'strength' of passwords and the 'perceived risk associated with the site' on which the password will be used. When posed with several possible future situations and requiring respondents to indicate which of these will, may or will not lead to a possible change of their passwords, it was also clear that security was not the foremost concern. Indifference, that is a lack of motivation to apply secure practices, is thus an important aspect to address in order to improve users' poor password practices.

9. Addressing poor password performance

An important departure point to address poor password performance is to recognise that proper password security involve both human and technological aspects (Brostoff and Sasse, 2002:41). Yet, technologies incorporated into security systems, although an important part of mitigation, are of little value if users aren't educated or don't understand the measures, risks or consequences associated with poor password practices. To improve password performance one of the most common suggestions made by researchers is the education of computer users through improved security education, training and awareness programs (Riley, 2006; Conklin *et al.* 2004:5; Adams and Sasse, 1999:43 and 46; Butler, 2007:250; Furnell *et al.* 2007:417).

The results of this study indicated a willingness among respondents to improve their password practices if they had more knowledge on password-related matters. In fact, 65,9% of the respondents indicated that they will definitely, and 29,3% may, change their passwords if they realized that their current password was not very secure. In addition an overwhelming 72% of the respondents indicated that they would like to receive a copy of the guidelines for safer online password practices that are to be compiled and distributed based on this research in an effort to improve their password-related knowledge.

This willingness of users to acquire knowledge suggests an opportunity for those who define the learning outcomes to design a process that addresses all the underlying causes of poor password performance. As literature indicates that training programs do not necessarily address all the issues that should be dealt with (Anderson and Agarwal, 2010:614 and 616-617), education and training programs can thus be improved to take cognisance of the determinants of password performance. Besides sharing knowledge on secure password practices, password vulnerability, threats and consequences of violations, these programs should focus on users' ability to apply these practices as well as address the motivational issues.

According to Pfleeger and Caputo (2012: 597) a key element to improve security is 'acknowledging the importance of human behaviour when designing, building and using cyber security technology'. When the usability by users is neglected by designers of technology it leads to increased pressure on the users to enforce security (Brostoff and Sasse, 2002:41). Researchers (Furnell, 2005b:274; Furnell, Jusoh and Katsabas, 2006:27; Furnell *et al.* 2007:416) recommend improving the usability of security features as users often don't apply these features because they have problems to find, understand and use these security features. Inglesant and Sasse (2010) advise greater emphasis on human computer interface (HCI) principles to increase the usefulness and effectiveness of password security.

10. Conclusion

Passwords, often in combination with others methods, will remain the most common authentication method used by computer systems for the foreseeable future. The human factor associated with password systems is an important consideration to ensure security. This research suggests that the password performance of users is dependent on the user's Knowledge, Capability and Motivation concerning passwords. It is suggested that initiatives to improve password security should address all aspects of poor password performance. Poor password practices among South African online consumers can be improved through greater attention to the human computer interface and relevant education, training and awareness programs.

11. References

Adams, A. and Sasse, M.A. (1999), "Users are not the Enemy", *Communications of the ACM*, Vol. 42, No. 12, pp40-46, December.

Anderson, C.L. and Agarwal, R. (2010), "Practising Safe Computing: A Multimethod Empirical Examination of Home Computer User Security Behavioral Intentions", *MIS Quarterly*, Vol. 34, No. 3, pp613-643, September.

Anderson, N.H. and Butzin, C.A. (1974), "Performance = Motivation X Ability: An integrated-theoretical analysis", *Journal of Personality and Social Psychology*, Vol. 30, No. 5, pp598-604.

Brostoff, S. and Sasse, M.A. (2002), "Safe and Sound: a Safety-critical approach to security", Proceedings of the New Security Paradigm Workshop 2001, http://hornbeam.cs.ucl.ac.uk/hcs/people/documents/Angela%20Publications/unsorted/p41-brostoff.pdf, (Accessed 10 April 2014).

Brown, A.S., Bracken, E., Zoccoli, S. and Douglas, K. (2004), "Generating and Remembering Passwords", *Applied Cognitive Psychology*, Vol. 18, pp641-651, June.

Butler, R. (2007), "A framework of anti-phishing measures aimed at protecting the online consumer's identity", *The Electronic Library*, Vol. 25, No. 5, pp517-533.

Campbell, J., Kleeman, D. and Ma, W. (2007), "The good and not so good of enforcing passwords composition rules", *Information Systems Security*, Vol. 16, No. 1, pp2-8.

Carstens, D.S., McCauley-Bell, P.R., Malone, L.C. and DeMara, R.F. (2004), "Evaluation of the human impact of password authentication practices on information security", *Informing Science Journal*, Vol. 7, pp67-85.

Chiasson, S. and Biddle, R. (2007), "Issues in User Authentication", CHI Workshop: Security User Studies: methodology and best practices, April.

Conklin, A., Dietrich, G. and Walz, D. (2004), "Password-based Authentication: A System Perspective", Proceedings of the 37th Annual Hawaii International Conference on System Sciences, pp1-10.

Florencio, D. and Herley, C. (2007), "A large-scale study of Web Password Habits", Proceedings of the 16th International Conference on World Wide Web, pp657-666, May.

Furnell, S.M. (2005a), "Authenticating ourselves: will we ever escape the password?", *Network Security*, pp8-13, March.

Furnell, S.M. (2005b), "Why users cannot use security", *Computers and Security*, Vol. 24, pp274-279.

Furnell, S.M. (2007), "An assessment of website password practices", *Computers and Security*, Vol. 26, pp445-451.

Furnell, S.M., Bryant, P. and Phippen, A.D. (2007), "Assessing the security perceptions of personal Internet users", *Computers and Security*, Vol. 26, pp410-417.

Furnell, S.M., Dowland, P.S., Illingworth, H.M. and Reynolds, P.L. (2000), "Authentication and Supervision: A survey of User Attitudes", *Computers and Security*, Vol. 19, pp529-539.

Furnell, S.M., Jusoh, A. and Katsabas, D. (2006), "The challenges of understanding and using security: A survey of end-users", *Computers and Security*, Vol. 25, pp27-35.

Gehringer, E.F. (2002), "Choosing passwords: Security and human factors", *Technology and Society*, pp369-373.

Inglesant, P. and Sasse, M.A. (2010), "The true cost of unusable password policies: password use in the wild", Proceedings of CHI 2010 (ACM Conference on Human Factors in Computing Systems), 10-15 April.

McCloy, R.A., Campbell, J.P. and Cudeck, R. (1994), "A Confirmatory Test of a Model of Performance Determinants", *Journal of Applied Psychology*, Vol. 79, No. 4, pp493-505.

Notoatmodjo, G. and Thomborson, C. (2009), "Passwords and Perceptions", Proceedings of the Australasian Information Security Conference (AISC2009), Wellington, New Zealand, *Conferences in Research and Practice in Information Technology*, Vol. 98, pp71-78.

Pfleeger, S.L. and Caputo, D.D. (2012), "Leveraging Behavioral Science to Mitigate Cyber Security Risk", *Computers & Security*, Vol. 31, No. 4, pp597-611.

Riley, S. (2006), "Password Security: What Users Know and What They Actually Do", *Usability News*, Vol. 8, No. 1, February, http://psychology.wichita.edu/surl/ usabilitynews/81/Passwords.asp, (Accessed 19 March 2013).

Stallings, W. (1995), *Network and Internetwork Security Principles and Practice*, Prentice Hall, Englewood Cliffs, New Jersey.

Tam, L., Glassman, M. and Vandenwauver, M. (2010), "The psychology of password management: a tradeoff between security and convenience", *Behaviour and Information Technology*, Vol. 29, No. 3, pp233-244, May-June.

Weber, J.E., Guster, D., Safanov, P. and Schmidt, M.B. (2008), "Weak password security: An empirical study", *Information Security Journal: A Global Perspective*, Vol. 17, No. 1, pp45-54, January.

Weinstein, N.D. (1980), "Unrealistic optimism about future life events", *Journal of Personality and Social Psychology*, Vol. 39, pp806-820.

Wessels, P.L. and Steenkamp, L. (2007), "Assessment of current practices in creating and using passwords as a control mechanism for information access", *South African Journal of Information Management*, Vol. 9, No. 2, June, www.sajim.co.za, (Accessed 15 May 2013).

Yan, J., Blackwell, A., Anderson, R. and Grant, A. (2004), "Password memorability and Security: Empirical results", *Security and Privacy*, IEEE, Vol. 2, No. 5, pp25-31, September-October.

Zviran, M. and Haga, W.J. (1999), "Password security: An empirical study", *Journal of Management Information Systems*, Vol. 15, No. 4, pp161-185.

Linking Student Information Security Awareness and Behavioural Intent

B. Ngoqo[1] and S.V. Flowerday[2]

[1]Applied Informatics Department, Walter Sisulu University, East London, South Africa
[2]Department of Information Systems, University of Fort Hare, East London, South Africa
e-mail: bukelwa.ngoqo@gmail.com

Abstract

This study analysed existing theories from the social sciences in order to gain a better understanding of factors which contribute to student mobile phone users' poor information security behaviour. Two key aspects associated with information security behaviour were considered, namely: awareness and behavioural intent. Researchers have identified the most common cause of poor security practices on the part of mobile phone users, and which cause them to fall victim to social engineering techniques such as phishing, is their lack of awareness of existing security threats, vulnerabilities and risks. However, an increasing number of researchers consider human behaviour to be another cause of security breaches. Zhang *et al.* (2009) concur with this view and state that understanding human behaviour is important when dealing with the problems caused by human errors. Harnesk *et al.* (2011) expressed a concern that existing research does not address the interlinked relationship between anticipated security behaviour and the enactment of security procedures. Existing researchers in the field of information security still grapple with the 'knowing-and-doing' gap, where user information security knowledge/awareness sometimes does not result in safer behavioural practises. This paper proposes that the knowing-and-doing gap can possibly be reduced by addressing both awareness and behavioural intent. This paper explores the relationship between student mobile phone user information security awareness and behavioural intent in a developmental university in South Africa.

Keywords

Mobile phone information security, information security awareness, information security behavioural intent

1. Introduction

The field of information security management for organisations is pervaded with policies, standards and frameworks. However, for application to the student mobile phone user context, this paper adopts the definition of information security management suggested by Parakkattu *et al.* (2010:318) which simply states that information security management is concerned with "ensuring the security of information through the proactive management of information security risks, threats and vulnerabilities". Although the information security environment of private mobile phone users is not regulated by standards, mobile phone users as owners of a technological asset (phone) which contains or is used to transmit information (asset)

162

should be concerned with ensuring the security of this information. Humans have been repeatedly identified as the most important factor to be considered in the securing of information assets. People use technology in one of two environments, namely: the workplace and home (Talib, Clarke and Furnell, 2010). The mobile phone user considered in this study falls into the latter group of technology users. A unique attribute of these students is that they are registered in a newly restructured South African educational entity referred to in this study as a 'developmental university'.

In 2002 the Higher Education Restructuring Proposal (Ministry of Education, 2003) for the consolidation of higher education institutions through mergers and incorporations was approved by the government and resulted in the higher education system comprising eleven universities, six comprehensive universities and six universities of technology. The participants in this study are students from a comprehensive university structure which was formed in 2005 by merging three 'historically black' institutions. The Draft National Plan for Higher Education in South Africa (Department of Education, 2001) justly makes references to the demographic profile of the student body with the teaching of under-prepared students being an inherent characteristic associated with the 'historically black' institutions. These students are second language English speakers in an environment where instruction and teaching materials are presented in English and access to technological resources (e.g. computer labs, Internet) is limited. Arguably, in this developmental environment students are more vulnerable to information security threats than their counterparts in more well established universities.

Van Niekerk and Von Solms (2010) mention two primary human related factors in information security, namely: knowledge and behaviour. They caution that adequate security measures may be rendered inadequate if there are low levels of user cooperation or knowledge. For example, mobile phones have a password lock feature which requires the user to enter a password prior to accessing any information on the phone; however, if the mobile phone user does not activate the password, it cannot serve its purpose of protecting the information asset. For the purposes of this paper, the primary human related factors are considered to be awareness and behaviour. To determine participant information security threat knowledge/awareness ('know'), this paper firstly discusses how the level of awareness was calculated using Kruger and Kearney's (2006) method. Following this, a discussion of participant information security behaviour ('doing') and an explanation on how participant behavioural intent levels were calculated using similar methods follows. Finally, a discussion of the findings and concluding remarks is presented.

2. Measuring mobile phone information security awareness

In view of the poor levels of knowledge about the information security threats to which they are exposed in their environment, mobile phone users pose the biggest threat to information security (Chen, Medlin and Shaw, 2008; Talib *et al.*, 2010) with some security breaches (virus infections, identity theft, dumpster diving) being a direct result of what Chen *et al.* (2008) consider to be user carelessness or a lack of action. There is little evidence which proves that mobile phone users are knowledgeable about or are, in fact, practising information security (Talib *et al.*, 2010). This study adopted Chen *et al.'s* (2008) definition of information security awareness who consider the ultimate goal of information security awareness to be an awareness of security threats, an understanding of the way in which these threats work, and the ability to predict/anticipate potential outcomes if the threats are ignored.

Awareness campaigns are aimed at improving user knowledge, attitude and behaviour towards information security and were used as the interventions in this action research study. Kruger and Kearney (2006) identified a set of factors which contribute to information security awareness as knowledge (related to what users know), attitude (what they think) and behaviour (what they do). "Each dimension was then divided into focus areas" (Kruger and Kearney, 2006:291).

This study adopts the awareness measurement tool proposed by Kruger and Kearney (2006) for the purpose of measuring the level of student mobile phone user information security awareness. However, the following considerations must be noted:

- The dimension weights were kept at the percentages calculated by Kruger and Kearney (knowledge (30), attitude (20) and behaviour (50)).
- Due to the longitudinal nature of the study, different measurements were taken over a period of time. The initial calculated values were only important for checking the degree of observed changes between each subsequent measurement taken.
- The original measurement tool (Kruger and Kearney, 2006) refers to user actual behaviour. Users gave an indication of how they behaved by answering a set behaviour related questions. However, Kruger and Kearney (2006) acknowledge that users are not always truthful when answering such questions and as a result the measurement for actual behaviour may not be accurate. In lieu of this, this study substitutes the 'Behaviour' dimension with questions addressing 'Perceived Behavioural Intent'.
- Perceived Behavioural Intent helps to mitigate the impact of this possible inaccuracy by acknowledging the calculated value is based on what the mobile phone user professes.

Factoring the comments above, the tool was adapted for application in the student mobile phone user environment of a developmental university. The level of awareness map is then modified as follows:

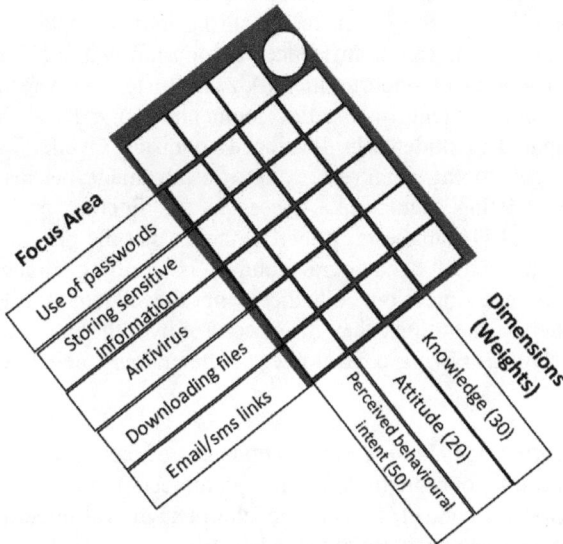

Figure 1: Level of Awareness map (adapted from Kruger and Kearney, 2006)

Recognising the limitation of undertaking an awareness campaign and its potentially poor impact on user behaviour, this study attempted to use information security awareness to stimulate security compliant student mobile phone user behaviour. While Furnell (2010) recognises that raising awareness is an important step, he does not consider it to be sufficient to overcome all the information security hurdles/challenges and concedes that it does not always result in improved security behaviour. Behavioural intent and how it can be applied to the student mobile phone user context is discussed in the next section.

3. Measuring mobile phone information security behavioural intent

The poor information security awareness of mobile phone users has a direct impact on their information security behaviour. To gain a better understanding of mobile phone user information security behaviour, this study relied on the Theory of Planned Behaviour (TPB) formulated by Ajzen (1991). The TPB outlines the interaction between a person's attitude, subjective norms, perceived behavioural control and their behavioural intentions. The TPB suggests that an individual's behaviour is determined by the person's intention to perform that behaviour and that intention is a function of their attitude, subjective norms and the perceived behavioural control which are important to the individual. Attitude looks at the individual's negative or positive feelings about performing the behaviour. Ajzen (1991) suggests that people are inclined to have a positive attitude towards behaviours believed to yield desirable consequences, while a negative attitude will be present where the consequences are believed to be negative. Ajzen (1991) describes subjective norms as the individual's perception about whether people important to the individual think the behaviour should be performed, and considers perceived behavioural control to be the extent to which the individual feels they are able to enact the behaviour. This can be influenced by non-motivational factors such as the availability of resources or opportunities (Ajzen, 1991). As a result of these non-motivational factors, students in the developmental context are faced with added challenges compared to students in developed countries. Oyedemi (2011) mentions that students in developing countries are at a disadvantage because they are faced with challenges relating factors like access to the Internet or limited access to computers. Ajzen (1991) makes a further argument that the person's perceived, and not necessarily the actual behavioural control, is a strong enough motivator for influencing behavioural intention. Whether or not the student mobile phone user has actual (or as much as they think they have) control over the given behaviour, if they perceive themselves as having control over the behaviour, their intention to act will increase.

Regarding the correlations between the components of the TPB model, Ajzen (1991) notes that the more favourable the attitude and subjective norms and the greater the perceived behavioural control, the stronger the behavioural intention and the more likely the person is of enacting the given behaviour.

The TPB has found wide application in the information security context, having been applied to computer abuse problems (Lee and Lee, 2010), security policy compliance (Pahnila *et al.*, 2007), and insider security contravention (Workman and Gathegi, 2007). This study relies on the TPB for determining factors which influence mobile phone users' information security behavioural intent. Based on the same focus areas used in measuring level of awareness, the dimensions considered in calculating behavioural intent are (*attitude, subjective norms* and *perceived behavioural control*) adopted from the TPB. However, unlike the *'perceived behavioural intention'* referred to used when calculating level of awareness, a critical difference exists in how the terms *'perceived behavioural intent'* (*cf* section 2 above) vs *'behavioural intent'* are defined and applied in this study. Behavioural intent is a calculated value based on the mobile phone users' scores in response to questions relating to their attitude, subjective norms and perceived behavioural control over information security related behaviour. On the other hand, the level of perceived behavioural control is a value solely based on the mobile phone users' scoring on answers to questions relating to their information security behaviour.

For the purposes of determining baseline figures, equal weights were allocated to each dimension. The findings will be used to determine how these weights can be adjusted for future application. For the purposes of this paper, the degree of the change between iterations of the study cycles is deemed to be a sufficient indicator for purposes of reviewing the relationship between awareness and behavioural intent.

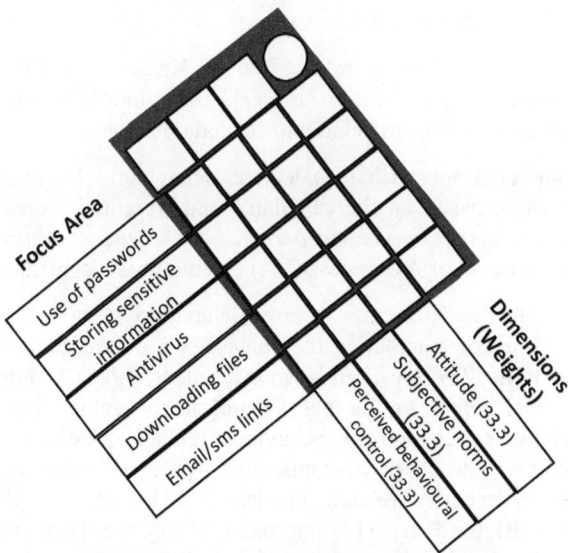

Figure 2: Level of Behavioural intent map
(adapted from Kruger and Kearney, 2006)

The level of behavioural intent was determined by using the scorecard approach (see Figure 2) based on mobile phone users' responses to information security behaviour related questions. While the focus areas remained the same (see Figure 1), the dimensions considered (attitude, subjective norms and perceived behavioural control) are the main difference between the Level of Awareness map (Figure 1) and the suggested Level of Behavioural intent map in Figure above. The relationship between awareness and behavioural intent is discussed in the next section.

4. Relationship between awareness and behavioural intent

This paper suggests that there is a relationship between the student mobile phone user information security awareness levels and their levels of information security behavioural intent. While studies have been undertaken to assess levels of awareness in an organisation, the field of information security behavioural intent is rarely researched with most of the focus being on actual behaviour. While interventions like awareness campaigns result in an observable change in levels of what people 'know', sometimes a difference exists between what people 'know' and what they 'do'. Using the TPB, this paper acknowledges that behavioural intention is a predecessor to actual behaviour which is used as a proxy measure of actual behaviour for the purposes of this study. The following similarities and overlaps exist between the factors used to calculate level of awareness and those used to calculate behavioural intent:

- *Attitude* is a common factor.

- The factor *Behaviour* is referred to in Kruger and Kearney's level of awareness model (*see section 2 above*). Behaviour is determined by scoring participants responses to behaviour related questions.

- Using the TPB approach to calculate Behavioural Intention (BI), BI is a derived value based on the calculated and weighted scores of the factors: *attitude, subjective norms* and *perceived behavioural control*. Whereas in calculating Level of Awareness (LA) behaviour is a contributing factor.

- To highlight the distinction in how Behaviour/ Behavioural Intent is used differently in the calculating the values for the main components (LA and BI), the term *'Perceived Behavioural Intent'* (PBI) is introduced in this study. PBI refers to the behavioural intent value obtained by asking participants to respond to behaviour related questions. The answers provided are how the participants think ('perceive') they would respond to information security related incidents. This PBI is different to the calculated BI used the TPB approach. Using the TPB approach, BI is a calculated value based on the participant's score on questions relating to attitude, subjective norm and perceived behavioural control.

With the evident overlapping of factors from the underlying theories used in defining level of awareness and behavioural intent in this study, serious consideration was given to the existence of a relationship or inter-dependence between the two components.

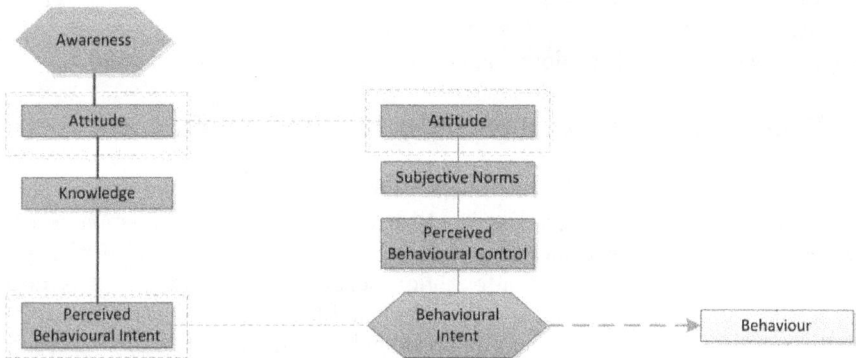

Figure 3: Mobile phone information security constructs

Figure 3 provides a graphic representation of identified associations between information security awareness, behavioural intent and actual behaviour. Behavioural intention influences actual information security behaviour. A survey was conducted using action research principles amongst 90 students from a developmental university in South Africa. Information security awareness interventions were implemented during the three cycle data collection process and a baseline survey (before any intervention was implemented) and subsequent surveys were taken after the completion of each intervention. The findings from the administered surveys are summarised below.

5. Findings

The main focus during analysis of the study findings remained on observing any changes to constructs awareness and behavioural intent. Correlation analysis tests were conducted to determine whether relationships existed between the different factors. The correlation coefficients give an indication of whether the relationship is a positive relationship (changes to constructs increase or decrease in the same direction) or a negative relationship (constructs respond in opposite directions). This section concludes by analysing the relationship between overall awareness and behavioural intent. Level of awareness is presented below.

Level of Awareness (LA)

Awareness factors (Knowledge (K), attitude (A), behaviour (PBI)). Relationships between factors are presented below:

		K	PBI	A
K	Pearson Correlation	1	.022	-.176
	Sig. (2-tailed)		.844	.117
	N	81	81	81
PBI	Pearson Correlation	.022	1	.219
	Sig. (2-tailed)	.844		.050
	N	81	81	81
A	Pearson Correlation	-.176	.219	1
	Sig. (2-tailed)	.117	.050	
	N	81	81	81

Table 1: Correlation (K, A, PBI)

Knowledge and attitude

As shown in Table 1, Pearson's correlation coefficient was used to investigate the relationship between knowledge and attitude of student mobile phone users. It was found that there was a low degree of negative correlation between knowledge and attitude at [$r = -0.176$, $n = 81$, $p = 0.117$].

Knowledge and perceived behavioural intent

Table illustrates how Pearson's correlation coefficient was used to investigate the relationship between knowledge and perceived behavioural intent of student mobile phone users. It emerged that there was a low degree of positive correlation between knowledge and perceived behavioural intent at [$r = 0.022$, $n = 81$, $p = 0.844$].

Attitude and perceived behavioural intent

As presented in Table above, Pearson's correlation coefficient was used to investigate the relationship between attitude and perceived behavioural intent. It was found that there was a low degree of positive correlation between attitude and perceived behavioural intent at [r = 0.219, n = 81, p = 0.050].

Correlation between the factors *knowledge/attitude* and *knowledge/perceived behavioural intent* was determined to be non-existent or negligible. Therefore based on the findings, no relationship can be assumed between these factors. However, a weak positive relationship is shown between *attitude/perceived behavioural intent*. It can therefore be inferred that a more positive student mobile phone user information security attitude is associated with an increased information security behavioural intention. The relationship was found to be weak; its significance is also negligible with p=0.050.

Behavioural Intent (BI)

Behavioural intent factors (Attitude (A), subjective norms (SN), perceived behavioural control (PBC)). Relationships between factors are presented below:

		A	SN	PBC
	Pearson Correlation	1	.399	.185
A	Sig. (2-tailed)		.000	.098
	N	81	81	81
	Pearson Correlation	.399	1	.337
SN	Sig. (2-tailed)	.000		.002
	N	81	81	81
	Pearson Correlation	.185	.337	1
PBC	Sig. (2-tailed)	.098	.002	
	N	81	81	81

Table 2: Correlations (A, SN, PBC)

Attitude and subjective norms

As illustrated in Table 2 above, Pearson's correlation coefficient was used to investigate the relationship between attitude and subjective norms of student mobile phone users. A moderate degree of positive correlation exists between attitude and subjective norms at [r = 0.399, n = 81, p = 0.000]. With p < 0.05 this correlation is statistically significant with high scores for attitude associated with high scores for subjective norms.

Attitude and perceived behavioural control

As shown in Table 2 above, Pearson's correlation coefficient was used to investigate the relationship between attitude and perceived behavioural control for student mobile phone users. It was found that there was a low degree of positive correlation between attitude and perceived behavioural control at [r = 0.185, n = 81, p = 0.098].

Subjective norms and perceived behavioural control

As shown in Table 2, Pearson's correlation coefficient was used to investigate the relationship between subjective norms and perceived behavioural control for student mobile phone users. It was found that there was a moderate degree of positive correlation between subjective norms and perceived behavioural control at [r = 0.337, n = 81, *p* = 0.002]. With p < 0.05 this correlation is statistically significant with high scores for subjective norms associated with high scores for perceived behavioural control.

With the exception of *attitude/perceived behavioural control* which showed a non-existent or negligible relationship, moderate positive relationships which were determined to be statistically significant were found between *attitude/subjective norms* and *subjective norms/perceived behavioural control*. The findings show that it can be anticipated that a more positive student mobile phone user information security attitude is associated with positive information security behaviour subjective norm propositions. The tests for significance show the result is not due to chance.

Awareness and Behavioural intent

Correlation analysis tests performed also confirmed the existence of relationships between two of the constructs used in the model. A key assumption made in developing the proposed model in this study was that a relationship exists between level of awareness and the level of behavioural intent.

Overall effects of Awareness **(LA)** on Behavioural Intent **(BI)** – is there a negative or positive relationship?

		LA	BI
LA	Pearson Correlation	1	.374
	Sig. (2-tailed)		.001
	N	81	81
BI	Pearson Correlation	.374	1
	Sig. (2-tailed)	.001	
	N	81	81

Table 3: Correlations (LA, BI)

As shown in Table 3 above, the value of Pearson's product between the two factors (LA and BI) was r=.374 (p<0.05). The results show a moderate positive correlation between level of awareness and level of behavioural intent with statistically significant result (p < 0.05).

The statistical tests confirmed the existence of a positive relationship between the constructs (LA and BI). The main inference which can be made based on this determination is that the more aware the student mobile phone users are about information security threats, their intention to follow safe information security practices will also increase.

6. Discussion and concluding remarks

Due to their usage of mobile phones and more specifically mobile phone applications, students in a South African developmental university are faced with the same threats as students in a better developed university. However compared to their global counterparts from more developed countries, they are more vulnerable to threats because of the developmental university environment where students have limited access to sources of information (e.g. Internet) that could help improve their awareness. Thus the findings of this study are important by providing better insight on the awareness and behavioural intent related factors which must be considered to influence a change in South African students' mobile phone information security behaviour.

Statistical tests conducted to determine the extent to the factors that contribute to mobile phone user information security awareness confirmed the levels of influence between the factors knowledge and attitude; knowledge and behaviour and between attitude and behaviour are not significant. Based on the study findings, no claims can be made on the relationships between the individual Level of Awareness (LA) factors.

In reviewing the results obtained from exploring the relationships between the factors which contribute to mobile phone user information security behavioural intent, significant influences were recorded between the following factors: attitude and subjective norms and subjective norms and perceived behavioural control. However, the influence between attitude and perceived behavioural control was found not to be significant. In a similar pattern uncovered in the relationships between the awareness factors, mobile phone users' information security attitude will influence or be influenced by their subjective norms and perceived behavioural control. The extent to which mobile phone users feel they have control over information security behaviours/actions is also influenced and influences the mobile phone users' perceptions about what they think their family or peers deem to be acceptable information security behaviour.

The significant positive correlation found between Level of Awareness (LA) and Behavioural Intention (BI) was a key finding which confirmed this study's premise, which suggests that a relationship exists between information security awareness and behavioural intent. The most common efforts aimed at addressing the 'knowing-and-doing' gap have concentrated on improving awareness, and this paper suggests that this gap can be reduced by addressing awareness in conjunction with behavioural intent.

7. References

Ajzen, I. (1991). The theory of planned behavior. *Organizational Behaviour and Human Decision Processes,* 50, 179-211.

Chen, C.C., Medlin, B.D. and Shaw, R.S. (2008). A cross-cultural investigation of situational information security awareness programs. *Information Management & Computer Security,* 16(4), 360-376.

Department of Education, "National Plan for Higher Education in South Africa", *Ministry of Education,* South Africa, February 2001.

Furnell, S. (2010). Jumping security hurdles. *Computer Fraud & Security,* 1074.

Harnesk, D. and Lindstrom, J. (2011). Shaping security behaviour through discipline and agility: Implications for information security management. *Information Management & Computer Security,* 19(4), 262-276.

Kruger, H.A., Kearney, W.D. (2006). A prototype for assessing information security awareness. *Computers & Security,* 25, 289-296.

Lee, H. and Lee, S. (2010). Internet vs mobile services: comparisons of gender and ethnicity. *Journal of Research in Interactive Marketing,* 4(4), 346-375.

Ministry of Education. (2003). *Higher Education restructuring. Guidelines for mergers and incorporations.* Retrieved November 11, 2013, from http://www.education.gov.za/LinkClick.aspx?fileticket=Fk0AzO7hgqA%3D&tabid=95&mid =507

Oyedemi, T.D. (2012). Digital inequalities and implications for social inequalities: A study of Internet penetration amongst university students in South Africa. *Telematics and Informatics,* 29(2012), 302-313.

Pahnilla, S., Siponen, M. & Mahmood, A. (2007, 14-16 May). Employees adherence to information security policies an empirical study. *IFIP TC-11 22nd International Information Security Conference.* Johannesburg, South Africa.

Parakkattu, S. and Kunnathur, A.S. (2010, March). A framework for research in information security management. *Northeast Decision Sciences Institute Proceedings,* pp. 318-323.

Talib, S., Clarke, N.L. and Furnell, S.M . (2010, 15-18 February). An analysis of information security awareness within home and work environments. *Conference on Availability, Reliability and Security, ARES'10 International conference,* (pp. 196-203). Krakov.

Van Niekerk & Von Solms. (2010). Information security culture: A management perspective. *Computers & Security,* 29, 476-486.

Workman, M. & Gathegi, J. (2007). Punishment and ethics deterrents: a study of insider security contravention. *Journal of the American Society for Information Science and Technology,* 58(2), 212-222.

Zhang, J., Reithel, B.J. and Li, H. (2009). Impact of perceived technical protection on security behaviours. *Information Management & Computer Security,* 17(4), 330-340.

Towards an Education Campaign for Fostering a Societal, Cyber Security Culture

R. Reid and J. Van Niekerk

Institute of ICT Advancement, Nelson Mandela Métropolitain University
e-mail: S208045820@nmmu.ac.za; johanvanniekerk@nmmu.ac.za

Abstract

The need for information security has moved beyond its traditional organizational boundaries. It is becoming a requirement for all information technology users. Many countries are recognizing this need for their citizens to be cyber aware and secure. Consequently these countries are beginning to implement national cyber security campaigns and efforts. Literature advocates that these campaigns should aim to foster a national (societal) cyber security culture to be truly effective. Currently there are no guidelines for how to foster a cyber security culture at a *societal* level. One of the elements required in a culture fostering process is education. This education needs to be effectively conducted to have a foreseeable, positive result which is measurable. Therefore a scalable, culture fostering campaign is needed. This paper reports a study of an annual cyber security educational campaign which aims to begin fostering a cyber-security culture amongst the youth in the Nelson Mandela Metropolis in South Africa. The objective of studying this campaign is to establish a baseline campaign from which suitable guidelines for a future campaigns (at any scale) may be abstracted.

Keywords

Cyber Security Education, Cyber Security Culture, Youth, Case Study, Awareness

1. Introduction

People, also known as the "human factor", have been established as one of the weakest links in many information or cyber security solutions. These security solutions consist of technologies, processes and people. The technologies and processes within security can be created or drafted to be theoretically secure. However, how truly secure the technologies and processes are depends on whether the people use the technologies securely and/or follow the secure procedures.

People can consciously or unconsciously become a threat to any information security solution (Thomson et al., 2006). When they become a conscious threat it may be with a specific intent or via negligence. Alternatively when they become an unconscious threat it may be for a range of reasons including: a lack of knowledge of security practices; an inability to properly apply their knowledge to their own work role or environmental context; or common negligence. Regrettably as a result of this it is more likely that a breach within an information security solution will occur because of a human fault (the "human factor"), not a technical fault (Mitnick and Simon, 2002).

Within organizations the establishment of an information security culture (hereinafter "ISC") has been widely accepted as a viable counter to this "human factor" threat (Van Niekerk and Von Solms, 2010). The fostering of a culture attempts to address two primary dimensions of the human factor: knowledge, and behaviour (Van Niekerk and Von Solms, 2010).

The establishment of an ISC has traditionally occurred within organizations. This is because in the past the integration of IT into daily activities, and the subsequent need for information security was considered more of an organizational issue. However, the perceived exclusivity of this issue is no longer a valid belief.

The world beyond organizations has become progressively more information-oriented. As a result information security principles have become more applicable to information use in a personal context. Thus at present *all Internet and ICT users* need a basic level of cyber security awareness and knowledge to securely perform their daily activities (Chen et al., 2008; Furnell, 2013).

Security issues relating to the cyber-world now require a coordinated and focused effort from the national and international society, governments and private sectors (Dlamini, 2009). To suit this broader security context a security solution with a greater scope than information security is required. Cyber security is such a solution.

Information security is a process involving the protection of the *confidentiality, integrity, and availability* of *information* from a wide range of threats in order to ensure business continuity, minimize *business* risk and maximize return on investments and *business* opportunities (*ISO/IEC 27002*, 2008). Cyber security also principally involves the protection of information and ICT; however, its scope also extends much further (*ISO/IEC 27032*, 2012).

Cyber security involves the protection of the interests of a person, society or nation, including their information and non-information based assets, which need to be protected from risks relating to their interaction with cyberspace (*ISO/IEC 27032*, 2012; Von Solms and Van Niekerk, 2013). Within this definition humans and their societies are part of the assets needing protection.

Many security specialists and nations are acknowledging the need for populaces to be aware of and educated about being more cyber secure. To achieve this within the current population, and ensure that it continues within the future populaces a "self-renewing" belief which affects behaviour is needed. In an organizational context this need is met through the fostering of an ISC. Similarly in a societal context a parallel cyber security culture ought to be fostered.

This paper represents an initial cycle in a larger action research approach. The paper begins to examine how a cyber security culture could be fostered via education. The findings of this study will begin to demonstrate how to structure a cyber security education campaign which targets needs of a subset of society. The next section will provide further context and rationalisation for this study. This will be followed by the presentation of the study results, findings and conclusions.

2. Background

Culture is broadly considered to be the overall, taken-for-granted assumptions that a group has learned throughout history (Schein, 2009). ISC builds upon this premise. Many current authors deal with the topic of ISC (Schlienger and Tuefel, Da Veiga and Eloff, Van Niekerk and Von Solms). Most of these authors define ISC in terms of its underlying constituent components. This paper will use the definition offered by Van Niekerk and Von Solms (2010). ISC as an omnipresent concept understood by the people involved in the information security solution(Van Niekerk and Von Solms, 2010). They argue that over simplifying the ISC could be dangerous as an ISC consists of four information security related components:

1. Artefacts: The actual happenings within the organization's daily tasks. This dimension includes the visible structures and processes which were deemed to be "measurable but hard to decipher";
2. Espoused Values: The guidelines (strategies, goals) for what to include in a policy, and consequent ISC to adequately address the business's needs;
3. Shared Tacit Assumptions: The beliefs and values of an individual and collective employees. This includes their unconscious beliefs, perceptions, thoughts and feelings;
4. Knowledge: The necessary and required levels of information security specific knowledge needed to perform the daily business tasks in a secure manner (Van Niekerk and Von Solms, 2010).

The accumulation of how these components develop and interact is considered to be an ISC's effect (Van Niekerk and Von Solms, 2010). Each of these levels can either positively or negatively influence the overall ISC. It may be theorized that a *cyber* security culture would have similar components and behaviors, although the exact details would differ to some extent due to the practices differences in implementation details and context. The method by which the culture is fostered would be important.

A culture can be fostered through either coercion or education. Woodall (1996) argues that, if used, an equitable balance should exist between the degree of coercion used and the reward given, however, generally coercion should be avoided. Within an organizational context, users can be coerced into following security policies and procedures. This can lead to a forced organizational ISC. In a national context it is also possible to use coercion. However, due to ethical and implementation considerations it is a more difficult undertaking and thus less desirable as an approach. Within a national context the educational approach for fostering a culture is preferred. Educational campaigns to teach all of society's users about cyber security issues and practices are thus required.

Many countries have recognized this need to become cyber secure. Part of the process of cyber-securing a country would be the education of the countries citizens about cyber issues and security practices. Many countries have acknowledged this need for citizen education in their national cyber security policies (Klimburg, 2012 ,pp. 47). However, detail about how this education is to be provided to each society is not provided. This has led to a search for existing guidelines for such an endeavour.

A comprehensive literature review revealed that there are currently no widely accepted, documented guidelines for how to educate users at a societal level about cyber security. There are few generic guidelines for implementing cyber-security and societal educational campaigns even as separate subjects. This leads to two questions: "How can an effective cyber security educational campaign be developed?" and "How can this campaign be made suitable for educating an entire society?"

The first question's solution can begin to be found through adopting some of the fundamental practices from the implementation of past (similarly purposed) informations security campaigns. However, most information security education campaigns occur within organizations therefore the scope and its implementation would have definite difference. For example, in an organisational context education may often be formally (possibly mandatorily) conducted by security experts or human resources. Comparatively in a societal context such a practice would not be well-received. Therefore to answer the second question other methods are necessary. Some methods may be abstracted from the practices of other educational campaigns (of any subject-domain) which aim to educate or raise awareness in general society. Using these premises a number of "trial by error" attempts may be necessary to determine a suitable approach for a societal, cyber-security educational campaign.

The next sections will present a case study of a specific set of such attempts. The next section presents the methodology followed during this study.

3. Methodology

The paper presents a case study (as defined by Creswell (2007)) which spans several years. During these action-research-like cycles of continuous improvement of the process based on lessons learned in previous research cycles is followed. The study follows the case of the annual South African Cyber Security Academic Alliance (SACSAA) educational campaign since 2011. The ultimate aim of the campaign is to foster a cyber security culture via education. This campaign's target audience is the South African youth. However, the presented results were only successfully gathered and analysed from the youth in the Nelson Mandela Metropolis area.

The campaign itself consists of two parts: an education campaign and a poster contest. The campaign aims to first raise the youth's awareness of a number of important cyber safety and security topics specific to the practice of cyber security (humans form part of the assets to be protected). These topics cover the issues commonly acknowledged as being relevant to their own cyber activities and existence. The topics covered the following cyber security issues: stranger danger; browsing, downloading and online activities; cyber citizenship; cybercrime; social networking; cyberbullying; password and hardware security; viruses and malware; cyber –bullying, -harassment and –stalking; cybersex and finally cyber identity management. The contest is secondly used as an instrument to measure the campaign's impact on the involved youth's awareness levels. Learners are invited to voluntarily create and submit posters (hand-crafted or digitally-created) which promotes awareness of campaign's covered security issues.

To aim of this study is to create an educational campaign component which *effectively* and *measurably* educates the target audience about cyber issues. The researchers selected three measurements to determine the effective impact of the campaign: learner participation; learner internalization of the lessons; campaign memorability through brand association. The first measurement is self-explanatory. It was measured through the empirical data available in the number of entries. The second measurement of internalization, refers to learning which impacts on knowledge, attitudes and behaviour (KAB). An analysis of the posters and the messages/scenarios they depict indicates how educational lessons was perceived and the degree to which they had been internalized (Van Niekerk et al., 2013). The brand association sought to determine whether the campaign itself as an entity was associated with its message. Inclusion of branding into the posters was an indicator.

This section described how the research has been conducted. The next section will present the overviews, results and analysis of each campaign conducted since 2011.

4. Campaigns and Competitions: Results and Analysis

Each campaign formed an iteration of the research cycle which aimed to improve upon the results of its predecessor. This is attempted through the modification of the existent education campaign based on lessons learned in the previous cycles. This section will discuss the implementation and lessons learned in each year's campaign.

4.1. Campaign 1 (2011)

The first campaign was run as a voluntary, distance education campaign. It was a "trial run". The campaign was advertised using professional, promotional flyers. These flyers were distributed via 'snail mail' to schools in the Nelson Mandela Metropolis; and posted on the Nelson Mandela Metropolitan University's campus noticeboards. The pamphlets named topics of interest and encouraged learners to self-study and then participate. Generous cash prizes were offered for the winners.

In total, 3 poster entries were received from NMMU students. Lessons learned were: firstly learners may need to be personally convinced and motivated to become involved. Secondly, to attract school and user attention so as to educate them, a more involved education approach was required. Finally learners may have been more interested in participating if less self-study had been required. Due to the low number of entries no further analysis of the posters was conducted.

4.2. Campaign 2 (2012)

This campaign refocused on solely educating the youth within primary and secondary schools. The invitations were issued via post. Additionally to further attract participants, the researcher personally visited many schools to advertise the campaign and explain its purpose to teachers and learners. The teachers were asked to encourage learner participation in the campaign and competition. Generous prizes were offered for participation in competition.

Several changes were made to the previous campaign approach. To reduce self-study requirements, children were: firstly given a cyber awareness talk by the researcher, and secondly were provided access to relevant material in the form of pamphlets and online topic summary sheets relating to the chosen cyber security issues. Additional resources and reinforcement materials was provided in the format of pedagogically sound games which taught cyber security principles to children through play (Reid and Van Niekerk, 2013). Finally to make the campaign lessons more memorable for the learners, the learners were encouraged to make a cyber safety pledge to themselves and Cyber Sid (a SACSAA partner's campaign mascot).

This campaign was more successful than its predecessor. A total of 217 poster entries were received. Primary school children accounted for 94 of the entries. The remaining 123 entries were from secondary school children. All of the entries received were from the Nelson Mandela Metropolitan area. This is despite having many requests from schools located all across South Africa for competition flyers, educational material and additional information regarding how to enter. In fact, all entries were received from schools that were personally visited by the researcher. Upon analysis of the posters it was found that 66.18% of all of the participants had (in the researcher's opinion) successfully internalized the taught messages.

This campaign showed that a more proactive education approach combined with pedagogically-sound supporting educational material and fun activities engaged more participants. The prizes also potentially attracted participants. Additionally it was found that mascots and other branding should be carefully chosen. Several of the children related the mascot to the topic. Many learners included Cyber Sid in their posters. Finally it was found that the teachers in their support role were vital in assisting to promote the campaign to the children. In future campaigns teachers should be asked to participate more actively in the research.

4.3. Campaign 3 (2013)

This campaign implemented almost all of the previous campaign's procedure. However, a few superficial changes were made. Firstly the Cyber Sid mascot was replaced by the SACSAA logo on all the provided material. Secondly the lectures and support material presented by the researcher was further customised for each school. Upon the teachers' request particular emphasis was placed on the topic/s which most related to problems learners at that particular school had faced. Cyberbullying was considered a prominent issue by many of the schools. Thirdly the teachers were provided with access to more support material. They could incorporate these resources into their own classes to reinforce the researcher's guest lectures. Finally, less generous prizes than previous years were offered.

This campaign was the most successful thus far. In total 468 poster entries were received. Of these entries 275 were from primary school children and 193 were from secondary school children. The analysis of the posters showed that 84.22% of the participants had (in the researcher's opinion) well internalized the taught messages.

The results of this campaign showed a definite increase in the number of participants. The aggregate of total learners who internalized the message also increased. Unfortunately the number of learners who identified with the mascot/logo decreased.

The analysis of this campaign's results confirmed most of the previous year's observation. Firstly it showed that personalization of the material to emphasize each school's pertinent issues was particularly impactful. For each school that had made a personalization request, the majority of their learners chose that issue as their poster topic. Secondly it showed that increased teacher involvement led to a rise in the percentage of learners who internalized the message. However, this finding is accompanied by a new issue. The level of customization to education material (done by the researcher) cannot be maintained indefinitely using the current educational delivery model. A campaign model which is more scalable is needed.

This section examined the basic results and findings of each year's campaign. The next section will discuss the aggregate findings in terms of the selected impact measurements described in the methodology.

4.4. Overall Analysis and Discussion (Lessons learned)

The ultimate goal of this research is to determine how to educate society and foster a societal cyber security culture. Thus far this study has shown that the campaign is becoming more effective at achieving this objective for the youth societal sub-group. However, the campaign is not as of yet ideal sustainable, scalable and measurably effective. Furthermore some old and new campaign problems are still being resolved. Some campaign success indicators and problems will now be discussed.

The first indicator of campaign effectiveness is the number of participants each year. Due to the various changes incorporated into the campaign participation has annually increased from 3 entries in 2011 to 463 entries in 2013.

This improvement is encouraging, however, it has resulted in a few new issues being identified. The issue of the limited scalability of the current education campaign model is of particular concern. With the current education model's delivery methods and degree of customization (done by the research) only a portion of the total target audience is being reached. This is unacceptable therefore a more scalable education delivery model is required to improve the campaigns advancement.

The percentage of learners who internalized the campaign's lessons are the second indicator of campaign effectiveness. Overall this percentage has increased each year (see Figure 1). The current approach is therefore gaining the learner's attention and explaining the lessons well enough that the learners are adopting the lessons and considering how the issue affects themselves and others around them.

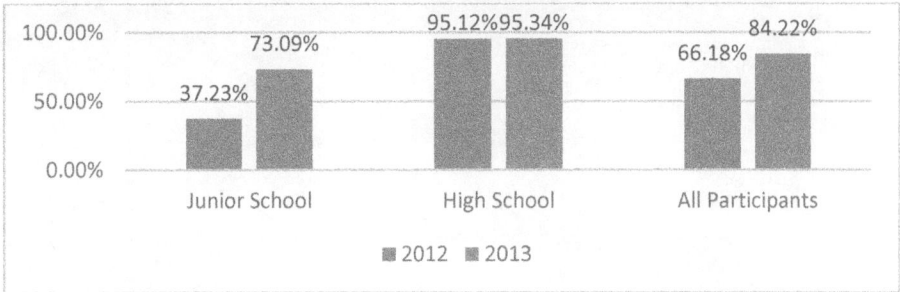

Figure 1: Learner internalization of the taught campaign message

The third indicator of campaign effectiveness is the campaigns memorability through brand association. This is being established through the use of pedagogy and strategic marketing e.g. the use of a mascot. Thus far, each year the brand association has fluctuated based upon the type of branding logo/mascot used (see Figure 2).

This indicator's findings show that the selected branding/mascot must be appropriate for the audience. More of the younger children associated with the character mascot than with logo. The older children displayed the opposite tendency. This indicates that to enable a diverse target audience to associate with the campaign, a more flexible but consolidated branding strategy is necessary.

Overall this study has resulted in four principal lessons being learned. Firstly distribution (logistics) definitely impacts how/if the message is received. The current distribution model is not sustainably scalable. Therefore more suitable model should be sought. Secondly teacher involvement is even more crucial than previously supposed. Teacher involvement caused the levels of internalization and participation to increase. If their involvement becomes more focused, the scalability of the campaign could improve. Security experts are capable of communicating the security material however, the results of their methods are not as successful as those obtained when educationalists are involved. Thirdly suitable, official and age appropriate branding is necessary for campaign memorability and relatability. Fourthly the content of the course is well-chosen, however, the presentation and delivery of the course continuously requires improvement. Involvement from appropriate experts should possibly be sought.

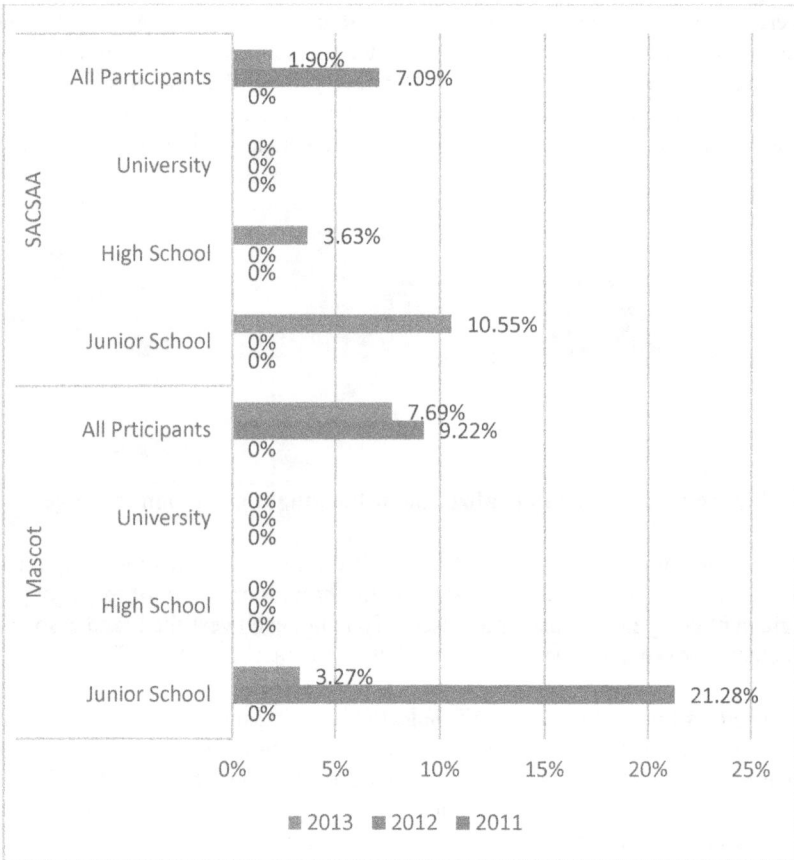

Figure 2: Brand Association for the cyber security education campaign

4.4.1. Upcoming 2014 campaign (future work)

The will be altered to take into consideration the lessons learned in 2013's campaign. An attempt to improve the scalability of the campaign by increasing the educational role of the teachers and decreasing the security expert's presentation role. This year the campaign will follow an adaption of a top-down, organisational culture change approach. Experts will obtain principle top-management support and allow existing hierarchies to further communicate the campaign message. For youth sub-group of society this will be one by getting principal buy in via DOE. Then the security experts will educate the teachers about the campaign topics. The experts will also provide the information about the campaign topics as well as previous campaigns successfully used resources. The researcher will have no contact with the children. The teacher will be expected to customize and present the material to suit their classes and students. Finally lessons learned from this campaign will be used and adapted to guide the development and launch of a parallel campaign which will target another societal subgroup (possibly the organisational sector).

5. Conclusion

The fostering of a societal cyber security culture is vital to educate society about cyber security issues and practices. The lessons learned indicate that to be effective all decisions and implementations of the critical aspects of such a campaign need have a solid theoretical basis. This is particularly important for the selecting and presenting the campaign message.

In this case the most suitable people to ensure that the message is clear is the cyber security subject-domain experts. However, these experts are not necessarily skilled or constantly available enough to any of the other aspects of producing an effective cyber security educational campaign. Therefore the researchers advocate that security expert should determine what to teach users, however, the education and other aspects of the campaign should be done by relevant domain experts. Ultimately the findings or this research strongly suggest that an interdisciplinary approach to education is needed for a cyber-security education needs of a society.

The significance of recognising this need for an interdisciplinary approach could enable the improvement of scalability, quality manageability and continuity possible for a course. Therefore this will aid in developing a culture fostering process which will endure and adapt to change. Further research will focus on developing a framework to enable all involved subject domain specialists to integrate their contributions to create and manage a cyber-security education course which aims to foster a societal cyber security culture.

6. Acknowledgements

The financial assistance of the Vodacom/NMMU and National Research Foundation (NRF) scholarships towards this research is hereby acknowledged. Opinions expressed and conclusions arrived at are those of the author and are not necessarily to be attributed to the sponsors.

7. References

Chen, C.C., Medlin, B.D. and Shaw, R.S. (2008), "A cross-cultural investigation of situational information security awareness programs", *Information Management & Computer Security*, Vol. 16 No. 4, pp. 360–376.

Creswell, J.W. (2007), *Qualitative inquiry and research design, Qualitative inquiry and research design*, Sage Publications, Inc, Vol. Second Edi, pp. 73–84.

Dlamini, M. (2009), "Information security: The moving target", *Computers & Security*, Elsevier Ltd, Vol. 28 No. 3-4, pp. 1–10.

Furnell, S.M. (2013), "Security Education: The Challenge beyond the Classroom", *8th World Conference on Information Security Education*, Auckland, New Zealand, pp. 33–38.

ISO/IEC 27002. (2008), *Change*, Organization International Standards.

ISO/IEC 27032. (2012), *Order A Journal On The Theory Of Ordered Sets And Its Applications*, Organization International Standards.

Klimburg, A. (Ed.). (2012), *National Cyber Security Framework Msnual, Strategies*, NATO CCD COE Publicaions.

Mitnick, K.D. and Simon, W.L. (2002), *The Art of Deception: Controlling the human element of security*, Wiley Publishing Inc.

Van Niekerk, J. and Von Solms, R. (2010), "Information security culture: A management perspective", *Computers & Security*, Elsevier Ltd, Vol. 29 No. 4, pp. 476–486.

Van Niekerk, J., Thomson, K.-L. and Reid, R. (2013), "Cyber Safety for School Children: A Case Study in the Nelson Mandela Metropolis", *8th World Conference on Information Security Education*, Auckland, New Zealand.

Reid, R. and Van Niekerk, J. (2013), "Back to basics: Information security education for the youth via gameplay", in Dodge, R.C. and Futcher, L. (Eds.),*8th World Conference on Information Security Education*, Springer, Auckland, New Zealand, pp. 1–10.

Schein, E.H. (2009), *The corporate culture survival guide*, Jossey-Bass Publishers, San Francisco, California.

Von Solms, R. and Van Niekerk, J. (2013), "From information security to cyber security", *Computers & Security*, Elsevier Ltd, Vol. 38, pp. 97–102.

Thomson, K., Von Solms, R. and Louw, L. (2006), "Cultivating an organizational information security culture", *Computer Fraud & Security*, No. 10, pp. 7–11.

Woodall, J. (1996), "Managing culture change: can it ever be ethical?", *Personnel Review*, Vol. 25 No. 6, pp. 26–40.

Towards Cyber Safety Education in Primary Schools in Africa

S. von Solms[1,2] and R. von Solms[3]

[1]Council for Scientific and Industrial Research, Pretoria, South Africa
[2]North West University, Potchefstroom, South Africa
[3]Nelson Mandela Metropolitan University, Port Elizabeth, South Africa
e-mail: svsolms@csir.co.za; rossouw@nmmu.ac.za

Abstract

Cyber safety has become critically important to all who are active in cyber space. In most African countries no coordinated activities in this regard are taking place, even though many children are already active on cyber space. This paper presents an introductory, but usable, guide to empower primary school teachers, specifically in Africa, to impart the basic principles of cyber safety to their learners. A set of very usable, self-explanatory, publicly available online video cartoons were identified for use as resources by teachers in discussing and stimulate cyber safety principles to primary school learners.

Keywords

Cyber safety, cyber security, cyber awareness, cyber education.

1. Introduction

Internet usage has increased significantly across Africa in the past few years through the increase in bandwidth, wireless technologies and infrastructure. In fact, Africa has the fastest growing market in terms of information technology growth (TeleGeography, 2013). This increase in Internet usage throughout Africa offers a wide range of advantages, but also increases users' vulnerability to malware infection, cyber-bullying, identity theft and cyber terrorism (Dlamini, Taute, & Radebe, 2011). Africa mainly consists of developing countries which are characterised by limited knowledge, expertise and understanding regarding cyber safety (Dlamini, Taute, & Radebe, 2011), (e4Africa, 2011). Young children especially are at risk as they may not know the dangers associated with cyber space.

Many developing countries in Africa do not currently have comprehensive cyber safety initiatives in place (Kortjan & von Solms, 2013); this is exacerbated by the fact that schools have no available curricula or extramural for cyber safety education (Kritzinger, 2011). Teachers' limited knowledge regarding cyber safety, together with limited budgets and resources make the education of children on cyber safety issues extremely challenging. School children in Africa are becoming ever more active in cyber space and few schools are offering any cyber safety education to teach these children safe practices whilst online. Along with this, almost all teachers are ill equipped to understand and offer assistance in and hardly any resources are available to schools and teachers in this regard. Further, hardly any African governments are providing any governmental support in attempting to raise the levels of cyber safety amongst school children. Thus, cyber safety among the youth in most African countries is becoming a growing problem.

The objective of this paper is an attempt to empower African school teachers to educate children on cyber safety by learning along with their learners and by identifying freely available resources on the Internet. This paper aims to provide a guide or basic syllabus to empower teachers in primary schools to teach children to protect themselves when exploring the online world by means of safe and responsible online behaviour and in the process teachers will also educate themselves in this regard.

The next section describes the modern cyber space, its growth, the services it offers as well as the risks associated with it. Section 3 discusses education towards a cyber secure culture and Section 4 will look at the problem of cyber safety education in schools. Section 5 discusses the methodology followed to form a basic syllabus, which is proposed in Section 6. Section 7 will conclude this paper.

2. Modern Cyber Space

It is projected that Africa's demand for Internet access will grow by an average of 51% every year until 2019 (TeleGeography, 2013) and that there will be approximately 1 billion mobile cellular subscribers in Africa by 2015 (Reed, 2012).

Access to the Internet through mobile phones in Africa is becoming more widely available, consequently impacting on the lifestyle and well-being of communities (PWC, 2012). This includes the improvement of banking, healthcare, farming and many other practices. M-Pesa, the international money transfer service launched by Safaricom in Kenya in 2007, has enabled Kenyans to transfer and receive funds and conduct other basic banking transactions using their mobile phones (Safaricom, Relax, you've got M-Pesa, 2012). By March 2012, the number of active M-Pesa users was approximately 14,6 million (Migrant, 2013). Farmers are utilising their mobile phones to get daily updates on the weather, the directions of locust swarms and commodity prices. They also use mobile applications, like iCow by Safaricom, which enable dairy farmers to monitor their cows, receive farming advice and veterinary assistance (Safaricom, iCow, 2012). Mobile phones greatly assist healthcare in rural areas, as people can enjoy access to medical specialists and services from clinics without the need to take long journeys on foot to the nearest health care centre (Mars & Erasmus, 2012). As can be seen, the use of the Internet has greatly enhanced living standards in many respects.

The rapid growth in Internet usage also, unfortunately, makes African countries vulnerable to cyber-attacks and threats owing to high levels of computer illiteracy and ineffective or insufficient legislation (Grobler & Dlamini, 2012). All users of ICT, which includes the private and the public sectors, government, and the general public, including school children (de Lange & von Solms, 2012), are vulnerable to these attacks and threats. Internet users may be exposed to a range of threats, including (de Lange & von Solms, 2012), (Atkinson, Furnell, & Phippen, 2009):

- Technology-focused threats, i.e. hacking, malware and spyware.
- Content-related risks, i.e. exposure to illicit or inappropriate content.
- Harassment-related threats, i.e. cyber-bullying, cyber-stalking and other forms of unwanted contact.
- Risk of exposing information, i.e. children exposing their personal information through phishing or sharing information on social networking platforms.

In many cases, people tend to think that all these potential risks can be eliminated completely by means of technology-based solutions, like blocking or filtering software to restrict what children access online. There are several technologies that can greatly assist in keeping users safe online, but the use of the Internet can never be completely safe (Atkinson, Furnell, & Phippen, 2009), (Byron, 2008). Thus users of cyber space need to be educated to develop safe and responsible online behaviour in order that they will be empowered to protect themselves while exploring the online world (Becta, 2009).

3. Education towards a Cyber Safety Culture

Children can be especially vulnerable to cyber threats as most children are curious and enthusiastic to explore new technologies and environments. In addition, they are naive and unaware of the dangers they may face. As children are educated by parents, guardians and teachers to make wise decisions when dealing with their daily life, like not talking to strangers, walk in unsafe places or to give away personal information, they should be taught how to make wise decisions online as well. This includes using a cell phone, searching the web and using social networking platforms in a safe and responsible manner (Miles, 2011).

The education of children regarding cyber safety threats is vital in order to establish a cyber secure culture (Kortjan & von Solms, 2013). It is stated that the education of children on safe Internet usage will encourage support and knowledge sharing among peers, which would instil the confidence in children to practise safe online behaviour (Atkinson, Furnell, & Phippen, 2009), (Becta, 2009). Today's youth is the guardians and teachers of the future, and teaching them to be responsible digital citizens will have a massive impact on the establishment of a cyber secure culture. Thus the establishment of a culture of cyber safety through education and empowerment is therefore a vital part of addressing the growing threats of Internet usage.

The fact that there are several role players in the cyber safety education of children is widely supported. These role players include (Kortjan & von Solms, 2013), (de Lange & von Solms, 2012), (Atkinson, Furnell, & Phippen, 2009), (Becta, 2009), (Miles, 2011):

- *Government.* Government should develop structures to adequately support cyber safety, establish and promote a cyber safety culture through support and funding toward research and education of cyber safety initiatives and encourage compliance with cyber safety standards.
- *Law enforcement.* Legislation relating to cybercrime toward children is critical to protect them against cyber-bullying, cyber-stalking, online harassment and so on.
- *Parents/guardians.* Parents or guardians have the most direct influence on children and play a vital role in cyber safety education and awareness, which includes education on safe and responsible usage, rules and assistance when using the Internet.
- *Schools.* Cyber safety strategies should be developed and implemented in schools.
- *Teachers.* Teachers should be knowledgeable in the field of cyber safety, act as advisors to children, deliver the cyber safety messages and act as observers in noticing changes in a child's behaviour.
- *Peers.* Peer mentoring is a very effective way of encouraging children to stay safe online. Encouragement, support and sharing of knowledge give children more confidence to practise safe online behaviour.

According to the Africa Child Online Protection Education and Awareness (ACOPEA) centre there is no concrete PAN-African child online protection education and awareness model in Africa (ACOPEA, 2012) and limited cyber security awareness and education initiatives in developing African countries (Kortjan & von Solms, 2013). A summary of selected African countries' cyber safety efforts toward education and awareness is shown in Table 1:

Country	National cyber safety awareness and education
Uganda	×
Sudan	×
Tunisia	√ (Cole, Chetty, Larosa, Rietta, Schmitt, & Goodman, 2008)
Rwanda	√ (Kanyesigye)
Egypt	×
Morocco	×
Kenya	×
Cameroon	×
Ghana	√ (Antwi-bekoe & Nimako, 2012)
Mauritius	√ (Dlamini, Taute, & Radebe, 2011)

Table 1: Cyber safety efforts by selected African countries

With the lack of comprehensive cyber safety initiatives in many African countries, the increase in Internet usage is not matched with sufficient education and awareness (Dlamini, Taute, & Radebe, 2011), (e4Africa, 2011). This greatly affects the manner and effectiveness in which the abovementioned role players can assist in creating a cyber aware culture.

During a discussion on cyber safety at the African Internet Governance Forum (AFIGF) in Nairobi in September 2013, it was stated that one of the best strategies for implementing cyber safety and combatting cybercrime in Africa is for African governments to introduce cyber safety curriculums in schools (Sato, 2013). In order to assist in cyber safety education and awareness in schools, this paper focuses on teaching cyber safety to primary school learners through resources freely available on the Internet.

4. The Problem of Cyber Safety in Schools

In addition to the lack of comprehensive cyber safety initiatives in many African countries, the education of primary school children is extremely difficult owing to a lack of expert knowledge, funding and resources. Teachers may be unaware of the threats associated with cyber space as they lack experience and knowledge themselves. Schools may also not have the available funding and resources to formulate and offer a cyber safety curriculum. In addition to limited resources, technology is constantly changing and with it comes new risks and solutions. Teachers may have trouble keeping up to date with the rapidly changing landscape of the online world, the associated cyber safety threats as well as the various methods to keep them safe (Atkinson, Furnell, & Phippen, 2009), (Miles, 2011). This presents a major obstacle for teachers as they have limited access to learning material and must keep pace with the changing technological advancements.

Even though schools and teachers are faced with the abovementioned challenges, they are often faced with scenarios where children are the victims of cyber threats. Therefore, it is vital for schools to equip children with the knowledge and skills they require in order to use the Internet safely and responsible.

One method that can assist schools and teachers with limited resources is open educational resources (OER). OER are teaching and learning materials that are freely available on the Internet. This educational material can include lectures, games, assignments, videos as well as full courses and modules. All of these educational resources are available to learners and teachers without the need to create accounts or to pay royalties or licence fees (Jisc, 2012), (OER_Africa, 2013).

The utilisation of OER by African schools and teachers can greatly assist in the acquisition of relevant, current learning material. By creating a basic cyber safety syllabus from material freely available online, teachers may be empowered to educate children on using cyber space safely. The advantages of using freely available educational material include the following:

- *Material is free.* No budget is needed by schools to access this material with the exception of data fees.
- *Material can be easily accessed.* By using videos posted on YouTube and other open platforms, teachers do not have to create accounts to view or use the material.

- *Material is developed for educational reasons*. There is no need for schools to develop their own curriculum.
- *Material is up to date*. The curriculum can be updated regularly to keep children aware if the latest cyber threats and solutions.
- *Material covers a range of subjects*. The wide variety of videos available enables teachers to educate children on a wide range of current subjects.
- *Material covers age ranges*. The available videos are designed for children of various ages.

In the following 2 sections, a methodology and basic cyber safety syllabus for primary school children are presented. This syllabus is assembled from publicly available videos on YouTube and other open platforms. This syllabus can form a baseline for the future development of a complete curriculum that can be added to dedicated OER websites. In this manner, more schools can obtain easy access to a much-needed, comprehensive cyber safety education curriculum.

5. Methodology

The objective of this paper is to identify a set of effective, self-explanatory, publicly available online resources that can be used by teachers in a class situation to spread the cyber safety message to their learners. It is also assumed that these teachers are not necessarily very knowledgeable in the field of cyber safety. For this reason the material proposed also needs to educate the teachers along with the learners. Therefore, it was decided to choose a set of online videos, all readily and publicly available, to form the core of the educational resources to be used in this proposed syllabus for cyber safety for primary school learners.

On 15 November 2013 the online video-sharing website, YouTube, was searched for various cyber safety related videos. On searching the word 'e-Safety', 141 million possibilities were identified. A search for the phrase 'e-Safety for children' produced 11 million videos and the phrase 'e-Safety for children cartoon' indicated that more than 1,8 million possible cartoon videos exist. Similar searches for phrases with 'cyber safety' and 'Internet safety' revealed similar high numbers of possible videos. See Table 2 for details.

	Safety	For children	Cartoons
e-	141 m	11 m	1,8 m
Cyber	2,1 m	305 k	285 k
Internet	19 m	2 m	244 k

Table 2: YouTube searches (15 November 2013)

As the target audience for this proposed syllabus for cyber safety is restricted to primary school children, aged 7 to 13, it was decided that cartoons should be utilised as far as possible as primary school learners are very attracted to cartoons. With this in mind, 47 possible videos were initially identified. It was also decided to use the knowledge and experience of a primary school teacher with 25 years of experience to conduct a content analysis to assist in analysing and classifying the videos. This teacher helped to analyse the contents of respective videos for suitability of use, which videos would be most suitable for which ages and which videos would have the most impact in stimulating a subsequent cyber safety discussion. At a later stage, the teacher was again used as an expert to assure that the proposed 'syllabus' was indeed usable in a typical African primary school, where Internet access was available.

The proposed methodology should ensure that a set of publicly available, online cartoon-based videos, with a clear message aimed at specific ages, forms a basic primary school syllabus that can be used in a class situation. It must be noted that the objective is not to establish a detailed syllabus with extensive lesson plans, workbooks, discussion topics, and so forth. The objective to develop a detailed syllabus is seen as future work.

6. The Video-based Syllabus for Cyber Safety for Primary School Learners

Having determined that primarily cartoon-based videos with a clear cyber safety message would be used, it was decided to analyse and categorise the 47 videos initially identified. It should again be noted that all of these videos are readily available on YouTube. Further, whilst analysing these videos, the Internet browsers, Google Chrome and Internet Explorer, did identify and suggest other possible sites for finding cyber safety related resources. One such suggestion subsequently identified a series of very popular cyber safety videos, that of Hector's World (Think_U_Know, 2008). These videos were thus also used.

All of these initially identified videos were watched, analysed and categorised with the aid of the experienced teacher. It was decided that the learners should be divided into three groups according to age, that is, 7 to 9 years of age, 10 to 12 years of age and 13 years and older. According to the experienced teacher, these are the age groups in which learners in general perform certain functions and activities online, for example, from 10 years and older, social networking and instant messaging become widely used.

The videos were categorised according to the age groups previously determined. In many cases a specific cyber safety topic is advocated by more than one video, like the message; 'Do not share your personal details.' In such cases, the videos were classified according to the most suitable age group. Most of the videos do reflect more than one cyber safety topic, but only the main topics were recorded. In Table 3, a list of cyber safety topics, the number of videos that portrayed those messages and the age groups for which such a cyber safety message is ideally suited, are reflected.

Safety topic	Number of videos	Applicable to age groups
Do not share personal information	11	7–13+
Be careful what you post online	6	10–13+
Do not be nasty to others online	1	7–13+
Choose a secure, strong password	1	10–13+
Online people are not always who you think	3	7–13+
If you feel uncomfortable, tell a responsible adult	8	7–13+
Games can be addictive	1	10–13+
Information posted online never disappears	5	10–13+
Be careful who you accept as friends	2	10–13+
A bad online profile can count against you	2	10–13+
Use privacy settings, e.g. with Facebook	3	10–13+
Cyber bullying	5	7–13+
Sexting	1	10–13+
Information spreads very fast online	1	10–13+

Table 3: Cyber safety topics

In many cases videos were part of a series of videos, and as such it is important that such a series of videos is kept and used together. Based on these assessments, three syllabus tables, one for each age group, were drafted. Each of these syllabus tables (Tables 4 to 6) reflect a lesson number, a main topic area or video focus and the URL of the video. It will be noted that videos that form a series are grouped together with the same numerical lesson value, but different alphabetical characters.

It is suggested that teachers spread these lessons over a period of six or even twelve months to periodically instil the required cyber safety lessons and messages. Following below are the tables showing the three syllabuses: Table 4 for 7 to 9 year olds, Table 5 for 10 to 12 year olds and Table 6 for learners of 13 years and older.

Children ages 7–9		
	Topic areas	**URL**
Lesson 1a	Basic cyber safety	*http://www.youtube.com/watch?v=-nMUbHuffO8*
Lesson 1b	Summary of Lesson 1a	*http://www.youtube.com/watch?v=vmqNg-7QrDk*
Lesson 2a	Sharing personal information	*http://www.youtube.com/watch?v=M-njh8mFvVk*
Lesson 2b	Summary of Lesson 2a	*http://www.youtube.com/watch?v=VhThfiQ7FRA*
Lesson 3	Hector's World 1	*http://www.thinkuknow.co.uk/5_7/hectorsworld/Episode1/*
Lesson 4	Hector's World 2	*http://www.thinkuknow.co.uk/5_7/hectorsworld/Episode2/*
Lesson 5	Hector's World 3	*http://www.thinkuknow.co.uk/5_7/hectorsworld/Episode3/*
Lesson 6	Hector's World 4	*http://www.thinkuknow.co.uk/5_7/hectorsworld/Episode4/*
Lesson 7	Hector's World 5	*http://www.thinkuknow.co.uk/5_7/hectorsworld/Episode5/*
Lesson 8	Hector's World 6	*http://www.thinkuknow.co.uk/5_7/hectorsworld/Episode6/*

Table 4: Syllabus for learners of 7 to 9 years of age

Children ages 10–12		
	Topic areas	**URL**
Lesson 1a	Phishing and viruses	*http://www.youtube.com/watch?v=svb6d55e29k*
Lesson 1b	Information on web not always true	*http://www.youtube.com/watch?v=GNf3OmUKWmk*
Lesson 1c	Sharing personal information	*http://www.youtube.com/watch?v=HiyqFwXnMZo*
Lesson 1d	Cyber bullying	*http://www.youtube.com/watch?v=ipD0IS4EUcI*
Lesson 1e	Summary of above	*http://www.youtube.com/watch?v=HI0US7LgGeQ*
Lesson 2a	Protect password	*http://www.youtube.com/watch?v=T0Q5b-pzhD8*
Lesson 2b	Do not open suspicious files	*http://www.youtube.com/watch?v=nlx4wRkssRo*
Lesson 2c	Beware of online friends	*http://www.youtube.com/watch?v=j88SddAk--I*
Lesson 2d	Tell a trusted adult	*http://www.youtube.com/watch?v=oXNsXKgJw0c*
Lesson 2e	Cyber safety rules	*http://www.youtube.com/watch?v=xp9H01BKL2Q*
Lesson 2f	Summary of above – Part 1	*http://www.youtube.com/watch?v=MDvhiwMwdO4*
Lesson 2g	Summary of above – Part 2	*http://www.youtube.com/watch?v=E3vVbAitTDY*
Lesson 3a	Accepting friend requests	*http://www.youtube.com/watch?v=KGr_KFiCX4s*
Lesson 3b	Privacy settings	*http://www.youtube.com/watch?v=-Dn1Jmqecvk*
Lesson 3c	Cyber bullying	*http://www.youtube.com/watch?v=elYv-pZVgvo*
Lesson 4a	Do not meet online friends in real life	*http://www.youtube.com/watch?v=gPse7dcXwrU*
Lesson 4b	Online game addiction	*http://www.youtube.com/watch?v=hGfjyDALM2Q*
Lesson 4c	Illegal downloads	*http://www.youtube.com/watch?v=N1xFUw3bW10*
Lesson 4d	Cyber bullying	*http://www.youtube.com/watch?v=RKi9FybL-Og*

Table 5: Syllabus for learners of 10 to 12 years of age

Children ages 13+		
	Topic areas	**URL**
Lesson 1a	Accepting friend requests	*http://www.youtube.com/watch?v=KGr_KFiCX4s*
Lesson 1b	Privacy settings	*http://www.youtube.com/watch?v=-Dn1Jmqecvk*
Lesson 1c	Cyber bullying	*http://www.youtube.com/watch?v=elYv-pZVgvo*
Lesson 2a	Online privacy	*http://www.youtube.com/watch?v=vYIfnjgn_eY*
Lesson 2b	Cyber bullying	*http://www.youtube.com/watch?v=Hfi8811ONSk*
Lesson 2c	Sharing of private information	*http://www.youtube.com/watch?v=vijhpQsxnQM*
Lesson 3	Think before you post information online	*http://www.youtube.com/watch?v=dT1GvPQG904 &list=PLB5E270C7C30E3079*
Lesson 4a	Safe social networking	*http://www.youtube.com/watch?v=Esj-PBmXjCU*
Lesson 4b	Cyber privacy	*http://www.youtube.com/watch?v=9bhHaVxo3i0*
Lesson 4c	Cyber bullying	*http://www.youtube.com/watch?v=xGKmlTtZnSk*
Lesson 4d	Online postings can haunt you in the future	*http://www.youtube.com/watch?v=V3DlVkOAPVQ*
Lesson 4e	Be careful of online friends	*http://www.youtube.com/watch?v=y4nyluaXoFY*
Lesson 5	Sexting	*http://www.youtube.com/watch?v=AL5Y6rJwTuQ*

Table 6: Syllabus for learners of 13 years and older

It should be noted that each of the three tables above reflect a number of publicly available online videos most suitable to the ages mentioned. The content and basic cyber safety message(s) of each of these videos are clear and self-explanatory. It is recommended that the teacher, before presenting the lesson to the class, look at the video and identify its main message. It would be easy to find more related information, from Google for example, on the topic to prepare the teacher for some discussion with the learners afterwards. It would be ideal if the video lesson were discussed as a group afterwards. A discussion will ensure that the cyber safety message is clearly understood by the learners and subsequently entrenched.

As mentioned earlier, no lesson plans or discussion questions are included in each of the lessons and the individual teachers will have to contextualise the message based on their individual circumstances. It was clearly not the objective of this paper to prepare a fully-fledged syllabus with lesson plans and associated learning and discussion material, but it should be noted that the Hector's World environment has a complete set of such material available, ready for the teachers to use (Think_U_Know, 2008). On the other hand, the authors and the expert teacher are of the opinion that the attached 'syllabus tables' can be used with much success in any classroom.

From a technical point of view, it is obviously important that the teacher is able to show the individual videos to the class using an Internet link, a computer and ideally a data projector with audio. If a computer facility is available, the children can watch the videos individually or in groups of two or three. None of these videos are longer than 10 minutes; therefore the time to stream them should be reasonable even if the Internet connection is fairly slow. It was also found that Google Chrome was the best browser for viewing the videos.

7. Conclusions

Cyber space is growing by the day. More and more services appear in cyber space every day and more and more people are becoming absolutely dependent on cyber space for entertainment, social networking, e-commerce, finding information etc. It is also known that, along with all these advantages of cyber space, a number of ever-increasing risks are present. For this reason it is important that the users of cyber space should be properly schooled in using these services in a secure and safe manner. Internationally, many governments are taking the lead or at least ensuring that some form of cyber safety or security training is conveyed to their general population, whether young or old, private or professional, as everybody needs to be cyber smart to protect themselves as well as commercial and governmental assets. Most countries envisage a cyber safe culture as the ultimate goal in this regard.

Although Africa in general is seen as a developing region, it is important to note that Africa is active in cyber space and similar cyber safety awareness and education programmes are just as applicable to Africa as to the rest of the world. It is also noted that very few African countries have really introduced organised and coordinated measures for ensuring such a cyber safe culture. In few schools in Africa such efforts are taking place.

Although everybody active in cyber space needs to be made aware of the risks and be educated on ways and means to protect themselves, this paper set out to address the specific needs of young, primary school learners. The objective of this paper was to identify some publicly available online resources, which can be used in a class situation by a teacher to educate and train young 7 to 13 year old learners. Three different 'syllabus tables' were prepared for three different age groups. Each of these syllabus tables present a set of videos with cyber safety related messages in a genre most applicable to that particular age group involved. Using these, teachers should be empowered to play an important role in preparing and equipping primary school learners for their activities in cyber space.

8. Acknowledgement

The input and contribution of Mrs Hester von Solms, an experienced teacher, is hereby acknowledged.

9. References

ACOPEA. (2012). "African Child Online Protection Education \& Awareness Centre," *available online from: http://www.cto.int/media/events/pst-ev/2013/CTO%20Forum/African%20Child%20Online%20Protection%20Education%20\&%20Awareness%20Centre.pdf, Accessed on [12 November 2013].*, 2012.

Antwi-bekoe, E., and Nimako, S.G. (2012). "Computer Security Awareness and Vulnerabilities : An Exploratory Study for Two Public Higher Institutions in Ghana," *Journal of Science and Technology*, vol. 1, pp. 358-375, 2012.

Atkinson, S., Furnell, S.M., and Phippen, A. (2009). "Securing the next generation: enhancing e-safety awareness among young people," *Computer Fraud \& Security* , vol. 2009, no. 7, pp. 13-19, 2009.

Becta. (2009). "AUPs in context: Establishing safe and responsible online behaviours," *available online from: http://education.qld.gov.au/studentservices/behaviour/qsaav/docs/establishing-safe-responsible-online-behaviours.pdf, Accessed on [10 November 2013].*, 2009.

Byron, T. (2008). "Safer Children in a Digital World," *available online from: http://webarchive.nationalarchives.gov.uk/20130401151715/https://www.education.gov.uk/publications/eOrderingDownload/DCSF-00334-2008.pdf, Accessed on [5 November 2013].*, 2008.

Cole, K., Chetty, M., Larosa, C., Rietta, F., Schmitt, D.K., and Goodman, S.E. (2008). "Cybersecurity in Africa : An Assessment," *available online from: http://s3.amazonaws.com/zanran_storage/www.cistp.gatech.edu/ContentPages/43945844.pdf, Accessed on [22 November 2013].*, 2008.

de Lange, M., von Solms, R. (2012). "An e-Safety Educational Framework in South Africa," *Proceesing of the Southern Africa Telecommunication Networks and Applications Conference (SATNAC)*, 2012.

Dlamini, I., Taute, B., and Radebe, J. (2011). "Framework for an African policy towards creating cyber security awareness," *Proceedings of Southern African Cyber Security Awareness Workshop (SACSAW)*, pp. 15-31, 2011.

e4Africa, "Technology in schools – for better or for worse," *available online from: http://www.e4africa.co.za/?p=3516, Accessed on [20 November 2013].*, 2011.

Grobler, M., and Dlamini, Z. (2012). "Global Cyber Trends a South African Reality," *IST-Africa 2012 Conference Proceedings*, 2012.

Jisc. (2012). "A guide to open educational resources," *available online from: http://www.jisc.ac.uk/publications/programmerelated/2013/Openeducationalresources.aspx Accessed on [20 November 2013].*, 2012.

Kanyesigye, F. (2013). "New drive to fight hackers, New Times," *available online from: http://www.newtimes.co.rw/news/index.php?a=66437&i=15343, Accessed on [22 November 2013].*, p. 2013.

Kortjan, N., and von Solms, R. (2013). "Cyber Security Education in Developing Countries: A South African Perspective," *Lecture Notes of the Institute for Computer Sciences, Social Informatics and Telecommunications Engineering*, vol. 119, pp. 289-297, 2013.

Kritzinger, E. (2011). "Cyber Awareness Implementation Plan (CAIP) for schools," *Presentation for Southern African Cyber Security Awareness Workshop (SACSAW)*, 2011.

Mars, M., and Erasmus, L. (2012) "Telemedicine can lower health care costs in Africa," *Innovate*, vol. 7, pp. 32-33, 2012.

Migrant. (2013). "M-PESA International Money Transfer Service, Safaricom," *available online from: http://www.ilo.org/dyn/migpractice/migmain.showPractice?p_lang=en\&p_practice_id=70, Accessed on [12 November 2013].*, 2013.

Miles, D. (2011). "Youth protection: Digital citizenship - Principles and new resources," in *Second Worldwide Cybersecurity Summit (WCS)*, 2011.

OER Africa. (2013). "Understanding OER," *available online from: http://www.oerafrica.org/understandingoer/UnderstandingOER/tabid/56/Default.aspx, Accessed on [20 November 2013].*, 2013.

PWC. (2012). "Telecoms in Africa: innovating and inspiring," *Communications Review*, 2012.

Reed, M. (2012). "Press release: Africa mobile subscriptions count to cross 750 million mark in fourth quarter of 2012," *Informa Telecoms \& Media*, 2012.

Safaricom. (2012). "iCow," *available online from: http://www.safaricom.co.ke/personal/value-added-services/social-innovation/icow, Accessed on [12 November 2013].*, 2012.

Safaricom. (2012). "Relax, you've got M-Pesa," *available online from:* *http://www.safaricom.co.ke/personal/m-pesa/m-pesa-services-tariffs/relax-you-have-got-m-pesa, Accessed on [12 November 2013].*, 2012.

Sato, N. (2013). "ICT stakeholders discuss emerging issues on African cyber security," *available online from: http://www.humanipo.com/news/32773/ict-stakeholders-discuss-emerging-issues-on-cyber-security, Accessed on [21 November 2013].*, 2013.

TeleGeography, "Africa's international bandwidth growth to lead the world," *TeleGeography: Global Bandwidth Forecast Service,* 2013.

Think U Know. (2013). "Welcome to Hector's World," *available online from: http://www.thinkuknow.co.uk/5_7/hectorsworld/, Accessed on [15 November 2013].*, 2008.

Users can't be Fooled – The Role of Existing vs. Fictitious Third Party Web Assurance Seals on Websites

N. Bär and J. Krems

Chemnitz University of Technology, Chemnitz, Germany
e-mail: {nina.baer; josef.krems}@psychologie.tu-chemnitz.de

Abstract

For secure online behaviour, individual attitudes like the users' trust in websites are just as important as technical security means. One possibility to accomplish trust in the web environment is the use of third party web assurance seals. Still, the effects of such security indicators are discussed controversially. Previous studies indicated that online users are vulnerable to visual deception; therefore might misleadingly place trust in insecure websites. In order to check the effectiveness of existing web assurance seals in comparison to fictitious graphical elements that could fool users, an online study (N = 131) was conducted. The participants had to estimate the trustworthiness of four different German websites which were equipped with either typical existing, fictitious or no web assurance seals. Results show that the existing seals provoked the highest level of users' trust while the fictitious seals did not yield any significant trust-promoting effects compared to the control group. However, qualitative feedback indicated that the users' knowledge about web assurance seals is rather unspecific which makes them vulnerable to manipulation.

Keywords

Web assurance seals, users' trust, user behaviour, website

1. Introduction

Security in online interactions is of major concern for users, website providers and governmental institutions. Implicitly, online users demand high security standards when they conduct any types of online business to prevent, e.g. unauthorized access to their personal information by unknown third parties, deception by phishing websites or similar. The possibility that negative consequences will arise from insecure online actions is both closely connected to the actual security provided on the website and the subjective evaluation of the situation by the user. Objective properties of the interface - like browser warnings, https identification or web assurance seals and certificates awarded by independent third parties - influence the subjective evaluation of the security on the website and can help to trigger the establishment of users' trust. Trust is an essential aspect for users' engagement in online actions (e.g. Bélanger and Carter, 2008; Beldad *et al.* 2010). It is defined as an "attitude that an agent will help to achieve an individual's goal in situations characterized by uncertainty and vulnerability." (Lee and See, 2004, p. 51). Depending on the perceptions during the interaction, a user might form the conviction that the interaction partner will support the user in achieving his or her goals. Mainly in transactional websites, when users are asked to disclose their

198

personal information or transfer money or any tangible objects, security ought to be of crucial importance for the achievement of the users' goals. To improve perceptions of security on transactional websites and therefore perceptions of trustworthiness, objective website elements like third party web assurance seals are used. Such security indicators should assure quality, serve as an independent recommendation and enhance trust. However, the effectiveness of such indicators is discussed controversially, as online users are vulnerable to visual deception (Dhamija *et al.* 2006). Therefore, users might even base their trust on spurious security indicators on websites. Considering the economic aspects of third party certification, the question if existing web assurance seals create higher users' trust than fictitious graphical web elements, is of particular relevance for website providers. Especially for small online shops or start ups it is crucial to know if expensive web assurance seals are effective in establishing a good reputation within their users. The aim of this study was to check if existing web assurance seals are effective when evaluating the trustworthiness of a website or if users can be fooled by any fictitious graphical elements. In an online study on different types of transactional websites, the effectiveness of existing web assurance seals in evoking users' trust was compared to fictitious web assurance seals as well as to a control condition without any security indicators.

2. Related work

Users are the key factor when it comes to online security. Especially young people – digital natives - feel secure and educated about e-safety risks (Atkinson *et al.* 2009). They even feel very confident in online security-related decisions although their subjective impression does not always correspond to the actual correctness of the decision. For instance, when differentiating phishing websites from real websites, participants were confident in their decisions, whether they were correct or incorrect (Dhamija *et al.* 2006). So, at a surface level users' confidence in online security issues appears to be high by all means. Looking closely at the users' awareness of online security threats and their resulting security practice, problems occur not only with novice users but also with those who consider themselves as experienced (Furnell *et al.* 2007). Even sophisticated users are not immune to attacks like visual deception (Dhamija *et al.* 2006). For everyday use and applicable for a large scale of online users, third party web assurance seals are one way of assuring certain standards in service and security. They can contribute to estimations of the trustworthiness of a website (e.g. Kim and Benbasat, 2010). However, only few users seem to check if the presented seals are genuine (Kimery and McCord, 2002). Recognition rates of third party web assurance seals are rather low, and even fictitious seals were recognized as familiar (Moores, 2005). Assuming that fictitious web assurance seals were mixed up with existing seals and the tendency of users to rely on the graphical image instead of the underlying certificate of approval, one could expect that fictitious seals might also induce users' trust. This would limit the meaning of third party web assurance seals as a way of generating trust in a website.

3. Method

The study was conducted in Germany as an online survey. Between three groups of participants the type of third party web assurance seals was manipulated. Participants were randomly assigned to one of the groups, facing four screenshots of different transactional website that either contained existing web assurance seals ('Existing Seals'), fictitious web assurance seals ('Fictitious Seals') or no trust inducing element that implied recommendations of third parties ('Control group'). In both experimental groups the manipulated third party web assurance seals were placed in the same spot where they had been in the original version of the website. In the control group the spot was not left blank but was covered by other elements of the website to keep a consistent design.

Participants. Of 149 people starting the online survey, N = 131 completed it and were included in the analysis. The sample consisted of 34 men and 97 women. All but one were psychology or sensor systems students of Chemnitz University of Technology, aged from 18 to 45 years (M = 22.2, SD = 4.1). All of them were well grounded in Internet use. 41% of the participants reported to have had bad experiences in the Internet, which have mostly been related to delivery problems of purchased products (no delivery or defect products delivered) and overlooked fees for website use. The most frequently used information to assess the trustworthiness of websites was recommendations of friends (87%). Another large proportion of 73% stated to use experience reports. Information by media was an important source of information for 53% of the participants, while ratings of previous users were relevant for 39%. Third party web assurance seals were the least frequently used trust cue (19%). The sample largely knew about the idea of web assurance seals to be awarded by independent third parties. However, about 20% of the participants stated to know nothing or only little about such seals. An equal proportion was aware of the limited meaning of assurance seals. The participants had also difficulties in recognizing third party web assurance seals. 55% of the sample recognized the fictitious 'Fairtrade' seal as an existing one and only 9% knew about the (existing) 'EHI' seal. The groups did not differ in control variables like system trust, propensity to trust, Internet usage habits or bad Internet experiences.

Material. In the online survey the participants saw four screenshots of websites where transactions or the disclosure of private data were requested: an online pharmacy, an online shop for electronic products, a travel website and a dating agency. Each of the websites contained at least one in Germany well-established third party web assurance seal in the original version. In the experiment, the original versions of the websites were equipped with only one existing assurance seal: the seal of 'Trusted Shops' or the 'TÜV' seal. Two of the four websites were equipped with the same seal, i.e. the participants saw each of the seals twice. The fictitious seals were designed using official-looking graphics such as a stamp of product testing, to ensure a certain plausibility of use. Still, they resembled the existing seals in appearance, form and size (Figure 1).

Figure 1: Existing (left) and fictitious seals (right)

Procedure. A 15 minutes online survey was implemented. In the beginning, participants were advised that this study was on security indicators. They were instructed to explore the screenshots and imagine a scenario where they were interested in what the single websites offered. After the presentation of the screenshot questions were asked if they noticed a third party web assurance seal on the website and for their intention to start a transaction at the website they had just seen. Then perceived trustworthiness and trusting intentions as well as system trust and propensity to trust were assessed using modifications of the Items of McKnight *et al.* (2002). At the end of the experiment general items on the user's knowledge about third party web assurance seals and their online habits were administered before demographical data was collected.

4. Results

To check for possible differences between the control and experimental group we analyzed the mean scores for perceived trustworthiness (Figure 2) and trusting intentions of those participants, who corresponded to the instruction and correctly identified the presence/ absence of the third party web assurance seals (N = 64). A two-way analysis of variance (ANOVA) for mixed designs revealed a significant main effect of the type of web assurance seals in trust scores (F (2,61) = 4.04, p = .022, η^2=.12) with a power of 91%. In post-hoc multiple comparisons the Bonferroni correction was used to reduce the chances of obtaining false-positive results when several statistical tests are being performed simultaneously on a single data set. A significant difference between the control group and the group that saw the existing third party web assurance seals was detected (p = .032). The ratings on perceived trustworthiness for the fictitious seals did not differ from both the other groups.

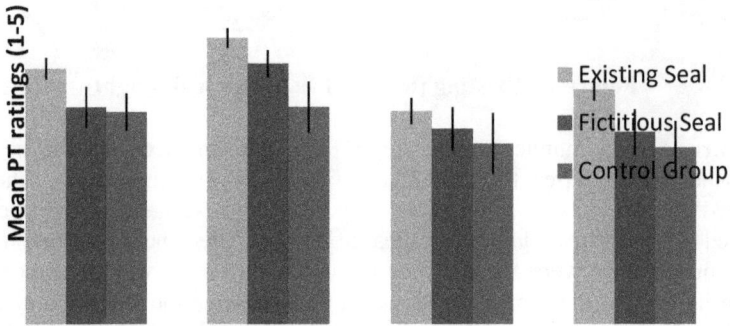

Figure 2: Mean scores in trust ratings (error bars indicate standard error)

Furthermore, a significant main effect of the type of website was found (F (3,183) = 13.24, p < .001, η^2=.18, power = 1.0). All websites differed significantly in their scores on perceived trustworthiness apart from the dating website compared to the travel website (pairwise comparison, Bonferroni-corrected, all p < .001). The dating agency obtained the lowest ratings while the online shop for electronic products scored highest. The results for trusting intentions confirm the pattern found for perceived trustworthiness only for main effect for the website (F (3,183) = 13.54, p < .001, η^2=.18). Except for the online pharmacy and the travel website all websites differed significantly from each other (pairwise comparisons, Bonferroni-corrected, all p < .007). There was no significant difference between the groups (F (2, 61) = 2.86, p = .065, η^2=.09, power = .80). The participants' intention to engage in a transaction at the websites did not differ between the experimental groups (F (2,61) = 2.95, p < .060, η^2=.09, power = .80) but for the websites (F (3,183) = 32.64, p < .001, η^2=.35, power = 1.0). The online pharmacy did not differ from the travel website while the intentions to engage in a transaction for all other websites differed significantly from each other (pairwise comparison, Bonferroni-corrected, all p < .001). For none of the variables a significant interaction between the two factors could be detected.

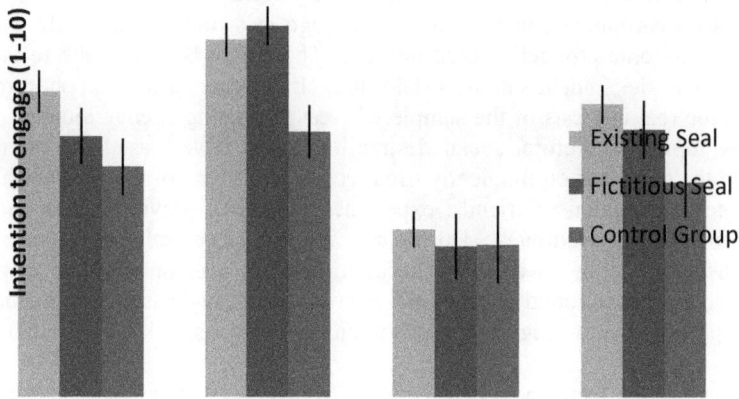

**Figure 3: Mean scores in intention to engage in a transaction (error bars
indicate standard error)**

5. Discussion

The existing seals induced significantly higher scores of perceived trustworthiness
than the websites in the control group without any seals of approval as security
indicators. This supports the general positive effect of third party web assurance
seals on perceived trustworthiness (e.g. Kim and Benbasat, 2010; Noteberg *et al.*
2003; Rifon *et al.* 2005). Fictitious seals did not yield any significant trust-
promoting effects even when they were explicitly noticed as web assurance seals
compared to the control group. The participants were instructed to pay attention to
security-inducing website elements to make sure they did not overlook the
manipulation. According to the Prominence-Interpretation Theory (Fogg, 2003) a
website feature has firstly to be perceived to be interpreted and potentially influence
appraisals of the website. Therefore only the data sets of participants who indicated
to have noticed a third party web assurance seal were included in the analysis. This
approach considerably reduced the sample size. Still, the calculated power was large
enough to detect the effects in spite of the small sample size. For the existing seals
the conscious perception did influence the ratings of perceived trustworthiness while
the fictitious seals did not. This finding is somehow encouraging. Still, the
participants were unsure in recognizing existing and fictitious seals of approval when
asked if a seal was familiar to them. The general idea of third party web assurance
seals was known by the majority of the participants while the knowledge appeared to
be unspecific ("Seals signal quality"). Only a few participants stated that the criteria
for awarding a third party seal are sometimes vaguely defined and seals are easily
manipulable. A little percentage of participants reported that they knew about the
possibility to check for the genuineness of seals of approval. For the trusting
intentions and the intention to engage in a transaction at a certain website the
different types of seals of approval did not make any difference. So, even when seals
of approval positively affect users' appraisals of a website the actual behaviour is

motivated by various factors and the influence of the trustworthiness of a website is limited. For all experimental groups, the dating agency obtained the lowest ratings of both trustworthiness and intentions to engage in a transaction, while the online shop for electronic products scored highest. This might be due to the relevance of both topics in the student sample's daily life. It is assumed that the shop might be close to the real interests of the sample whereas the dating agency touches a highly sensitive topic. Therefore, social desirability might have biased the ratings. As stated in the questions on frequently used recommendations of the trustworthiness of a website, the opinion of friends, experience reports of previous users and media reports are the preferred ones. Third party web assurance seals are considered only little when estimating a website. The importance of peer opinion and a website's reputation have been found to be crucial for website usage decisions even when users possess profound knowledge about information security risks (Kline *et al.* 2011).

In summary, the effectiveness of existing third party web assurance seals as security indicators in promoting trustworthiness on websites could be confirmed. However, the method used in this study entails certain limitations. The sample size was rather small and only a few websites were investigated. Therefore, the generalization of the results is limited. Still, the effects that were found were large enough to be detected, even with the number of participants. It is assumed, that a replication of this study with a larger sample size would strengthen the findings. The fact that the participants have almost exclusively been students should not be a disadvantage of the study, as students are typical Internet users. Furthermore, most studies on online users' trust report student samples, which makes the results comparable to previous studies. Further studies on the effectiveness of web assurance seals could extend to samples with different demographics. Then, the experimental surrounding could be complemented by a field study to gain a higher real-life correspondence.

6. Conclusion

In summary, third party web assurance seals have a positive effect on perceived trustworthiness compared to no seals used. Fictitious seals do not obtain any trust-promoting effects compared to websites without such graphical elements. This supports the system of third party approval. For website providers who want to improve their reputation and communicate trust cues to their users, third party web assurance seals seem appropriate. Still, the users reported to have difficulties in differentiating between existing and fictitious seals. That circumstance makes them vulnerable to manipulation. To prevent manipulation of third party web assurance seals, more transparent information about third party approval is needed.

7. References

Atkinson, S., Furnell, S., & Phippen, A. (2009). Securing the next generation: enhancing e-safety awareness among young people. *Computer Fraud & Security, 2009*(7), 13–19. doi:10.1016/S1361-3723(09)70088-0

Bélanger, F., & Carter, L. (2008). Trust and risk in e-government adoption. *The Journal of Strategic Information Systems, 17*(2), 165–176. doi:10.1016/j.jsis.2007.12.002

Beldad, A., de Jong, M., & Steehouder, M. (2010). How shall I trust the faceless and the intangible? A literature review on the antecedents of online trust. *Computers in Human Behavior, 26*(5), 857–869. doi:10.1016/j.chb.2010.03.013

Dhamija, R., Tygar, J. D., & Hearst, M. (2006). Why phishing works. In *Proceedings of the SIGCHI conference on Human Factors in computing systems* (pp. 581-590).

Fogg, B. J. (2003). Prominence-interpretation theory: Explaining how people assess credibility online. In *CHI'03 extended abstracts on Human factors in computing systems* (pp. 722–723).

Furnell, S. M., Bryant, P., & Phippen, A. D. (2007). Assessing the security perceptions of personal Internet users. *Computers & Security, 26*(5), 410–417. doi:10.1016/j.cose.2007.03.001

Kim, D., & Benbasat, I. (2010). Designs for effective implementation of trust assurances in internet stores. *Communications Of The ACM, 53*(2), 121-126.

Kimery, K. M. & McCord, M. (2002). Third Party Assurances: Mapping the Road to Trust in eRetailing. *Journal of Information Technology Theory and Application* 4(2).

Kline, D., He, L., & Yaylacicegi, U. (2011). User perceptions of security technologies. *International Journal of Information Security and Privacy, 5*(2), 1-12

Lee, J. D., & See, K. A. (2004). Trust in automation: Designing for appropriate reliance. *Human Factors, 46*(1), 50–80.

McKnight, D. H., Choudhury, V., & Kacmar, C. (2002). Developing and validating trust measures for e-commerce: An integrative typology. *Information Systems Research, 13*(3), 334–359. doi:10.1287/isre.13.3.334.81

Moores, T. (2005). Do consumers understand the role of privacy seals in e-commerce? *Communication of the ACM, 48*(3), 86–91.

Noteberg, A., Christiaanse, E., & Wallage, P. (2003). Consumer trust in electronic channels: the impact of electronic commerce assurance on consumers' purchasing likelihood and risk perceptions. *E-service Journal, 2*(2), 46-67.

Rifon, N. J., LaRose, R., & Choi, S. (2005). Your privacy is sealed: effects of web privacy seals on trust and personal disclosures. *Journal of Consumer Affairs, 39*(2), 339-362.

Exploring the Human Dimension in the Beneficiary Institutions of the SANReN Network

Y. Mjikeliso, J.F. Van Niekerk and K.L. Thomson

Institute for ICT Advancement, Port Elizabeth, South Africa
e-mail: {s209039445@; Johan.vanniekerk; Kerry-lynn.thomson}@nmmu.ac.za

Abstract

One of the factors that play a major role in information security is people. People are the drivers of most processes and procedures in information security. However, many researchers agree that human aspects are not given enough attention; more focus is given to the technical security. This is especially true in the security of the underlying network infrastructure which is often seen as a technical issue and not a human issue. It is senseless to have good solid technical security without considering humans because most security breaches are caused by human mistakes. Regardless of all the technical and physical controls implemented for network security, which underpins information security, there will always be human vulnerabilities to the security of the network. Therefore, attention should be given to the human factors as it is widely acknowledged as the biggest vulnerability in network security, which impacts on information security. In South Africa there is an important network infrastructure known as the South African National Research Network (SANReN) which provides vitally important Internet access to research and educational facilities throughout South Africa. The SANReN network has the potential to provide many opportunities and benefits to the people of South Africa. It is therefore extremely important that the SANReN network is highly secured at all times in order to ensure continued availability of the network. This paper will focus on human factors that could affect the security of the SANReN beneficiary networks. Policies governing the use of the SANReN network will be investigated in order to establish whether human factors, which could pose security risks to the SANReN network, have been addressed in the policies.

Keywords

Human Factors, SANReN Beneficiary Networks, Policies

1. Introduction

The management of information security depends on technology, processes and people. However, more emphasis is often placed on strengthening the technological aspects and processes, while less attention is given to the human aspects (Ashenden, 2008). Even security surveys commonly acknowledge that the human aspects, such as policy, training and education, are more likely to be given less attention than the technical controls, such as firewalls, antivirus and intrusion detection (Furnell & Clarke, 2012). Regardless of all the technical and physical controls implemented for network security, which underpins information security, there will always be human vulnerabilities to the security of the network. Information security is about the protection of information and its critical characteristics (confidentiality, integrity, availability), as well as the systems and hardware that use, store and transit that

206

information (Whitman & Mattord, 2011). Network security is one underlying component of information security without which it may be difficult to achieve information security. This paper will firstly determine whether human factors are considered or addressed in the security of the SANReN beneficiary networks. The paper presents content analysis of the existing policies used to govern the SANReN network, in order to determine whether human factors which could affect the security of the SANReN network have been addressed in the policies.

2. Methodology

The paper utilises a combination of content analysis of policies, as well as interviews with SANReN network engineers and a network administrator from one of the SANReN beneficiary institutions. All current policies governing the SANReN network were gathered by collecting documents from the TENET (discussed in Section 2.2) website, through email correspondence with SANReN personnel, as well as through interviews with network administrators at beneficiary institutions. The main focus of the content analysis of the policies was to identify whether or not human factors or human aspect issues were currently being addressed within the SANReN policies.

3. NREN

A National Research and Education Network (NREN) is a specialised Internet service provider for the research and educational communities within a country (TERENA, 2010). It provides research institutions and educational institutions with services and access to the Internet. Other than just providing connectivity to the Internet, the NREN should also provide a number of important services such as a Network Operations Centre, performance monitoring and management, incident response (TERENA, 2009). The way in which the NRENs are managed from country to country differs, as the organizational and ownership model for each NREN varies (TERENA, 2010).

3.1. SANReN

SANReN is a high speed communication network that is designed primarily for research institutions and organizations. The main purpose of the SANReN network is to provide the South African research institutions and organizations with Internet access and related services, as well as connecting them to research networks all over the world. The SANReN network together with the Centre for High Performance Computing (CHPC) and Very Large Databases (VLDB) create the key components of the cyber infrastructure in South Africa (Meraka Institute, 2007). The major role players of the SANReN network are:

- Department of Science and Technology (DST)
- Council for Science and Industrial Research (CSIR) Meraka Institute
- Tertiary Education and Research Network of South Africa (TENET)
- SANReN beneficiary institutions

The SANReN network is a South African DST project, implemented by the CSIR through the Meraka Institute (Meraka Institute, 2007). The project is part of the South African government's approach to cyber infrastructure to ensure the successful participation of South African researchers in global knowledge (SANReN, 2014). The CSIR is the governing body of the SANReN network and the operational services of the SANReN network to all beneficiary institutions is provided by TENET on behalf of the CSIR (SANReN, 2014). A *beneficiary institution* is an institution that is defined by the DST as institutions that are allowed to be connected to the SANReN network. These beneficiary institutions are the current TENET institutions, such as universities and research councils (SANReN, 2014). The following subsection will provide more detail on TENET which is one of the SANReN role players.

3.2. TENET

TENET is a specialized ISP for higher education and research sector, which provides Research and Education Networking services "REN services" like Internet and related services to about 160 campuses of 54 institutions, including universities, research councils and other associated institutions (UbuntuNet Alliance, n.d.). All the public universities and science councils in South Africa qualify to be a part, or a member, of the TENET network (Martin, 2012). The South African NREN is formed by SANReN together with TENET. The roles and responsibility of the South African NREN (SANReN) are given to both the SANReN team and to the TENET team. The SANReN team build the network and the TENET team operates the network (Martin, 2012). The following subsection will focus on how the SANReN network is being rolled out.

3.3. SANReN Network Implementation

The SANReN project is being rolled out in a phased manner and will eventually connect up to 204 sites across South Africa, and connecting over 3 000 education and research organizations from all over the world (SANReN, 2014). The South African universities, research councils such as the CSIR, National Research Foundation (NRF) , and various other research institutes are the beneficiary institutions of SANReN (SANReN, 2014). These beneficiary institutions form the SANReN national network backbone. The SANReN network backbone consists of a 10Gpbs 7-stretch backbone ring between the South African major cities. The SANReN Point of Presences (PoPs), are placed in all the connected institutions. The rolling-out of SANReN is still progressing to other beneficiary institutions and will eventually also connect remote towns (Martin, 2012). SANReN has the potential to provide many opportunities and benefits to the people of South Africa. Rural areas will have increased accessibility to the Internet, which could help in addressing the digital divide (SANReN, 2012). The SANReN network is one of the cyber infrastructures attempting to close the digital gap between those who have access to the Internet and those who do not have, and will connect a wide variety of people. Therefore, it is important that the SANReN network is secured at all times in order to ensure the continued availability of the network.

4. Securing the SANReN Network

Many NRENs have Computer Security Incident Response Teams (CSIRTs) in place in order to respond to security incidents of the network (Moller, 2007). As a result, the SANReN team is also in the process of establishing a SANReN / TENET CSIRT team which will be responsible for managing the security incidents of the SANReN network. CSIRT is a team of people who are responsible for receiving and responding to network security incident reports and activities (Mooi, 2013). The need for the SANReN / TENET CSIRT was identified through a survey conducted in May 2012 (Mooi, 2012a). The survey was sent out to all the beneficiary institutions of the SANReN network. The purpose of the survey was to investigate whether the beneficiary institutions would be interested in an incident response team, as there is no central point, or a central managing party, for incident handling on the SANReN network at present. The TENET NOC (Network Operations Centre) is responsible for incident handling. However, there may be restricted resources and the TENET team may lack effectiveness since they may be the only ones responsible for incident handling (Mooi, 2012a). When the SANReN / TENET CSIRT team is established it will be responsible for protecting against all types of malicious activities on the SANReN network such as; spam, denial of service attacks or hacking attempts. Their responsibility will be to receive, review and respond to the network security incidents (Mooi, 2012b). From a technical point of view, the SANReN network may be more secure as a result of the SANReN / TENET CSIRT team. However technical controls should not be the only concern for addressing security on the SANReN network – human factors should also be of concern, as will be discussed in section 4. The SANReN network may be vulnerable to risks posed by human factors even if technological controls exist on the network.

5. Human Factors on the SANReN Network

"Don't rely on network safeguards and firewalls to protect your information. Look to your most vulnerable spot. You'll usually find that vulnerability lies in your people" (Mitnick & Simon, 2002). There are technical solutions for solving what is seen as a technical issue. However, having technical solutions can create a false perception of security. Even though technical security is very important and without it networks would be vulnerable, there is still a vulnerability that remains because of negligence and the malicious acts of human beings. Negligence, ignorance, anger or even curiosity are human elements which can increase security incidents (PricewaterhouseCoopers, 2010). Human beings are a more challenging problem to address because there is no easy way to target them; there are no product-based solutions for people, unlike technical solutions (Furnell & Clarke, 2012).

Many researchers agree that human factors are one of the most significant vulnerabilities in information security and are often overlooked in organizations (Thomson & von Solms, 2006; Kraemer & Carayon, 2007). People are said to be the greatest threat to information security, and are often the 'point of failure', whether intentionally or through negligence or a lack of knowledge. However, people could represent the key element in achieving security (van Niekerk & von Solms, 2010;

Furnell & Clarke, 2012).Human factors play a role on the SANReN network just like in any other network. The rolling out of the SANReN network has started for various beneficiary institutions and a number of people have been involved with this project. There are people involved in configuring the network devices, creating policies and using the network as end-users. It is important to understand that, by nature, people have limited attention and accuracy - they make mistakes and errors (Ashton, 2009). Therefore, SANReN must properly address the human vulnerabilities. The mistakes and errors that people make could result in security vulnerabilities (Kraemer, Carayon, & Clem, 2009). The greatest vulnerability to the security of the SANReN network may be the people that the network connects or the employees.

An interview was conducted with one of the network administrators at the Nelson Mandela Metropolitan University (NMMU), which is a beneficiary institution of the SANReN network. The interview was conducted in order to identify whether issues related to human factors could pose security risks to the SANReN network. The network administrator was completely certain and confident about the technical and physical security of SANReN network. "We believe that the management of SANReN is being done by some of the best IT professionals in South Africa, so in my opinion, I believe that the network configuration is as secure as necessary". According to the network administrator, the beneficiary institutions host the network devices and the TENET team remotely accesses the devices or sends someone from SANReN / TENET when they need to make configuration changes on the network devices. There are no people working for SANReN / TENET at the beneficiary institutions and the connected institutions have no management or configuration access to the SANReN networking devices. However, the network administrator also mentioned an incident where on one or two occasions the SANReN network administrators from TENET managed to lock themselves out of the remote configuration session. They required local assistance from IT staff at the NMMU and the local IT staff had to make the configuration changes to the network device of SANReN. The fact that the TENET people were able to lock themselves out of the configuration session indicates there was a human mistake or error. Therefore, through this human error, members of the local IT staff at the NMMU were given access to network devices that they should not usually have access to. From this incident it could be implied that even though the network might be seen as technically and physically secured, human factors could be the weakest link in the security of the SANReN network.

For example, here in South Africa there are institutions from disadvantaged areas which might lack highly trained IT professionals. What if a low-level skilled individual was asked to perform these changes on the SANReN network devices and ended up misconfiguring the devices creating more problems on the network? Having been granted access to the networking devices and, for example, knowingly or unknowingly connecting a device which contains viruses and worms which may be distributed throughout the network could have a severe impact on network security. Therefore, the SANReN / TENET network may be exposed to many security risks by allowing access to the wrong individuals. SANReN / TENET are not aware of how skilled or qualified the individuals are that they are giving access to the network. This may present a good opportunity for an insider threat to manifest. An insider threat poses a security risk to the network because of the legitimate access to facilities, information, and knowledge of an organization and the location of valuable assets (Williams, 2008).

Another possible threat would be to apply a security related patch to incorrect software or failure to secure the correct port making it a target for network attackers. Most network attackers usually start by looking for vulnerabilities or weaknesses of the individual or computer they can communicate with on the network targeted. Many software packages will never be free of vulnerabilities because of human errors (Grobler & Bryk, 2010). Any network will have some level of vulnerabilities as it is impossible to completely eliminate vulnerabilities (Ritchey & Ammann, 2000). It is, therefore, very important that networks such as SANReN properly address the vulnerability of human factors. In other words, their end-users and IT staff must know their roles and responsibilities and adhere to correct behaviour to protect the network. In order for people to adhere to correct behaviour there must be organizational policies from management dictating the appropriate behaviour of the employees (von Solms & von Solms, 2004). As mentioned previously, information security, to a large extent, relies on the security of the underlying infrastructure or network. The management direction, rules, regulations and procedures regarding the protection of information assets must be part of an information security policy. In order to change or influence the behaviours of people in an organization the information security policy and procedures must be properly communicated to all parties, such as employees of the organization and business partners (von Solms & von Solms, 2004). Employees of an organization would, of course, include IT staff. People could be the greatest threat to information security, and the related network security especially if policies, education, training and awareness are not properly utilized to prevent people from accidentally or intentionally posing risks to the security of network (Whitman & Mattord, 2011). Vulnerabilities may come from employees who do not comply with information security policies (Siponen, Mahmood, & Pahnila, 2014). Therefore, it is important that organizations like SANReN have policies in place in order to dictate the appropriate employee behaviour and better control what people can and cannot do on the network or network devices.

An investigation into the existing policies which manage the use of the SANReN network was conducted. The authors consulted appropriate people from SANReN concerning the current policies between SANReN and the SANReN beneficiary institutions. The authors were directed to the TENET website where the policies between SANReN and the beneficiary institutions were located. From the policies the authors were specifically looking for the operational roles and responsibilities of people in the SANReN network. The following questions were used to focus the content analysis of the TENET policies:

1. Who is allowed to have physical access to the SANReN devices of the beneficiary institutions?
2. Who can configure SANReN devices in the beneficiary institutions?

3. What minimum skills or qualifications should the people who configure SANReN devices in the beneficiary institutions have?
4. Are there training programs or some form of education that is given to the beneficiary institutions connected to the SANReN network?

The following policies were examined in order to determine whether human related issues regarding the previous questions have been addressed in the TENET policies. These policies were the only ones that existed on the website and according to the people of SANReN these policies are the only ones in existence that currently govern the use of the SANReN network: Acceptable Use Policy (AUP), Connection Policy and Privacy Policy. All these policies are created by TENET as it is the operating entity of the SANReN network. These policies are to the authors' knowledge the only ones that manage the use of the SANReN network. An analysis of these three policies was done in order to identify whether human factors are addressed in the policies and will be discussed in the following subsections.

5.1. Acceptable Use Policy (AUP)

The purpose of the TENET AUP is to outline for the SANREN beneficiary institutions the things allowed and not allowed on the network. It defines rules and responsibilities of the SANReN beneficiaries or participating institutions. According to the TENET AUP the beneficiary institutions are allowed to use the REN services for any legal activity which furthers the goals and aims of the institution, and only if their activity does not include any unacceptable uses. If the beneficiary institution does what is unacceptable on the network, the provision of the REN services may be discontinued by TENET. A few of the unacceptable uses of the REN services that are listed on TENET AUP are:

"Any attempt to use the REN services in a way that breaches or would breach the security of another user's account or that gains or would gain access to any other person's computer, software, or data or otherwise threaten another person's privacy, without the knowledge and consent of such person"

"Any failure to secure a server that is connected via the REN services to the Internet against being abused by third parties as an open relay or open proxy"

"Any effort to use the REN services in a way that circumvents or would circumvent the user authentication or security of any host, network account ("cracking or hacking")"

These are some of the unacceptable uses of the REN services which are listed in the TENET AUP. With regard to the questions posed previously, the TENET AUP stated nothing regarding physical access to SANReN devices in beneficiary institutions. Nothing was stated regarding people who are allowed to configure the SANReN devices. There was nothing stated about the level of skills or qualifications of people configuring SANReN devices in the beneficiary institutions and there was nothing mentioned regarding any form of training program which may be provided to beneficiary institutions by SANReN / TENET.

5.2. Connection Policy

The Connection Policy lists all types of connections which are available when connecting a Research and Education Network (REN). This policy specifies the differences, rules and responsibility of each connection. The REN network connection types are; direct on-site connection, direct PoP connection and indirect connection. The direct on-site connection is a type of connection which is under TENET operational management where the hand-off location is at the connecting site not the connecting party (beneficiary institutions). Hand-off location is the point where operational responsibility changes between the beneficiary institution and TENET (TENET, 2014). For the direct PoP connection the hand-off location is at the Point of Presence and TENET does not operate the terminating equipment at the connecting site and does not operate the access circuit between the connecting site and PoP. The institutions which have direct connection can then provide an indirect connection to other smaller research and education organizations around them. Places such as education and training colleges, schools and public museums can connect to the beneficiary institution's direct connection in order to access the REN services. However, the indirect connection is the responsibility of the SANReN beneficiary institution that connects it not of TENET. With regard to the questions previously posed, the TENET Connection Policy does not mention anything regarding physical access to SANReN devices in beneficiary institutions and nothing was mentioned about configuring devices. There was nothing stated about the level of skills or qualifications of people configuring SANReN devices in the beneficiary institutions and there was nothing mentioned regarding any form of training program which may be provided to beneficiary institutions by SANReN / TENET.

5.3. Privacy Policy

The TENET Privacy Policy explains how the personal information which TENET collects from TENETs contacts is used. TENET contacts are the people who work with TENET, such as the representatives of the beneficiary institutions, suppliers and other contractors (TENET, 2014). The TENET Privacy Policy states that TENET respects the privacy of its contacts and will protect the confidentiality of the contacts' personal information. With regard to the questions previously posed, the TENET Privacy Policy does not state anything regarding the physical access to SANReN devices in beneficiary institutions and nothing was mentioned regarding people who are allowed to configure devices. There was nothing stated regarding the level of skills or qualification of people configuring SANReN devices in the beneficiary institutions and there was nothing mentioned regarding any form of training program which may be provided to the beneficiary institutions by SANReN / TENET.

After conducting the analysis of the TENET policies, it can be noted that the AUP, Connection Policy and the Privacy Policy do not adequately address the human factors which might pose risks to the security of the SANReN network. None of the policies state the operational roles, responsibilities and procedures on the SANReN network. There was no documented framework that deals with security vulnerabilities posed by the human factors on the SANReN network and no clear guidelines and procedures concerning things like access control and authorisation. There was nothing mentioned about accessing the network devices nor about locking the doors or monitoring the room where these devices are placed. In other words, there were no direct rules and responsibilities or operational procedures addressed in these policies. If there are no proper procedures which people can abide by, the security of the network may be at risk. It may make it easier for unauthorized individual to gain access to the devices and, intentionally or unintentionally misconfigure network devices. Once an unauthorized person gains access to the devices even the technical solutions will not help in protecting the network. It is, therefore, very important that a security policy addressing operational concerns, for example, an operational security policy is put in place in the SANReN network and enforced in all the beneficiary institutions. Policies which outline the responsibilities and roles of people in the beneficiary institutions should be in place to better secure and manage the SANReN network. There is definitely a need for a formalized approach such as a framework or guidelines for addressing human related behaviour on the SANReN network.

6. Conclusion

This paper examined the existing policies which govern the use of the SANReN network. The TENET policies were examined to determine whether the issues of human factors, which could threaten the security of the SANReN network, were adequately addressed. The paper outlined that there were no current policies which address human factors on the SANReN network. Therefore a formalized approach to addressing human factors in the SANReN network is recommended as human factors could be the greatest risk to the security of the network. Just as there are formal policies in place to govern the use of technical controls, there should also be formalized policies in place to address human factors in order to strengthen the security of the SANReN network. Formal documents, such as an operational security policy, outlining the roles and the responsibilities of people involved in governing the SANReN network should be created and enforced in the SANReN beneficiary institutions. These policies should address all possible human related security concerns, ranging from Bring Your Own Device (BYOD) policies to security awareness and training. Future research would include creating a framework or guidelines which will address human factors in the SANReN network. The framework or guidelines could address issues such as the identification of role players and their responsibilities, determination of skills and the provision of a formalized training program to the beneficiary institutions.

7. References

Ashenden, D. (2008). Information Security management: A human challenge?, *13*(4), 195–201.

Ashton, K. (2009). That'Internet of Things'Thing. *RFID*. Retrieved from http://www.rfidjournal.com/articles/view?4986

Furnell, S., & Clarke, N. (2012). Power to the people? The evolving recognition of human aspects of security. *Computers & Security, 31*(8), 983–988. doi:10.1016/j.cose.2012.08.004

Grobler, M., & Bryk, H. (2010). Common Challenges Faced During the Establishment of a CSIRT. *IEEE*, 2–7.

Kraemer, S., & Carayon, P. (2007). Human errors and violations in computer and information security: the viewpoint of network administrators and security specialists., *38*(2), 143–54.

Kraemer, S., Carayon, P., & Clem, J. (2009). Human and organizational factors in computer and information security: Pathways to vulnerabilities. *Computers & Security, 28*(7), 509–520. doi:10.1016/j.cose.2009.04.006

Martin, D. (2012). *Tertiary Education and Research Network of South Africa NPC* (pp. 1–4). Retrieved from http://www.tenet.ac.za

Meraka Institute. (2007). African Advanced Institute for Information and Communication Technology. Retrieved from http://www.meraka.org.za/Faqs

Mitnick, K. D., & Simon, W. L. (2002). *The Art of Deception.* (C. Long, N. Stevenson, & J. Atkins, Eds.). Robert Ipsen.

Moller, K. (2007). Setting up a Grid-CERT : experiences of an academic CSIRT, *24*. doi:10.1108/10650740710834644

Mooi, R. (2012a). *Security Incident Response for the South African NREN* (p. 9). Retrieved from   http://www.sanren.ac.za/wp-content/uploads/2012/11/IRT_background_survey_problem_SANReN.pdf

Mooi, R. (2012b). *Introduction to CSIRTs* (p. 5). Retrieved from http://www.sanren.ac.za/wp-content/uploads/2012/11/SANReN_CSIRT_Introduction.pdf

Mooi, R. (2013). *SA NREN CSIRC Model* (p. 14). Retrieved from http://www.sanren.ac.za/wp-content/uploads/2013/05/SA_NREN_CSIRC_Model-Published.pdf

Networking in South Africa.pdf. (n.d.).

PricewaterhouseCoopers. (2010). *Protecting your business. Veterinary Record* (Vol. 122). doi:10.1136/vr.122.17.421

Ritchey, R. W., & Ammann, P. (2000). Using Model Checking to Analyze Network Vulnerabilities. *IEEE*.

SANReN. (2012). *About SANReN* (pp. 1–11).

SANReN. (2014). SANReN Overview. Retrieved April 10, 2013, from http://www.sanren.ac.za/overview

Siponen, M., Mahmood, A., & Pahnila, S. (2014). Employees' adherence to information security policies: An exploratory field study. *Information & Management, 51*(2), 217–224. doi:10.1016/j.im.2013.08.006

TENET. (2014). TENET Standard Terms and Conditions. Retrieved January 22, 2014, from http://www.tenet.ac.za

TERENA. (2009). *TERENA COMPENDIUM*. Retrieved from www.terena.org/compendium

TERENA. (2010). Research and education networking FAQ. Retrieved from http://www.terena.org/activities/

TERENA. (2013). *TERENA COMPENDIUM*.

Thomson, K. L., & Von Solms, R. (2006). Towards an Information Security Competence Maturity Model. *Computer Fraud & Security*, 11–15.

UbuntuNet Alliance. (n.d.). TENET South Afrca. Retrieved from www.ubuntunet.net

UbuntuNet Alliance. (2013). *What is UbuntuNet?* Retrieved from www.ubuntunet.net

Van Niekerk, J. F., & Von Solms, R. (2010). Information security culture: A management perspective, *29*(4), 476–486.

Von Solms, R., & Von Solms, B. (2004). From policies to culture. *Computers & Security*, *23*(4), 275–279. doi:10.1016/j.cose.2004.01.013

Whitman, M., & Mattord, H. (2011). *Principles of Information Security*.

Williams, P. A. H. (2008). In a "trusting" environment, everyone is responsible for information security, *13*(4), 207–215.

Human Aspects of Information Assurance: A Questionnaire-based Quantitative Approach to Assessment

E.D. Frangopoulos[1], M.M. Eloff[2] and L.M. Venter[3]

[1] School of Computing, University of South Africa (UNISA), Pretoria, South Africa
[2] Institute for Corporate Citizenship, University of South Africa (UNISA), Pretoria, South Africa
[3] Institutional Director: Research Support and Extraordinary Professor: Computer Science and Information Systems, North-West University, Potchefstroom, South Africa
e-mail: vfrangopoulos@hol.gr; mmeloff@unisa.ac.za; lucas.venter@nwu.ac.za

Abstract

In work previously done by the authors, various human aspects of Information Assurance were identified. These comprise Social and Psychological aspects, the effects of Psycho-social risk at the workplace, the application of Influence techniques, user response to Social Engineering Methods and choices based on Economic considerations. Even though these aspects have been shown to gravely affect Information Assurance, the current level of their incorporation in the Plan-Do-Check-Act virtuous cycle of Information Security Management Systems, leaves a lot to be desired. In order to combine the findings of previous research and effectively provide quantified input that is usable in the context of an Information Security Management System (ISMS), an appropriate methodology must be introduced. This paper sets the framework and constraints for the methodology and by examining the merits and shortcomings of existing work in the field, proposes a questionnaire-based quantitative methodology that meets the set requirements. This will ultimately provide a tool for rapid, consistent and repeatable assessment of the Information Assurance level, as this is affected by the identified human aspects of Information Assurance.

Keywords

Information Assurance Assessment Tool, Questionnaire, Information Security, Quantitative vs, Qualitative, Human Aspects of Information Assurance, PDCA, ISMS, InfoSec.

1. Introduction

In the Information Security and Assurance literature it has been long established (Schneier, 2000) that the human factor is a most important component of Information Security / Assurance, perhaps even more important than the technical measures taken against threats that affect Information Assurance (IA). Even though methodologies exist that allow academics and professionals to assess the level of information-related risk in information systems in particular and information-processing organisational structures in general, it is still difficult to integrate the human factor in the Deming (or Plan-Do-Check-Act) virtuous cycle (Deming, 1986) of an effective Information Security Management System (ISMS).

In previous work, several areas of non-technical, human aspects of IA such as Social and Psychological aspects, the effects of Psycho-social risk at the workplace, Influence techniques, Social Engineering Methods and most recently, human choices that affect IA and are based on Economic considerations, as a potential source of risk per se, were identified (Frangopoulos, Eloff & Venter, 2008; 2010; 2012; 2014).

The obvious question arising from this research is how to efficiently incorporate these vague aspects (compared to the more easily quantifiable technical issues and measures) in the IA assessment process for a given information system or an information-processing organisational structure.

Due to the human nature of these IA aspects, there is none better equipped to provide the information necessary for an assessment, than these who constitute the human element of the information system/structure themselves. To this end, information-gathering approaches that are based on focus groups, individual interviews, questionnaire distribution etc, can be directed towards the people in the organisational structure under examination, whose actions affect the IA posture of the structure.

The aim of this paper is to describe the advantages of a questionnaire-based methodology and discuss its framework and constraints, by drawing on conclusions from the authors' past work on the human aspects of IA and by benefiting from extensive work carried out on the subject of questionnaire-based methods in the field of social sciences. By examining the merits and shortcomings of existing, well-researched methodologies, the most appropriate one that meets the set requirements, will ultimately be identified.

In the discussion that follows, the foundation of such a structured methodology will be laid. At this stage, only the structure of a methodology and its governing principles will be presented, mostly based on the merits and known deficiencies of existing social science practices and adapted for the task at hand. This is a crucial first step which paves the way for future work that will examine the practical issues of how such a methodology may be applied, its scope of application and the incorporation of its results to the ISMS' virtuous PDCA cycle. This foundation work constitutes the paper's contribution to the field of the Human Aspects of Information Security and Assurance research.

2. Scope and defining qualities of the assessment methodology

In order to avoid misconceptions, it is important to clarify exactly what is expected from the proposed assessment methodology:

- Quantification in the form of percentages will be necessary.
- The methodology should be driven by and provide feedback to the ISMS effort.

- The assessment results are not necessarily expected to provide an absolute measure of any particular IA quality of the information system/structure but should be used to initially establish a baseline, while subsequent iterations will provide input to the ISMS PDCA cycle by comparison.
- The assessment method should be flexible enough to incorporate new IA aspects as they are identified and modular enough that aspects that no longer need to be monitored can be removed without affecting the validity of other results.
- The methodology should be such that it can be easily, swiftly and periodically administered without overburdening the respondents.
- Different groups of respondents should be catered for.
- Respondents should be authenticated (for reasons that are discussed later in the text) but at the same time,
- Respondent anonymity must be protected.

3. Comparison of Qualitative and Quantitative approaches

For the purposes of the current work, in this section some thoughts are presented on qualitative vs. quantitative research methodologies. The question of the comparative merits of the two approaches constantly surfaces in the social sciences literature, as in Bowling (1997), Babbie (2013) and elsewhere. When an attempt is made to analyse and predict human behaviour, the traditional qualitative approach methods involve observation (Jansen, 2010), participation (Mack et al., 2005), interviews, open-ended questionnaires, closed questionnaires, and, finally, meticulous data analysis.

The detailed comparison of qualitative and quantitative methods is beyond the scope of this paper and it is a subject that has been thoroughly examined by the social scientists. Suffice it to say that a very rich bibliography already exists on the subject and it is constantly expanding. For our purposes, the main comparison aspects are tabulated in the work by Mack et al. (2005) and are being reproduced in Table 1.

	Quantitative	*Qualitative*
General framework	*Seek to confirm hypotheses about phenomena*	*Seek to explore phenomena*
	Instruments use more rigid style of eliciting and categorizing responses to questions	*Instruments use more flexible, iterative style of eliciting and categorizing responses to questions*
	Use highly structured methods such as questionnaires, surveys, and structured observation	*Use semi-structured methods such as in-depth interviews, focus groups, and participant observation*
Analytical objectives	*To quantify variation*	*To describe variation*
	To predict causal relationships	*To describe and explain relationships*
	To describe characteristics of a population	*To describe individual experiences and group norms*
Question format	*Closed-ended*	*Open-ended*
Data format	*Numerical (obtained by assigning numerical values to responses)*	*Textual (obtained from audiotapes, videotapes and field notes)*
Flexibility in study design	*Study design is stable from beginning to end*	*Some aspects of the study are flexible (for example, the addition, exclusion, or wording of particular interview questions)*
	Participant responses do not influence or determine how and which questions researchers ask next	*Participant responses affect how and which questions researchers ask next*
	Study design is subject to statistical assumptions and conditions	*Study design is iterative, that is, data collection and research questions are adjusted according to what is learned*

Table 1: Comparison of quantitative and qualitative research approaches (Mack et al., 2005)

From the comparison presented in table 1, it becomes evident that for the purposes of the proposed methodology as described in section 2 above, quantitative methods appear to meet the set requirements more appropriately.

Qualitative methods cannot effectively be used in the context of the proposed methodology for the following main reasons: 1) The resulting data will be textual and very difficult, if not impossible, to transform into numeric values that indicate the current state-of-play for the information system/structure in question. 2) Due to the open-ended nature of the replies, the resulting data will not be comparable between iterations, thus reducing the value of the exercise for the PDCA cycle. 3) If the qualitative assessment methodology is interview-based, a large number of interviewers who must be specialised/expert both in the field of IA and in interview techniques, will have to be engaged every time the assessment procedure is run, resulting in a serious logistics burden for the Human Resources department and a high overall monetary cost. 4) If the qualitative assessment methodology is questionnaire-based and open-ended, due to the fact that the respondents will have to write extensive answers, the additional burden will make the whole exercise unattractive to the respondents and this will either lead to inaccurate results from unanswered or hastily answered questions, or the whole process will be met with scepticism and, consequently, will not obtain the acceptance level and necessary support to provide usable results in the long run.

A quantitative, written questionnaire-based approach where a) the questions are pre-determined and are not adapted along the way, as they would be by an interviewer according to the progress of a qualitative interview process, b) the replies are pre-set (i.e. close-ended) and c) discrete numeric values are assigned to them according to a Likert scale (Bowling, 1997) -this is examined in detail later on-, will produce directly comparable results between respondents and between iterations. The variations in the numeric outcomes of the assessment that are caused by IA measures adopted between iterations can thus be quantified. In this manner, the results of the IA effort can be directly assessed, thus allowing for accurate tuning of the overarching ISMS processes. Furthermore, the questionnaires can be easily administered via the organisation's intranet computer network, using existing software tools. Most importantly, the data analysis can be automated to a large extent, immediately yielding directly usable results that can be fed back to the appropriate ISMS modules. Last but not least, all of the above can be done without the extensive engagement of experts that a qualitative approach would require.

Even though the quantitative approach is more appropriate for the work at hand, the value of qualitative research is nevertheless very important in identifying IA weaknesses caused by human behaviour and in providing the necessary groundwork for establishing the quantitative methodology. As already stated, the human aspects of IA identified in previous work by the authors, comprise Social aspects (Frangopoulos et al., 2008), Psychological aspects (Frangopoulos et al., 2010), Psychosocial risk at the workplace (Frangopoulos et al., 2012), Influence techniques and Social Engineering Methods (Frangopoulos, 2007) and choices based on Economic Considerations (Frangopoulos et al., 2014). Luckily, extensive qualitative research has been carried out in the context of the social sciences through well-established self-report methods, as far as the general psychological and social issues are concerned (Kelly, 1955; Llewelyn, 1988; Winter, 1992; Kvale, 1996; Taylor & Bogdan, 1998; Patton, 2002). Insofar the specific context of the human aspects of IA in information systems is concerned, the qualitative approach has been thoroughly examined by Albrechtsen (2007) and others. Thus, most of the necessary qualitative groundwork has already been done, providing a solid foundation for the proposed quantitative approach and the generation of appropriately formed sets of close-ended questions with pre-set, weighted replies.

4. Respondent Groups, authentication and anonymity

In order to carry out an assessment which will yield the best possible results, it will be important to get as many people from the organisation as possible involved in the proposed questionnaire process. Ideally, for 100% precision, the confidence level index "α" should be made equal to 1 (Jansen, 2010), i.e. the total population involved with IA, in any manner, should be included in the process. Apart from that, different groups of people must be questioned in order to include all of the stakeholders in the assessment process. Questionnaires for each of the groups must be different and the main groups that should be questioned are a) the end-users, b) the Information System administrators, c) the Information Assurance Office personnel, d) the Human Resources Department, and e) representatives of the Management. Although these are the most obvious groups that must be involved, the methodology can be extended to involve any other groups particular to an organisational structure, which might contribute to the assessment process at hand. Such groups could include the infirmary employees (in order to assess psychosomatic issues related to stress and thus the level of the collective psychosocial risk as described by Haubold B., 2008), location security personnel and even cleaning crews. The idea behind the diversity of the various groups is that their diverging activities, roles and responsibilities give them radically different points of view on the same subject. Thus by asking different groups cleverly formulated, but dissimilar, questions on the same subject, the objectivity and accuracy of one group's replies on a particular subject can be judged. Based on Berger & Luckmann's (1991) general position about the problems in communication and understanding between groups of the same structure, it was argued in previous work by the authors (Frangopoulos et al., 2008) that different groups within an information system or information-handling structure, perceive matters differently, thus leading to misconceptions about IA and to a lack of common understanding of IA concepts. This very serious argument is corroborated by the results of the research carried out on the subject by Albrechtsen & Hovden (2009).

To illustrate the necessity of questioning multiple groups, one could consider an example whereby analysis of the data provided by the Management group demonstrates the commitment towards IA, the Information Security Office group data confirm the existence of password policies, the IT administrators group results ascertain the existence of technical measures for password policy enforcement, the end-users group data show compliance to all of the above and, finally, bursting the proverbial bubble, the cleaners group may report workstations that are left logged-on to the system and unattended or sticky yellow notes with funny words written on them on monitors and inside half-open drawers.

A common source of problems in data gathered from questionnaires is the bias created by multiple factors which need to be controlled. Such bias can arise as respondents may choose their replies not based on practice and experience but according to their understanding of what would constitute a "proper" answer. This is described in Barker et al. (2002) as a tendency towards acquiescence (agree rather than disagree) and social desirability (answering in a way that is socially acceptable). In Jones & Nisbet (1971) and Fiske & Taylor (1991), two more potential sources of bias are described: The first is known as the "actor-observer effect" and it refers to people saying that their own behaviour is caused by situational factors and that other people's behaviour is caused by dispositional factors. The second is the "self-serving" bias and it corresponds to the tendency to take credit for success and deny responsibility for failure. Even though there are techniques that mitigate the described bias sources, it can easily be deduced that the error introduced by the above biases is especially grave when the respondent feels pressured or even threatened by questionnaires not being anonymous. The respondent must never feel that a given reply may have even the remotest chance of being used or interpreted in a way that will affect him/her negatively. The principle of respondent anonymity must thus be upheld at all cost and this must be made crystal-clear to the respondents themselves.

This paramount requirement for anonymity creates all sorts of problems with the administration of the questionnaires, especially when multiple respondent groups are involved. In order to both have respondents answer the proper questionnaire set out for their group and be able to fine tune the iterations of the questionnaire process, each respondent must be identified and authenticated. The authentication requirement has to do with being able to track the participation of respondents in the questionnaire process. As it has already been mentioned, the questionnaire process has to be run iteratively and its results fed to the ISMS. At the same time, it must not create peaks in the collective burden of the organisation. To achieve this, the exercise can be spread out in time as well as among people. The question that arises though is how it can be assured that all (or most) of the respondents participate when requested. This issue can only be dealt with by administrative measures. The necessity for continual awareness education is highlighted in all IA best practices and standards texts such as the ISO 27000 series (ISO/IEC, 2014). This creates, among other administrative difficulties, the problem of tracking each employee's educational record with respect to IA and calling him/her to participate in relevant seminars and other IA awareness actions when the time is due. One way of tackling this is by creating an "IA point system" whereby each employee/respondent must reach a yearly quota of points gained by participating in IA-related activities such as -but not limited to- awareness seminars and assessment procedures (including questionnaires). Such a point system is adopted by the Information Systems Audit and Control Association (ISACA) for allowing its members to retain their hard-earned certifications by remaining continually informed on matters related to Information Security (ISACA, 2014). For such a system to be adopted, it is obvious that the employee/respondent will have to be authenticated in order to have the points awarded to the proper person. This in turn antagonises the much needed concept of anonymity. It should by now be obvious that in order to have respondent authentication combined with anonymity, questionnaire administration will have to adopt specialised anonymisation techniques. The proposed procedure may perhaps be able to borrow elements from existing solutions such as the ones used for collecting sensitive data anonymously for longitudinal research (i.e. correlational research involving repeated observations of the same variables over time), as described in the social sciences literature (Carifio & Biron, 1982; Yurek, Vasey & Havens, 2008; Schnell, Bachteler & Reiher, 2010). This could be combined with solutions proposed in the context of voting systems (Ray & Narasimhamurthi, 2001; Gerck, 2003; Liaw, 2004) whereby the voter is authenticated and given the permission to vote once, his/her vote is recorded, the voting action can be verified, but the vote content is completely disjointed from the voter's identity. In a similar manner, the replies to the questionnaire must be disjointed from the respondent, while the respondent participation is recorded and acted upon, be it for the award of IA points, further iterations of the assessment procedure, the comparative analysis of group data or for any other action in the context of the IA effort. In this framework, the value of the questionnaire itself as an IA *awareness* tool must not be overlooked as the questionnaire can help the respondent (even at a subliminal level) make sense of the various IA aspects and what these involve, every time the respondent is exposed to a questionnaire's content.

Even with the anonymity of the respondent assured, and other measures against bias errors being in place, the respondents may still choose to answer questions in a "proper" rather than a truthful manner. This is where the matter of question composition comes into play were e.g. potentially sensitive questions should never refer to the respondent's person but rather to the group's general behaviour and characteristics. However, further analysis of this issue goes beyond this paper's scope and will follow in future work.

5. Questionnaire design and administration

It should be clear by now that in order to attain its objectives, the proposed process must be built around a set of very carefully designed questionnaires that take into account the nature of the survey and the individualities of the various respondents.

In order to obtain the required numeric results, a questionnaire based on questions with pre-set (or "close-ended") replies to each of which a discrete numeric value is assigned, must be used. This approach is known as a rating-scale type questionnaire and it is considered to be the central quantitative self-report method (Barker et al., 2002). A variety of rating-scales exist, such as "Thurstone", "Guttman", "Likert" and others (Nunnally & Bernstein, 1994). However, the Likert scale is considered to be the most commonly used in questionnaires of this type (Barker et al., 2002). A discussion of the Likert scale can be found in Bowling (1997) according to whom, when a Likert-type scale is used, the respondent is asked to make judgement on an issue and a discrete numerical value is assigned to that judgement.

Nunnally & Bernstein (1994) argue that the reliability of the result increases with an increase in the dynamic range of the scale, i.e. with more scale points. However, Barker et al. (2002) point out that a dynamic range of more than seven points makes it difficult for respondents to adequately discriminate between them, while Lissitz & Green (1975) consider it useless to have a scale with more than five points.

Likert-type questions can provide quantified results on issues that require the level of respondent agreement with a given statement such as:

How much do you agree with the statement that "you have received adequate Information Assurance training during the past 12 months"?

1	*2*	*3*	*4*	*5*
o	o	o	o	o
I strongly disagree	*I disagree*	*I neither agree or disagree*	*I agree*	*I strongly agree*

Similarly, an even more direct result on frequency or quantity can be obtained, as shown in the example below:

On a scale of 0 to 6 where 0 represents "never" and 6 "regularly", how often do you find notes with passwords written on them in plain view?

0	1	2	3	4	5	6
○	○	○	○	○	○	○
Never						*Regularly*

Barker et al. (2002) use the term "central tendency" to describe the phenomenon of respondents avoiding the extreme ends of scales. Thus if the scale ends are avoided, there is not enough dynamic range left in the middle area of the scale to have clearly distinct results. Barker et al. proceed by arguing against a scale of three or four points which may return too many responses in the middle. Hence it seems that the optimal number of points in a Likert scale should be between 5 and 7. Whether it should be an odd number (5 or 7) or an even one (6) has to do with whether a mid-point that represents neutral replies such as "I neither agree nor disagree" is required. The argument for having a mid-point is that respondents should be allowed to express their neutrality. The argument against having a mid-point is that people usually hold an opinion that is not neutral, but may need a little "push" in order to express it. This "push" is accomplished by not giving the respondent a centre point to settle upon (Barker et al., 2002).

It should be borne in mind that it is useful to adopt and use a single type of Likert-scale question throughout the questionnaire as otherwise the respondents may get confused. Thus, if the issues described above are resolved and the question format is decided upon, there are several other matters that must be considered in the design of a questionnaire, as brought to light by Babbie (2013):

a) Sufficient attention must be given to the general format of the questionnaire, in order to not confuse respondents, not cause them to miss questions or even not make respondents reject the whole exercise and throw the questionnaire away. Most importantly, clear instructions must be given to the respondents on what exactly is expected of them and how to reply to the questionnaire.
b) The wording of each question must be such that it does not predispose the respondent towards a particular answer. Additionally, the wording must be such that the question is clear, unambiguous and does not confuse the respondent in any way.
c) Questions should not have multiple parts. Such questions are known as "double-barrelled" and by having more than one parts, they do not allow the respondent to give a focused answer as the respondent may agree with one part of the question and disagree with another. Some conditional questions may also fall in this category and should thus also be avoided. As a practical rule, the word "and" in a question may be making it double-barrelled. That question should thus be broken in two or more distinct questions.
d) Questions should not be arranged in a way that previous questions affect the respondents' replies to subsequent ones.

All of the above must be carefully catered for in the creation of the questionnaires that will be used in the proposed methodology, irrespective of the respondent group that they are distributed to or of the phase during which they are administered. Careful questionnaire design is quintessential to the success of the methodology.

6. Principles and objectives of data gathering and analysis

This section's objective is to set the ground for the possible directions of the analysis of the data that the proposed methodology can provide. The present discussion should neither be seen as an exhaustive approach nor function in a restrictive manner.

It should be borne in mind that each group must be questioned, to the greatest possible extent, on the identified human aspects of IA. It is thus expected that there will be various sets of questions that pertain to each of the identified human aspects areas and to each of the respondent groups. Assuming a) that the questionnaires will be administered over the organisation's intranet and b) that they must not be very time consuming for the respondents, it would be reasonable to administer the questionnaires with only a limited number of different questions each time. Assuming that the questionnaire process has been executed enough times to have obtained a complete first iteration for all subjects from all designated groups, then: a) by comparing the numerical results from different groups on the same subjects, the relative divide on IA issues between groups can be assessed, b) by carefully selecting the questions, their order and the questionnaire phase/section in which they are presented to the respondents, the convergence of what is theoretically understood by the respondents and what their actions prove to have been internalised by them, can be assessed. (In order to do this properly, it is important to be able to attribute replies provided by respondents at different times/phases, to the same, albeit anonymous, individual), c) even from the first time the questionnaire is run in its entirety, several important conclusions about the general IA posture can be drawn, thus identifying the major IA issues that require immediate attention, d) depending on the outcomes of the first iteration, the questionnaire and its deployment can be modified to address newly identified problematic areas during the next iteration. (This must be done in such a controlled way that it does not affect the ability to obtain comparative results on existing, known issues between iterations).

Assuming that the questionnaire procedure has been run at least twice, comparisons between the results obtained from different iterations can be made. Thus, a) conclusions can be drawn on IA-related trends, b) the effects of corrective or preventive IA actions that took place between iterations can be assessed and c) problems of a more general nature may be identified before they become full-fledged IA issues (such as increases in work-related stress, developing conflicting interests among user groups, effects of organisational re-structure etc.).

These outcomes should be used to fuel the virtuous PDCA cycle of the ISMS and provide for changes that may be as important as organisational strategy or policy adjustments. Furthermore, the proposed questionnaire process allows for rapid internal adjustments, in order to shift its focus towards any issue that attracts the attention of the IA team, most importantly emerging ones. Finally, it should be noted that the expected outcomes described above, should not be seen as an exhaustive list.

7. Conclusions and way forward

In this work, a proposed questionnaire-based methodology is described. This shall form the core of a tool that can provide continuous assessment of the human aspects that affect the IA posture in an organisational structure. Thus, if the "Check" part of the PDCA cycle is visualised as a dashboard on which key parameters and indices, critical for the system at hand, are monitored, the proposed methodology will effectively add another gauge labelled "Human Aspects of IA" to the board. This quantitative methodology is based on sets of different, close-ended, Likert-scale questionnaires that are distributed to various employee groups within an organisation. The comparative analysis of the questionnaire results will provide continuous input to the PDCA virtuous cycle embedded in an ISMS and can help identify emerging human aspect trends before they become full-fledged IA issues. Future actions will include a) the construction of the particular sets of questions which must effectively address problems of respondent-induced bias and inherent questionnaire design difficulties, b) the choice and adaptation of questionnaire administration tools for use over the organisation's intranet and c) the resolution of the matter of respondent identification/authentication combined with anonymity.

8. References

Albrechtsen, E., 2007. A qualitative study of users' view on information security. *Computers & security.* 26(4) pp.276–289.

Albrechtsen, E. & Hovden, J., 2009. The information security digital divide between information security managers and users. *Computers & Security.* 28(6) pp.476–490.

Babbie, E., 2013. *The Practice of Social Research.* 13th ed. Belmont, CA: Wadsworth.

Barker, C., Pistrang, N. & Elliott, R., 2002. *Research Methods in Clinical Psychology: An Introduction for Students and Practitioners.* 2nd ed. Chichester, UK: John Wiley & Sons, Ltd.

Berger, P.L. & Luckman, T., 1991. *The social construction of reality. A treatise in the sociology of knowledge.* London: Penguin Books.

Bowling A., 1997. Questionnaire design. In: *Research Methods in Health.* Buckingham: Open University Press.

Carifio, J. & Biron, R., 1982. Collecting sensitive data anonymously: Further findings on the CDRGP technique. *Journal of Alcohol and Drug Education.* 27(2) pp.38-70.

Deming, W.E., 1986. *Out of the crisis.* Cambridge, MA: Massachusetts Institute of Technology , Center for Advanced Engineering Study.

Fiske, S.T. & Taylor, S.E., 1991. *Social cognition.* 2nd ed. New York: McGraw-Hill.

Frangopoulos, E.D., 2007. *Social Engineering and the ISO/IEC 17799:2005 Security Standard: A Study on Effectiveness,*. MSc Dissertation, University of South Africa.

Frangopoulos, E.D., Eloff, M.M. and Venter, L.M., 2008. Social aspects of Information Security. In: *Proceedings of the Information Security South Affrica (ISSA) 2008 Innovative Minds Conference*. Gauteng Region (Johannesburg), South Africa, 2-4 July 2008.

Frangopoulos, E.D., Eloff, M.M. and Venter, L.M., 2010. Psychological Considerations in Social Engineering – The Ψ-Wall as defence. *IADIS International Journal on Computer Science and Information Systems.* 5(2) pp.1-20.

Frangopoulos, E.D., Eloff, M.M. and Venter, L.M., 2012. Psychosocial Risks: can their effects on the Security of Information Systems really be ignored? In: Clarke N.L. and Furnell S.M. (ed.) 2012. *Proceedings of the Sixth International Symposium on Human Aspects of Information Security and Assurance (HAISA) 2012.* Crete, Greece, 6-8 June 2012.

Frangopoulos, E.D., Eloff, M.M. and Venter, L.M., 2014 (in press). Information Security Economics: Induced Risks and Latent Costs. In: *Proceedings of the 13th European Conference on Cyber Warfare and Security ECCWS-2014.* Piraeus, Greece, 2-4 July 2014. (Accepted for publication February 2014).

Gerck, E., 2003. Private, secure and auditable Internet voting. In *Secure Electronic Voting,* pp. 165-179. Springer US.

Haubold B., 2008. *Les risques psychosociaux. Identifier, analyser, prévenir les risques humains.* Paris: Éditions d' Organisation Groupe Eyrolles.

ISACA, 2014. *CISM Continuing Professional Education (CPE) Policy* [pdf]. ISACA. [online] Available at: <http://www.isaca.org/Certification/CISM-Certified-Information-Security-Manager/Maintain-Your-CISM/Documents/CISM-CPE-English.pdf> [Accessed 1 April 2014].

ISO/IEC, 2014. *International Standard ISO/IEC 27000:2014. Information technology - Security techniques - Information security management systems - Overview and vocabulary.* Geneva: ISO Copyright Office.

Jansen, H., 2010. The Logic of Qualitative Survey Research and its Position in the Field of Social Research Methods. In: *Forum: Qualitative Social Research,* 11(2).

Jones, E.E. & Nisbett, R.E., 1971. The actor and the observer: Divergent perceptions of the causes of behaviour. In Jones, E.E., Kanouse, D.E., Kelley, H.H., Nisbett, R.E., Valins, S. & Weiner, B. (eds). *Attribution: Perceiving the causes of behaviour.* Morristown, NJ: General Learning Press.

Kelly, G.A., 1955. *The psychology of personal constructs.* New York: Norton.

Kvale, S., 1996. *Interviews: An introduction to qualitative research interviewing.* Thousand Oaks, CA: Sage.

Liaw, H. T., 2004. A secure electronic voting protocol for general elections. *Computers & Security,* 23(2), pp.107-119.

Lissitz, R.W. & Green, S.B., 1975. Effect of the number of scale points on reliability: A Monte Carlo approach. *Journal of Applied Psychology,* 60, pp.10–13.

Llewelyn, S.P., 1988. Psychological therapy as viewed by clients and therapists. *British Journal of Clinical Psychology*, 27, pp.223–237.

Mack, N., Woodsong, C., MacQueen, K. M., Guest, G. & Namey, E., 2005. *Qualitative research methods: a data collectors field guide.* Research Triangle Park, North Carolina, USA: Family Health International [FHI].

Nunnally, J. C., & Bernstein, I. H., 1994. *Psychometric theory.* 3rd ed. New York, NY: McGraw-Hill.

Patton, M.Q., 2002. *Qualitative research and evaluation methods.* 3rd ed. Thousand Oaks, CA: Sage.

Ray, I., & Narasimhamurthi, N., 2001. An anonymous electronic voting protocol for voting over the internet. In *Advanced Issues of E-Commerce and Web-Based Information Systems, WECWIS 2001, Third International Workshop on,* pp.188-190.

Schneier, B., 2000. *Secrets & Lies.* USA: John Wiley & Sons Inc.

Schnell, R., Bachteler, T., & Reiher, J., 2010. Improving the use of self-generated identification codes. *Evaluation review*, 34(5), pp.391-418.

Taylor, S.J. & Bogdan, R., 1998. *Introduction to qualitative research methods: A guidebook and resource.* 3rd ed. New York: Wiley.

Winter, D.A., 1992. *Personal construct psychology in clinical practice.* London: Rutledge.

Yurek, L.A., Vasey, J., & Havens, D.S., 2008. The use of self-generated identification codes in longitudinal research. *Evaluation review*, 32(5), pp.435-452.

Author Index